Korean Cinema:
The New Hong Kong

**A Guidebook for the
Latest Korean New Wave**

Anthony C. Y. Leong

Front Cover: My Sassy Girl image courtesy of Mirovision.
Inside Cover: Joint Security Area image courtesy of CJ Entertainment; Il Mare image courtesy of Sidus.
Back Cover: My Wife is a Gangster image courtesy of Samsung Pictures; Failan image courtesy of Tube Entertainment; 2009 Lost Memories image courtesy of CJ Entertainment. All other images contained within courtesy of identified copyright holders and all rights reserved.

National Library of Canada Cataloguing in Publication

Leong, Anthony C. Y., 1969-
     Korean cinema : the new Hong Kong / Anthony C.Y. Leong.
Includes bibliographical references and index.
ISBN 1-55395-461-0

     1. Motion pictures—Korea (South) 2. Motion picture industry—Korea (South) I. Title.
PN1993.5.S68L46 2003   791.43'095195   C2002-905904-6

TRAFFORD

This book was published *on-demand* in cooperation with Trafford Publishing.
On-demand publishing is a unique process and service of making a book available for retail sale to the public taking advantage of on-demand manufacturing and Internet marketing. **On-demand publishing** includes promotions, retail sales, manufacturing, order fulfilment, accounting and collecting royalties on behalf of the author.

Suite 6E, 2333 Government St., Victoria, B.C. V8T 4P4, CANADA
Phone   250-383-6864   Toll-free 1-888-232-4444 (Canada & US)
Fax   250-383-6804   E-mail   sales@trafford.com
Web site www.trafford.com   TRAFFORD PUBLISHING IS A DIVISION OF TRAFFORD HOLDINGS LTD.
Trafford Catalogue #02-1176   www.trafford.com/robots/02-1176.html

10   9   8   7   6   5   4

Dedicated to 'My Sassy Girl', Michelle

Table of Contents

Acknowledgements

A lot of effort went into putting this book together, and I would like to express my appreciation to those people who provided me assistance along the way.

A very big thanks to my fiancée, Michelle, who in addition to suggesting that I write this book in the first place, has provided many tireless hours throughout the editorial process. The front, inside, and back covers are her handiwork, and she also helped prepare the production stills you see throughout the book. Michelle, you are truly an inspiration and I could not have done this without you.

I would also like to thank Darcy Paquet, the man behind what is probably the best web site on Korean cinema, KoreanFilm.org. In addition to helping me navigate the confusing Romanization of Korean names, his site was a rich source of research material for the book (you will see his name a few times in the Bibliography).

Thanks also to Tom Weisser, editor of Asian Cult Cinema, who has found it worthy to print my Asian film articles in his magazine over the past few years, and who pointed me in the right direction on some issues with this book.

Thank you to Phil Hall of Film Threat for passing along a screener of Kim Ki-duk's eye-opening film, "The Isle".

Another shout out goes to Yu Byeong-gwan, who made my web-based reviews of Korean films a permanent fixture on his CineKorea.com web site, and the folks over at AsianDB.com, who have put together the most comprehensive source of information and images for Korean films.

Of course, I would like to thank the filmmakers and producers of the latest 'Korean New Wave' for creating some of the most fascinating and engaging films I have seen in my life. Keep up the good work!

Finally, thank you to my family.

Introduction: South Korea Who?

You don't have to look very far these days to see the influence that the film industry of Hong Kong has had on moviemaking around the world. Hong Kong film stars, such as Jackie Chan, Chow Yun-fat, Jet Li, and Michelle Yeoh, have become household names headlining Hollywood blockbusters. So too have numerous Hong Kong directors, such as John Woo, Tsui Hark, and Wong Kar-wai, who are closing deals in Tinseltown and developing huge international followings. Western filmmakers are even employing the visual dynamic of Hong Kong movies, bringing hyperkinetic martial arts action, 'wire-fu', and graceful gun battles to mainstream audiences through films such as "The Matrix" and "Charlie's Angels".

However, despite achieving such recognition abroad, the luster on Hong Kong's homegrown film industry has faded quite a bit over the past decade. This gradual decline in Hong Kong cinema has been due to a number of reasons. There has been a considerable 'brain drain', with the best and brightest players departing for the bright lights of Hollywood, spurred in part by the uncertainty that surrounded the Handover back to Mainland China in 1997. Piracy, mostly through the VCD and now the DVD format, are putting films on the street as soon as they open in theaters, selling at a fraction of the cost of a movie ticket. And the 'shoot it fast, shoot it cheap' mentality of the local industry has not helped either, with studios continuing to churn out low quality 'disposable' offerings. Mind you, there have been a few bright spots over the years, such as the recent successes of Stephen Chow's "Shaolin Soccer" or Wong Kar-wai's "In the Mood for Love". But overall, the magic of Hong Kong's golden era, the so-called 'Hong Kong New Wave', is all but gone.

However, for those Hong Kong cinema aficionados who passionately followed the rise of the 'Hong Kong New Wave' during the Eighties and early Nineties, only to become increasingly disenchanted since then, like myself, I offer you two words: South Korea.

Over the last few years, particularly since 1998, South Korea's local film industry has undergone a remarkable transformation. The staples of Korean cinema, the staid melodramas and exploitation movies, have given way to a 'new wave' of filmmakers. Schooled abroad and influenced by their contemporaries around the world, this new generation of Korean moviemakers is revitalizing the industry with bold arthouse productions, big-budget actioners, thought-provoking dramas, and subversive satires. In some circles, South Korea is even being likened to the new 'Hong Kong', with its homegrown film industry on the verge of exploding onto the world stage, similar to how the 'Hong Kong New Wave' catapulted the former British colony and its groundbreaking directors into the international spotlight. Already, some Korean films have found success in the North American market through limited release (such as the groundbreaking blockbuster "Shiri"). Korean directors are being courted by major Hollywood studios for lucrative U.S. remake rights, such as with Dreamwork's recent deal for "My Sassy Girl".

When I first became hooked on Korean films just a little over a year ago, I was interested in learning more about Korean cinema and what its other standout offerings were. Unfortunately, I was disappointed to learn that there were few information sources I could tap. Instead, I had to rely on a hodgepodge of different information sources, such as entertainment trade journals, foreign-language newspapers, or academic textbooks. I also examined a number of web sites and on-line discussion forums dedicated to Asian cinema or Korean film, but the information was either not very well written or lacked the scope I was looking for (e.g., coverage of lesser-known Korean films). Alas, other than Darcy Paquet's excellent Korean film web site, KoreanFilm.org, there were no convenient and comprehensive information sources that dealt specifically with the latest 'Korean New Wave'.

"Korean Cinema: The New Hong Kong" is a guidebook for exploring this new and exciting treasure trove of cinema. It is the first book of its kind, covering this emerging cinematic powerhouse in an easy-to-read and leisure-focused fashion, bringing all the sought-after information on Korean cinema into one convenient package.

While it is not a comprehensive overview, detailing every single film of the latest 'Korean New Wave', it will provide the reader a flavor of what Korean cinema has to offer with some suggestions on which films to see, as well as which ones to avoid. It will be a must-read for the growing legion of Korean movie fans, whether they are seasoned veterans or have only been recently introduced to it. Other books on Korean film read like dry academic dissertations or spend far too much time detailing the exploits of obscure filmmakers who died prior to the outbreak of the Second World War. This is will not be the case with "Korean Cinema: The New Hong Kong". Though the reader will be provided with sufficient background and context where it merits, this book is primarily geared to be an entertaining read, providing a flavor of what is exciting in Korean moviemaking, and why, without relying on too much "Cineaste"-style jargon or obscure French words.

What Are the Highlights of This Book?

Within the pages of "Korean Cinema: The New Hong Kong", you will find:

- A brief history of South Korea and its film industry, which will help you understand the reasons behind the revolutionary changes in Korean cinema and what is influencing the country's directors
- A look at the present state of Korea's filmmaking industry and how it resembles the dot-com era (with the only difference being that these companies are actually making money, and lots of it)
- An examination of the characteristics, themes, and dominant genres of the films in this newest 'Korean New Wave'
- In-depth reviews and commentary of the top ten must-see films of this latest 'Korean New Wave'
- An overview of the top genres of Korean cinema, with reviews, commentary, and notes on availability for the good, the bad, and the ugly
- A look at the stars of Korean cinema, such as the Korean equivalents to Tom Cruise (Han Suk-kyu) and Julia Roberts (Shim Eun-ha).
- How moviegoers can go about seeing Korean flicks (with English subtitles too!)

The reviewed films are listed in each relevant chapter in order of decreasing rank. Thus, you will find the must-see entries of a particular genre at the beginning of the chapter, and the ones that are best avoided near the back. In addition, the book uses a five-star system to rate each film, which can be decoded as follows:

●●●●●	Absolute must-see (buy a Region 3 DVD player if need be)
●●●●	Highly recommended
●●●	Average effort that does have its moments
●●	Mediocre film with few redeeming qualities
●	Watching will result in a violent reaction (e.g., kicking yourself)

The reviews also provide information on availability on an English-subtitled home video format, specifically VCD and DVD. For more information on these formats, including region-coding of DVDs, be sure to read Chapter 12: Where to Get Your Fix of Korean Flicks.

Book Outline

This outline should give you an appreciation for the level of depth and breadth that this sourcebook on 'Korean New Wave' cinema will provide:

Who Should Use This Book?

Anyone interested in film, particularly Asian cinema, will find "Korean Cinema: The New Hong Kong" a worthwhile read, particularly:

- Fans of Hong Kong films who are looking for an alternative source for the type of innovative, unconventional, and visually exciting filmmaking that went out of style with the Gulf War
- The uninitiated who have recently been turned on to Korean cinema, yet don't have a clue in terms of what to watch
- Seasoned aficionados of Korean cinema who are interested in learning more about their favorite films

Chapter 1: A Brief History of South Korea and Its Film Industry

Right now, I have a feeling that some of you who picked up this book are wondering why the first chapter is a (yawn) history lesson. Some of you are also probably tempted to skip ahead to Chapter 4 to find out what DVDs are worth buying or renting. True, reading about wars, oppressive governments, and civil unrest is nowhere near as thrilling as watching espionage-actioner "Shiri", or as amusing as hanging out with "My Sassy Girl". However, in order to fully appreciate the uniqueness of South Korea films, as well as how they got to be that way, it is important to understand the history and culture of the country, which has shaped both the creativity of its filmmakers and the tastes of its moviegoers. Thus, this opening chapter provides some historical and cultural context to the films of South Korea, all of which have had a significant impact on the types of films we now see in the latest 'Korean New Wave'.

Looking back over the past one hundred years, the most striking aspect of modern Korean history is the amount of turmoil that the country has endured. Within ten decades, the people of what is now South Korea have seen the fall of the age-old Choson Dynasty, endured the oppressive rule of the Japanese, had their country divided by the Cold War, fought their former countrymen in the Korean War, struggled long and hard to establish a true democratic state, and suffered from the meltdown of the Asian economic crisis. However, as the old proverb goes (or at least how it was presented in Disney's "Mulan"), "The flower that blooms in adversity is the most rarest and beautiful of all".

The Growth of the Korean Film Industry Under Japanese Occupation

Prior to 1910, the Korean peninsula had been ruled by a single monarchy, the Choson Dynasty, a social and political order that had remained stable for over half a millennia. However, as Japan expanded its sphere of influence in Asia during the end of the 19th century, which included victories over China and Russia, Korea finally came under the direct control of its most eastern neighbor.

In 1905, the Protectorate Treaty was imposed upon Korea by Japan in the aftermath of the Russo-Japanese War. This was followed by formal annexation in 1910, after which Japan increasingly tightened its grip on the peninsula, assuming control over every aspect of Korean life. The Japanese government even went as far as trying to completely eradicate the Korean culture during the Thirties and Forties through the banning of the Korean language and the use of Korean family names.

During these four decades of Japanese rule, an infusion of money from Japanese business interests laid the foundation for Korea's film industry. In addition to building a number of theatres in the major cities, Japanese money financed some of the films, such as the first feature with sound, "Ch'yunhyang-jun", a filmed adaptation of a popular pansori folk tale (which also was the basis for Im Kwon-taek's "Chunhyang" from 2000).

However, a few enterprising Koreans were able to turn out features of their own during the time, some of which used the new artform for political purposes. Unfortunately, like other institutions around the country, the ruling Japanese government began to impose more and more restrictions on the production and exhibition of films, including censorship. As the years passed, the number of 'safe' genres that were approved for screening gradually dwindled until Korean-language films were completely banned by the Japanese government in 1942, and the local film industry became little more than an outlet for Japanese propaganda.

Postwar Partition, the Korean War, and the Golden Age

Japanese rule of Korea finally came to an end after four decades with the defeat of Japan by Allied forces in 1945. In order to expedite the surrender of the defeated Japanese forces to the armies of the United States and the Soviets, Korea was divided at the 38th parallel. Though this had initially been envisioned as an interim measure, this dividing line became a permanent fixture in the Korean political landscape as each side shepherded separate governments and attempts at reunification failed amidst the growing Cold War tension. In 1948, Korea was officially divided in two, with the Republic of Korea in the south and the Democratic People's Republic of Korea in the north, which ultimately led to the Korean War in 1950.

As part of the Cease-fire Agreement that ended the Korea War in 1953, a 4km-wide Demilitarized Zone (DMZ) was created to act as a buffer between the North and South. In addition, the two sides agreed to create a Joint Security Area (JSA) around Panmumjeom, the site where the Cease-fire Agreement had been negotiated, where both sides could meet face-to-face. With only the Cease-fire

Agreement between them, both North and South Korea are technically still at war. Over the years, there have been a number of cross-border incidents, both within the DMZ and elsewhere, with the potential to become the flashpoint of renewed hostilities.

Most of South Korea's production and exhibition infrastructure was destroyed during the Korean War. However, during the remainder of the 1950s, a combination of tax incentives and foreign aid helped rebuild the local film industry, launching Korean cinema's 'Golden Age' during the late Fifties and throughout the Sixties. During this time, the number of homegrown film productions skyrocketed, as did attendance at the country's movie theaters. A number of Korea's most well respected directors had their start during this period, such as Im Kwon-taek and Kim Ki-young.

However, while the film industry was enjoying a tremendous revival, changes in the political landscape were paving the way for censorship, the bane of the industry, to rear its ugly head again-- only this time, it would be the Korean government restricting what its people could and could not see. During this period, South Korea was gripped with sluggish economic growth and paranoia over the growing influence of pro-North leftist groups. Taking advantage of the political instability, Park Chung-hee instigated a military coup in 1961.

Censorship and the Decline of Korean Cinema

Over the next decade, Park's regime maintained an increasingly tight grip on the country through various means, such as declaring martial law, spying on and harassing political opponents, violently suppressing anti-government demonstrators, and manipulating of the country's constitution to allow for an indefinite term of office. As South Koreans increasingly had their freedoms curtailed, so did the film industry. Filmmakers faced increasing government censorship over films that criticized Park's regime, portrayed North Korea in a sympathetic light, or dabbled in sexual material. In addition, changes to the Motion Picture Law in 1973 placed controls on the companies entitled to produce films as well as the types of films they could make, such as a stipulation that their films had to reflect the ideology of Park's 'Revitalizing Government'. As a result, the film industry focused on 'safe' fare, such as action films and melodramas. Coupled with the growing popularity of television, audiences abandoned the country's movie theaters in droves during the Seventies, leading to widespread bankruptcies among Korea's production companies.

In contrast to measures aimed at stifling creativity, another initiative of the Park regime was the imposition of a quota system aimed at protecting the country's film industry. Under the quota system, the country's theaters were mandated to show Korean films, while limits were placed on how many foreign films could be imported and how many days of the year that they could be shown. Though this protectionist measure was lifted somewhat in 1988, to this very day, Korean theaters are still obliged to screen homegrown fare at least 106 days out of the year.

Reform and Revival in the Eighties

After a decade of increasing public dissatisfaction over his regime, the 1970s closed with the assassination of Park by Kim Jae-kyu, the director of the Korea Central Intelligence Agency, which plunged the country into chaos. General Chun Doo-hwan emerged victorious as the country's new president, however, instead of democratic reforms, Chun continued the 'revitalizing' initiatives of his predecessor, including the suppression of anti-government protests and the arrest of opposition politicians.

The new decade also brought the Kwangju Massacre (an event that figures prominently in Lee Chang-dong's "Peppermint Candy"). This important landmark in the South Korean democratic movement, in which a clash between government troops and student pro-democracy demonstrators resulted in 200 dead (mostly civilians), was a spectre that would haunt Korean politics for the next two decades, and ultimately result in the arrest and imprisonment of two former South Korean presidents. Furthermore, the Kwangju Massacre also triggered the rise of anti-American sentiment, as the Reagan administration had strongly endorsed the use of force in quelling the riot.

However, as the Eighties dragged on, President Chun's administration faced increasing opposition and mass demonstrations. Finally, in 1987, Chun finally caved in and delivered several democratic reforms, including a new constitution and open elections.

Similar to the gradual democratic reform gripping the country, South Korea's film industry enjoyed a modest revival during the Eighties, spurred by an infusion of new blood, increasing international recognition for Korean productions, and moviegoers returning to their local theatres. In addition, the country's new constitution of 1988 relaxed the country's strict censorship laws, providing filmmakers a more liberal venue for political expression.

However, this modest revival was tempered by another key legislative change that year. Import restrictions on foreign films were eased, forcing Korean filmmakers to compete directly against the slicker and more commercial Hollywood and Hong Kong productions. Unfortunately, the local film industry was slow in adapting to this new operating environment, and the market share of homegrown product plunged in the face of increased competition, reaching an all-time low of 16% in 1993.

The Long Road to Democracy

Though the following decade would bring South Korea renewed economic growth and membership in the United Nations, the young democracy would still be rocked by numerous challenges. Government corruption figured prominently, as the 'old ways' came under greater scrutiny in the nascent democracy, which included the arrest of former Presidents Chun and Roh Tae-woo for their roles in the 1980 Kwangju Massacre and allegations of bribery against President Kim Young-sam, who had himself spearheaded an anti-corruption campaign in the early Nineties.

But then in 1997, the Asian economic crisis hit the debt-ridden South Korean economy, which resulted in a rapid depreciation of the country's currency and a bailout by the International Monetary Fund. It would not be until 2000 that a semblance of stability would return to South Korea, as the local economy once again began to expand, and National Assembly elections brought veteran opposition leader and pro-democracy advocate Kim Dae-jung to power. At long last, the long five-decade long march was over, and democracy in South Korea had finally come of age.

During the early Nineties, South Korea's giant industry conglomerates, also known as *chaebols*, began making investments in the movie business, with Samsung being the first out of the gate. With these investments, the *chaebols* revamped South Korea's movie industry into a more professional and business-oriented infrastructure that integrated all production, distribution, and exhibition, and providing a solid footing for the country's filmmakers to compete on the world stage.

Interestingly (and ironically) enough, the 1997 recession in South Korea ended up helping the local film industry in the long run. As economic conditions in the peninsula became bleaker, the very same *chaebols* who had made substantial investments in the film industry only a few years earlier, such as Daewoo and Samsung, decided to divest their movie industry subsidiaries. The funding shortfall was then eagerly picked up by the private sector, which eschewed the conservatism of the past in favor of films that were more daring and in tune to audience tastes. In addition, this renewed entrepreneurial zeal provided many opportunities for novice directors (it has been estimated that 70% of productions are helmed by first-time filmmakers), whose unique worldview married their upbringing in Korean society with their exposure to Western education and filmmaking techniques.

Thus, it was in the 1990s that the final pieces of the puzzle fell into place, jump-starting the latest 'Korean New Wave': relaxed government censorship, investments in infrastructure, entrepreneurial zeal, and an iconoclastic attitude. As a result of these legislative, economic, and creative shifts, today's South Korea possesses one of the most successful and vibrant domestic movie industries in the world, and is rapidly becoming a key destination for those in search of the most exciting filmmaking today.

Chapter 2: Korean Moviemaking Today

The latest 'Korean New Wave' probably got its start sometime around 1997, when the industry began to reap benefits from significant investments in moviemaking infrastructure and a new entrepreneurial spirit. It was in this year that Chang Yoon-hyun's Internet romance "The Contact" became a hit with domestic audiences, and its success helped catalyze greater interest among Korean moviegoers for more homegrown fare. Other critical and financial success stories that would emerge during these early days of the latest 'Korean New Wave' include Lee Chang-dong's "Green Fish", Jacky Kang Je-gyu's "The Gingko Bed", and Hur Jin-ho's "Christmas in August" (all of which, interestingly enough, featured Korea's answer to Tom Cruise, Han Suk-kyu).

However, it would not be until 1999, a watershed year for South Korean cinema, that the latest 'Korean New Wave' became a creative force to be reckoned with. After spending many years taking a backseat to big-budget Hollywood imports, Korean filmmakers reclaimed the country's movie screens as nine homegrown productions earned a place in the box office top 20, such as "Shiri", "Attack the Gas Station!" and "Tell Me Something", which occupied the number 1, 3, and 8 positions among all the top-grossing films that year. South Korea's film industry no longer needed to rely solely on the country's quota system for financial viability, as a 'New Wave' of filmmakers, schooled abroad in Europe and the United States, returned home to

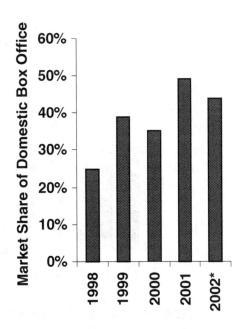

Since 1998, the market share of homegrown productions at South Korea's box office has grown by leaps and bounds (* Jan. to Sept. 2002) (*source: Korean Film Commission*)

create commercially-viable films that appealed to domestic audiences.

Explosive Domestic Growth

Since the start of the latest 'Korean New Wave', the market share for South Korean productions has been steadily climbing. In 1993, prior to the evolutionary changes in the country's film industry infrastructure, homegrown films only took in 15.4% of the domestic box office. In 1998, this number was up to 25%, which grew to 39% in 1999 and 35% in 2000. In 2001, homegrown films occupied 49.1% of the domestic box office, giving South Korea one of the healthiest local film industries in the world. In fact, seven of the top ten films of 2001, a group that accounted for almost half of the South Korean box office, were homegrown films, relegating American imports "Shrek", "Harry Potter & the Sorcerer's Stone", and "Pearl Harbor" to the sixth, seventh, and eighth spots, respectively. And once you factor in the fact that total admissions in South Korea surged from 54.7 million to 87.9 million tickets between 1999 and 2001, local fare is grabbing a larger piece of an ever-expanding pie.

Along with increased market shares, the new phenomenon of Korean blockbusters has propelled box office tallies to new record heights. "Shiri" was the first out of the gate, sinking the box office record set by "Titanic" back in 1997. However, in every year since then, the bar has been raised higher and higher, with "Shiri" giving way to "Joint Security Area", which then gave way to "Friend" for the title of all-time box office champ. The meaning of 'success', in terms of box office admissions, is also continuing to be redefined, as yesteryear's successes end up becoming the new baseline in an environment of heightened expectations.

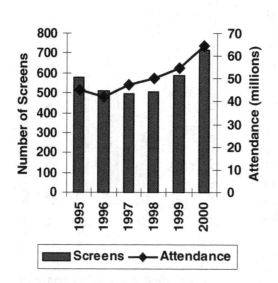

Since 1997, movie attendance and the number of movie screens in South Korea has grown (*source: Korean Film Commission*)

Another factor in the recent movie boom has been the growth in the country's movie screens, particularly through state-of-the-art multiplexes that feature stadium seating and digital sound systems. Similar to what happened during the Nineties in the United States and Canada, a theatrical building boom is helping to increase the capacity of the country's under-screened exhibition system, where moviegoers traditionally have to buy their tickets well in advance to avoid being confronted with the prospect of a sold-out show. Since 1996, the country's total number of screens has increased by 60%. Among the companies involved in the recent building boom include market leader CGV (which runs multiplexes with its business partners, Hong Kong's Golden Harvest and Australia's Village Roadshow), second-place Lotte Department Stores (which plans to have 100 screens in 10 theaters, all located within their stores, by 2003), and Megabox (which operates what is purported to be the largest movie theatre in Asia, which is located in a shopping mall in Seoul). In the spring of 2002, major studio Cinema Service threw its hat into the exhibition ring by announcing its plans to create its own chain of cinemas by the end of the year.

International Recognition and Expansion

In addition to finding critical and financial success at home, the films of this 'new wave' tapped the key element that catalyzed the phenomenal growth of Hong Kong's film industry during the Eighties and early Nineties-- international sales. Instead of being limited by the 600 screens of their native South Korea, filmmakers are reaching out to international audiences with more readily exportable films boasting pristine production values and more mainstream narratives. As an example of the explosive growth being enjoyed in the international market, total film exports grew 60% between 1999 and 2000 and 56% between 2000 and 2001, with its current level sitting just over $10 million US. So far, Japan, Hong Kong, and France have been the most receptive markets for Korean fare. However, some important in-roads are being made into the North American market, such as with theatrical releases (such as Im Kwon-taek's "Chunhyung" and Jacky Kang Je-gyu's "Shiri") and the selling of Hollywood remake rights (such as for Jo Jin-gyu's "My Wife is a Gangster" and Kwak Jae-young's "My Sassy Girl").

This international expansion has also been helped in part by the government of Kim dae-jung, which has supported a number of film festivals in Korea (such as the Pusan International Film Festival) where Korean filmmakers are given exposure to foreign buyers. In addition, Korean movie studios are increasingly entering into joint productions with foreign partners, such as from Hong Kong and Japan. Many of these co-productions involve leveraging film stars with broad pan-Asian appeal, such as Zhang Ziyi's ("Crouching Tiger, Hidden Dragon") appearance in historical epic "Musa" or Cecilia Cheung's ("Legend of Zu") appearance in the romance-drama "Failan".

Movie-mania Grips Investors

With Korea's homegrown film industry riding high in recent years, there is little difficulty for filmmakers to secure financing for their productions. In some respects, the funding environment in South Korea's film industry resembles the freewheeling days of the dot-com era, with venture capital firms and private investors lining up to get in on the action. As a testament to the investor fervor surrounding the country's film industry, the recent IPO by CJ Entertainment, a major film distributor, resulted in an initial doubling of the company's share price.

The more traditional players in the Korean film industry have been venture capital firms, who have been involved in funding productions since the *chaebols* began divesting during the Asian economic slump. Though a number of small venture capital funds have sprouted up since the start of the film investment boom, the biggest fish in this area are a number of established venture capital funds with billions of investments to their name, such as the privately held Korea Technology Bank, Terasource Venture Capital (which funded Lee Sung-gang's animated tale "My Beautiful Girl, Mari"), Unikorea (a relatively young firm that bankrolled Lee Chang-dong's "Peppermint Candy"), and Cinema Service (Korea's market leader in film financing and distribution).

However, the most unique financing tools to emerge during this latest 'Korean New Wave' are the so-called 'netizen funds'. Taking a concept that was developed during a 1999 film industry conference aimed at formulating new Internet-enabled marketing strategies, online start-up Intz.com created an online fund where anyone with an Internet connection could invest in upcoming films. For studios, these 'netizen funds' could be used to finance production and marketing activities, as well as encourage create greater consumer awareness and loyalty. Meanwhile, investors, in addition to earning a potentially lucrative return on their investment, could become an active participant in the excitement of the film industry.

The first film to benefit from a netizen fund was Kim Jee-woon's "The Foul King", which attracted 464 financiers and 101 million won ($77,500 US) of funds, with individual investments going as high as 2 million won ($1,500). When "The Foul King" was finally released in 2000, it became the fourth-highest grossing film that year, netting the private investors a 97% return on their investment.

Internet startups Simmani.com and Daum.net created yet another flavor of netizen funds by introducing free-market economics into the mix. In their models, investors buy 'shares' in a fund tied to a film property and are allowed to freely trade them on the open market. Once the fund reaches 'maturity', which is usually three months after the film's release on video, 'shareholders' are paid a return/loss on their investment based on the film's sales, which includes theatrical admissions, video rentals, and other ancillary sales. Among the films to have benefited from this 'stock market' model include the South Korean theatrical release of Wong Kar-wai's "In the Mood for Love" (which earned investors a 10% return) and Kwak Kyun-taek's "Friend" (which drew 190 investors and 100 million won within its first minute).

As the phenomenal returns of early netizen funding initiatives made headlines, public interest in this unique form of film financing escalated, as did the number of companies that joined the fray, creating an entirely new industry. By the end of 2001, this new speculative film investment market was estimated to comprise of 20 small-to-medium sized film investment associations with 90 billion won in investments, the Korean Film Commission with 30-40 billion won in investments, public film investment companies with another 30-40 billion won at stake, and the country's Ministry of Culture and Tourism and its 68.5 billion won in investments. In addition, the Ministry of Culture and Tourism has plans to up the ante in coming years by forming film investment associations worth 130 billion won every year to a total of 500 billion won by 2003.

Even banks have not been immune to the investor fervor over the film industry. At the tail end of 2001, Hana Bank, one of the country's top financial institutions, partnered with Cinema Service, a leading film distributor, to create the "Hana Cinema Trust Fund No. 1". This investment trust fund will raise 10 billion won by selling beneficiary certificates to individual investors, and then use the money to finance 10-15 film productions over a two-year period, creating returns for investors and an additional revenue stream for the bank in the form of percentage film profits.

Today, almost all major releases and a number of foreign imports make use of netizen funds in one way or another, and the practice is spreading to other areas of entertainment investment, such as for music and video games. However, like any speculative market, there has been a downside. While there have been a number of high-profile successes that have undoubtedly created unrealistically high expectations among would-be investors (such as Kim Sang-jin's "Kick the Moon" raising $150 million won in ten seconds of going to market), there have also been a number of failures, resulting in losses for investors, such as Oh Seung-ook's "Kilimanjaro" and Song Hae-seong's "Failan", and calls for more regulation. Thus, in the middle of 2001, the Korean government announced that its Financial Supervisory Service would start playing watchdog for all netizen funds.

Ready for the World

Since the first crests of the latest 'Korean New Wave' began washing ashore in the late 1990s, the South Korean film industry has been in a state of constant change. A new generation of Korean filmmakers, unconstrained by the government censorship that faced their predecessors, is being increasingly exposed to a receptive and growing audience, shattering box office records and expectations, both at home and abroad. This in turn has created a favorable climate for investment in the film industry, creating levels of investor fervor and market liquidity not seen since the halcyon days of dot-com mania. As a result, this potent concoction of renewed creative vigor, enthusiastic audience interest, and readily available financing has created a film industry on the verge of breaking out and fashioning its own unique identity on the world stage, not unlike what happened during the early Eighties in a former British colony known as Hong Kong.

Chapter 3: Korea's Latest Newest Wave

Over the last couple of chapters, you have seen how Korea's film industry has grown in fits in starts over the last century, with many of those years under the watchful eye of government censors. You have also seen how the relatively young country has struggled over the last five decades to create a working democracy, something that came to be in recent years. In addition, you have seen how the keys to success in Korea's film industry (new talent, top-notch infrastructure, eager investors, and enthusiastic audiences) have only come together in the past decade, laying the foundation for the latest 'Korean New Wave'.

All this then begs the question, "So what makes the films of this latest 'Korean New Wave' so special?" Indeed, why are they developing a loyal following around the world? Why are they creating buzz at whatever film festivals they appear in? And most interesting of all, why are Hollywood studios getting into bidding wars to emulate them?

In a nutshell, the magic qualities of the most recent batch of Korean films are their creativity, risk-taking, technical sophistication, and a unique cultural perspective. Aficionados of Asian cinema will note that these are the same qualities that were ascribed to Hong Kong films of the late Seventies and early Eighties (the 'Hong Kong New Wave') and even right on up into the early Nineties. It was these qualities that helped Hong Kong gain international recognition as a source of fresh and revolutionary filmmaking, and encouraged Hollywood studios to adopt their distinctive style into their own films.

Creativity

Though filmmakers of this latest 'Korean New Wave' have grown up with the films of Hollywood, Hong Kong, and other countries, they do not constrain themselves to telling the same tired stories, or rely on the same old well-tread clichés. Indeed, a number of filmmakers seem to go out of their way to break the rules as much as possible.

For example, Korean filmmakers seem quite content in mixing up elements from different genres to create unconventional takes on standard formulas. Given the affection of Koreans for melodrama (which, given the level of censorship filmmakers faced over the last century, was one of the few 'safe' genres), it is not surprising to find melodrama bolted into other genres. For example, Kim Jeong-kweon's "Ditto" and Lee Hyun-seung's "Il Mare" combine melodrama with science fiction (time travel), while Jacky Kang Je-gyu's box office behemoth "Shiri" creates a surprisingly good blend of melodrama with Jerry Bruckheimer-style pyrotechnics. However, Korea's filmmakers are not limiting themselves to melodrama when it comes to toying with genre—Kim Ji-woon's "The Quiet Family" mixes black comedy with straight-out horror, while Jo Jin-gyu's "My Wife is a Gangster" mixes 'fish out of water' humor with the other staple of Asian cinema, the gangland saga.

Even if filmmakers stay within the confines of a single genre, they end up making unforgettable films that bring a fresh perspective on what's been tried-and-true. For example, Hur Jin-ho's "Christmas in August" is for all intents and purposes a typical Korean melodrama, with the 'done to death' story of a hero is dying from a terminal illness. However, instead of the heavy-handed approach of lesser films, "Christmas in August" tells its story in a low-key manner, allowing the film's emotional pull come not from what the characters say, but what they don't say. The same could be said for Lee Jeong-hya's romantic comedy "Art Museum by the Zoo", which not only offers a more realistic perspective on budding romance, but also ends up mocking the genre.

Risk-taking

Hand-in-hand with creativity is the Korean filmmaker's flair for risk-taking. With many of the latest batch of filmmakers and film financiers belonging to a younger generation, it is not surprising to see their iconoclastic attitude spill out onto the screen. How else could films such as Bong Joon-ho's "Barking Dogs Never Bite" (a social satire where the protagonist does the unthinkable by killing a dog that is annoying him) or 1999's "Memento Mori" (lesbian drama meets ghost story) have been made?

And given the increased freedom of political expression in recent years, filmmakers are no longer afraid of tackling their own country's troubled history. For example, Lee Chang-dong's "Peppermint Candy" not only offers a harsh and uncompromising look at twenty years of recent South Korean history, but it also presents the material in an unconventional reverse chronological narrative. Meanwhile, other filmmakers are content on using the same newfound liberty to poke fun at their country's history and culture, such as Kim Sang-jin creates a microcosm of Korean culture in a gas station that is taken over by disaffected youths in "Attack the Gas Station!"

Technical Sophistication

On a less cerebral note, another striking aspect of the latest 'Korean New Wave' is the level of technical brilliance seen today. A combination of both the substantial investments made in film production infrastructure during the Nineties, as well as the fresh crop of visually oriented filmmakers (many of whom had earned their stripes in short films and overseas study), today's Korean films look, for lack of a better word, amazing.

From the live-action-meets-anime look of Lee Myung-se's actioner "Nowhere to Hide", to the urban sheen of Chang Yoon-hyun's "Tell Me Something", to the MTV-school-of-filmmaking exuberance of Kwak Kyung-Taek's gangland saga "Friend", South Korean films probably have the most striking visual dynamic in the world, on par with (or in some instances, even outdoing) the best that Hong Kong has to offer. Even South Korean moviegoers have noticed the difference in the current crop of films-- a survey conducted in 2001 found that 94.2% of those polled felt that the quality of homegrown films had improved over the last three to four years.

Korean filmmakers even have a gift in how they present snow on the big screen, accentuating scenes with the sedate image of big white fluffy flakes falling peacefully from the sky. "Shiri", Kim Sung-su's "Musa", and "Nowhere to Hide" are just some of the films that transform snow into a living, breathing 'character' on the screen.

Unique Cultural Perspective

During the mid-to-late Eighties, following the signing of the Sino-British Joint Declaration Agreement in 1984, a heavy cloud of uncertainty hung over Hong Kong. The British colony was to be handed back to Mainland China in 1997, and Hong Kong residents had mixed feelings in terms of how well the Chinese government would administer the promised 'one country, two systems'. Not surprisingly, this unease over the future had a profound effect on Hong Kong cinema during this period. A number of films preferred to bathe in the nostalgia of simpler times, triggering a resurgence in period dramas, such as Tsui Hark's "Peking Opera Blues" and Wong Kar Wai's "Days of Being Wild". In contrast, forward-looking films viewed the future with mistrust and cynicism, with a good example being John Woo's "A Better Tomorrow", where Chow Yun-Fat looks down at the neon-lit Hong Kong skyline and remarks, "I never realized Hong

Kong looked so good at night. Like most things, it won't last. That's for sure." Of course, the visions of doom-and-gloom only mushroomed following the events of Tiannamen Square in 1989, which galvanized the local film industry for a number of years with some decidedly anti-Mainland sentiments (witness Woo's "Bullet in the Head").

Like the filmmakers of Hong Kong's 'New Wave', South Korean filmmakers have not been immune to the social, cultural, and political forces that have shaped their lives. For example, the divided nature of the country has had a tremendous influence on filmmakers and the types of films that were made. Day-to-day realities of the ongoing Cold War (such as mandatory military service and spies invading from the North) and themes that speak to the divided nature of the country both figure heavily into the films produced since the end of the Korean War. Looking at the most recent batch of films to come out since the start of the latest 'Korean New Wave', quite a number either deal directly head on with the subject ("Shiri" and "Joint Security Area" for example) or make some reference to it (such as gags about the paranoia over North Korea spies in "The Quiet Family" or Shin Seung-soo's female road-trip comedy "A.F.R.I.K.A."). Furthermore, quite a number of romances deal with lovers having to overcome almost-impossible barriers to be together, such as the gender-bending love affair in Kim Dae-seung's "Bungee Jumping of Their Own", the geographical distance that separates the two main characters in E. J-yong's "Asako in Ruby Shoes", or any of the entries in the 'love across time' genre (see below).

Another remarkable influence has been the internal political upheaval that South Koreans have endured over the last few decades, as the country changed hands between successive military dictatorships before finally achieving a functioning democracy in 2000. Given that the South Korean people have made the painful transition from one political extreme to the other in the span of a single generation, it is not surprising that the country's filmmakers have been influenced by such upheaval. This is most apparent in what I dub the 'love across time' genre of South Korean melodrama.

Underlying the 'love across time' genre is the dichotomy between the lessons of the past and the understanding of the present, not unlike the themes addressed in the films of Hong Kong's Wong Kar-wai. All the characters in the genre's films struggle with trying to make sense of events in their past, which are often catastrophic, and using that knowledge to better understand themselves and their current circumstances. And like the growing pains experienced by South Korea over the last four decades, there is a realization that the trauma of past experience shapes and becomes an integral part of the individual (or a nation), wherein lies its acceptance. This perspective is readily demonstrated in the films of the genre, such as with Eun-joo (Jeon Ji-hyun) making sense of a broken relationship in Lee Hyun-seung's "Il Mare", or the dignity and comfort that Kang-jae (Choi Min-shik) finds in the letters from his late wife in Song Hae-sung's "Failan". And though these themes are most overt in the 'love across time' genre, they can also be readily seen in other films, such as the disintegration of Yong-ho (Sol Kyung-gu) in "Peppermint Candy".

The New Hong Kong

Though the hallmarks of the latest 'Korean New Wave' (creativity, risk-taking, technical sophistication, and a unique cultural perspective) lend themselves to the halcyon days of Hong Kong, today's South Korean cinema is carving out its own unique cinematic identity. Instead of being just another 'me too' by merely copying the groundbreaking efforts of their Hong Kong predecessors, South Korean filmmakers are advancing the art form with their own unique blend of daring and innovation, making today's Korean movies perhaps the most exciting development in world cinema since the Hong Kong 'New Wave'.

Chapter 4: Ten Korean Films Everyone Should See

Though the South Korean film industry only produces an average of 50 films per year, creating a list of the ten very best films of the newest 'Korean New Wave' was no easy task.

Unlike Hong Kong's film industry (or even Hollywood for that matter), the 'hit-miss' ratio for Korean cinema has been rather impressive over the last few years. The fact that homegrown films captured almost 50% of the domestic box office in 2001 is a testament to the emphasis of quality over quantity. In addition to whittling down a very short shortlist, another consideration was to pick films that would be accessible to non-Korean moviegoers, both in terms of being able to appreciate the material without having lived in Korea, and being able to actually watch the movies, such as via an English-subtitled all-region DVD release. Finally, in compiling the list, I tried to provide as wide a view into the diversity found within Korean film, choosing representative films across multiple genres, such as straight-out blockbusters, romantic comedies, horror, and even arthouse classics.

So, without further ado, here is a list of ten Korean films everyone should see. If you are not familiar with Korean cinema, watching these films will probably get you hooked. And if you are already a Korean movie aficionado, then your experience would be incomplete without having included these gems in your viewing repertoire:

Shiri (Swiri) - 1999

Starring: Han Suk-kyu, Choi Min-shik, Kim Yoon-jin, Song Kang-ho
Director: Jacky Kang Je-gyu
Availability: North American DVD, Hong Kong-import VCD, Korean-import DVD (multi-region)
Rating: ●●●●½

Shiri artwork (*Image courtesy of Samsung Pictures*)

No examination of the latest 'Korean New Wave' would be complete without a discussion of "Shiri", which marked an evolutionary turning point in South Korean cinema, heralding a move towards a more market-driven industry and the start of the Korean blockbuster era. Dubbed by the local press as the 'small fish that sank Titanic', "Shiri" was the most successful film in South Korean box office history in 1999 (though this record would eventually be eclipsed by "Joint Security Area" and "Friend" in subsequent years). With production values and visuals rivaling Hollywood action movies, the star power of popular Korean actors Han Suk-kyu and Choi Min-shik, and a story centered around the continuing Cold War tensions between North and South Korea, this espionage action-thriller has won audiences both at home and in international markets. In early 2002, "Shiri" enjoyed a limited theatrical run in the United States that eventually expanded to eleven theaters, as well as a subsequent DVD release in North America.

The film's prologue begins in 1992 at a training camp for assassins in the North Korean countryside. Using live ammunition and live targets, one soldier proves herself to be a superior killing machine, a young woman named Lee Bang-hee, who is promptly shipped off by her superior, Park (Choi) to take out political and military targets in South Korea. Fast-forward a few years later, and Bang-hee is still on the loose in South Korea, and the South Korean agents on her tail are Ryu (Han) and his partner Lee (Song Kang-ho). Unfortunately, Bang-hee's identity remains a mystery, since she has undergone plastic surgery to change her appearance.

However, Ryu and Lee have more pressing matters to attend to. Acting against orders from their own government, Park and a squad of North Korean commandos cross the border to steal a shipment of CTX, a powerful new explosive that is indistinguishable from water. The timing couldn't be worse, as the soccer teams of North and South Korea are about to partake in a symbolic game at the Seoul stadium, signaling a potential thaw in the long-running Cold War. To further complicate matters, the CTX heist brings Bang-hee out of hiding, whose superior sniping abilities wreak havoc on Ryu and Lee's attempts to foil Park's plans. In addition, it appears there is a leak within the South Korean intelligence service, which cause Ryu and Lee to suspect each other of being a double agent.

The film takes its name from a freshwater fish indigenous to the DMZ, the swath of land dividing Korea between the democratic South and the communist North. Like the fish which knows no borders or cares little for the rival ideologies on either side of the 38th parallel, writer/director Jacky Kang speaks to the hopes of reunification for his divided

Han Suk-kyu (*image courtesy of Samsung Pictures*)

country. Another reunification-minded fish-related symbol appears in the film in the form of *gourami*, the so-called 'kissing fish', which cannot live apart-- if one of a pair dies, the other follows suit soon after. Furthermore, according to marine biologists, the 'kissing' observed in the *gourami* is actually territorial behavior, mirroring the symbiotic yet adversarial relationship between the North and South. Kang even goes as far as portraying the North in a somewhat sympathetic light, as Park asks Ryu, "How can you, who grew up eating Coke and hamburgers, understand that your brothers in the North are starving?" This, of course, would have been unheard of a few years ago under South Korea's formerly draconian censorship laws. What is even more surprising is that despite the sympathetic tone towards the North, the South Korean military made "Shiri" required viewing for its troops, since its terrorist subject matter promoted the notion of eternal vigilance.

But aside from the political symbolism, the script for "Shiri" is a somewhat disappointing run-of-the-mill action-thriller, something not-too-far removed from the Jerry Bruckheimer school of filmmaking. Kang has studied the trappings of the American action movie to a fault, with its preponderance of terse and functional dialogue, unfunny comic relief characters, and overwrought 'ticking bomb' climax. And while Kang tries to add an emotional layer with a romantic subplot centered on Ryu and his fish store proprietor fiancée Hyun (Kim Yoon-jin), the poorly defined motivations he assigns to these characters ends up diminishing the emotional impact of the film's climax.

Choi Min-shik (*image courtesy of Samsung Pictures*)

That said, the film's action sequences are rather fun to watch. Though the film was made for a paltry $5 million U.S. (which is six times the typical budget for a typical Korean feature) and as a result, the production values, particularly in the action department, are top-notch. In order to bring such an ambitious project to life, both Kang and his two lead actors opted for Hollywood-type 'back-end deals', leaving more money up-front for the production itself, much of it can be seen on the screen. Fans of the Hong Kong 'SDU' action sub-genre will feel right at home, as there is plenty of hardware on display here, as the intrepid secret agents, North Korean terrorists, and dozens of MP5-carrying SWAT teams exchange blows in and around Seoul. Kang's cinematic action direction is more than competent, blending the 'hyper-reality' of Kirk Wong and the graceful slo-mo of John Woo in a number of memorable sequences. Highlights include a daring daylight heist of the CTX on a highway, a pitched exchange of gunfire through city streets, and the film's climactic and visually stunning showdown in Seoul stadium.

To its credit, "Shiri" boasts impressive action set pieces and production values that rival those of American action films. Unfortunately, it also suffers from a by-the-book script and half-baked characterizations that end up making it a 'fishy story'. But despite these shortcomings, "Shiri" will probably be remembered in the years to come as being one of the more influential works of the latest 'Korean New Wave', signaling when South Korean filmmakers finally learned how to compete on the world stage.

Joint Security Area (Gongdong Gyeongbi Guyeok JSA) - 2000

Starring: Song Kang-ho, Lee Young-ae, Lee Byung-heon, Kim Tae-woo, Shin Ha-kyun
Director: Park Chan-wook
Availability: Hong Kong-import VCD and DVD (multi-region), Korean-import DVD (multi-region)
Rating: ● ● ● ● ●

Lee Byung-heon, Lee Young-ae, and Song Kang-ho (*image courtesy of CJ Entertainment*)

If 1999's South Korean box office smash "Shiri" was dubbed by the local press as 'the little fish that sank Titanic', then "Joint Security Area" might as well be known as the blockbuster that ate "Shiri" for lunch. Within two weeks of its release during the fall of 2000, "Joint Security Area" took in one million admissions, a feat that had taken "Shiri" three weeks to accomplish, and went on to become the biggest box office draw in Korean history-- that is, until the gangland saga "Friend" bowed into theaters a few months later. And though it is not as action-oriented as "Shiri", "Joint Security Area" is an engaging and emotionally resonant military drama indicative of the continuing maturity of South Korean cinema.

Based on the Park Sang-yeon novel "DMZ", "Joint Security Area" centers on a modern-day cross-border incident between North and South Korea, specifically at the 'Bridge of No Return' in the middle of the Demilitarized Zone that separates the two countries. Swiss military officer Major Sophie Jang (Lee Young-ae), the daughter of a Korean expatriate and a Swiss mother, arrives in Panmumjeom, the village where the truce that ended the Korean War was negotiated and now serves as a neutral meeting place for both sides. Jang's assignment is to conduct an impartial investigation of the incident that has resulted in two deaths, and not surprisingly, both sides remain tight-lipped and treat her investigation with suspicion.

Based on the depositions filed by each side, two possible scenarios arise, which are told "Rashomon"-style. According to the South, South Korean Sgt. Lee Soo-hyeok (Lee Byeong-heon) was abducted by North Korean soldiers and dragged across the Bridge of No Return. During his escape, Lee killed two soldiers and wounded another. This runs counter to the account given by the wounded North Korean officer, Sgt. Oh Kyeong-pil (Song Kang-ho), who claims that Lee deliberately crossed the bridge and started a shooting spree.

As Jang's investigation develops, she uncovers evidence suggesting that neither account is correct, such as how the number of bullets recovered at the crime scene is inconsistent with the number fired by Lee. With the use of extended flashbacks, the truth about the incident, as well as the unlikely connection between sergeants Lee and Oh, gradually comes to light, revealing a tragedy borne of a divided country.

A tense standoff in the DMZ (*image courtesy of CJ Entertainment*)

One of the most striking aspects of "Joint Security Area" is its sumptuous cinematography, as it was the first Korea film to use the Super-35 format. This is most apparent in the flashback scenes, where director Park Chan-wook and cinematographer Kim Sung-bok (who also lensed "Shiri") have crafted a number of memorable scenes that drip in atmosphere, tension, and surprisingly, warmth, such as a night-time run-in between Lee and Oh amidst a field of billowing ferns and tall grass, or the well-staged firefight that ensues around Lee's escape. And though the story jumps back and forth between the past and present, Park's poised direction and technical prowess ensure that the transitions are not only eye-catching, but are also easily understood.

Though "Joint Security Area" may lack the firepower unleashed in "Shiri", it more than makes up for it with its compelling and emotionally resonant script. Like "Shiri", "Joint Security Area" offers complex North Korean characters and a tragic tale about a friendship doomed by the entrenched political distrust and fear that have divided Korea for almost fifty years. When the story finally comes full circle, revealing the truth about the shootings and the damage that it has wrought, the epiphany is devastating, which is best summed up in the poignant closing shot, a fleeting moment of friendship along the 38th parallel, forever frozen in time.

If there is a fault to be picked on, it would have to be the clumsy scenes conducted in English between Jang and her Swiss cohorts. Lee Young-ae's difficulties with the English language are readily apparent, which is both distracting and unintelligibly confusing (especially when she utters key expository dialogue). Likewise, the Swiss characters are occasionally difficult to understand with their thick accents and somewhat stilted line delivery. Thankfully, the Korean performances, including Lee's (who also has the distinction of playing a female character that is not a love interest in a Korean film), are much stronger. Lee Byeong-heon is convincing as a man torn by the truth, as is Kim Tae-woo, who plays his quiet but loyal sidekick. Shin Ha-kyun's turn as a North Korean soldier is also affecting, with the comic relief trappings of his character eventually giving way as he becomes the epicenter of the tragedy. However, the standout performance would have to go to Song Kang-ho, who demonstrates his considerable dramatic range as a North Korean soldier whose sense of duty and honor transcends all borders.

Song Kang-ho, Lee Byung-heon, and Shin Ha-kyun (*image courtesy of CJ Entertainment*)

"Joint Security Area" is one of the most expensive film productions in South Korean history, and it shows. In addition to the immaculate production values and lensing, Myung Film actually spent close to $1 million to build an almost-exact replica of the Panmunjeom to house the production. Despite its 'blockbuster' status and financial success, there is still a lot of heart in "Joint Security Area", making it one of the more memorable and moving films of the latest 'Korean New Wave'.

Friend (Chingu) - 2001

Starring: Yoo Oh-sung, Jang Dong-gun, Seo Tae-hwa, Jeong Un-taek
Director: Kwan Kyung-taek
Availability: Hong Kong-import VCD and DVD (multi-region), Korean-import DVD (multi-region)
Rating: ●●●●½

Friend poster (*image courtesy of Korea Pictures*)

Gangster movies are almost a dime-a-dozen in Asian cinema. A scan of the shelves of any Chinese video store will quickly net you at least two-dozen entries into the genre, such as the ever-popular "Young & Dangerous" franchise, the numerous offerings from Hong Kong über-producer Johnny To ("The Mission"), and even some parodies (such as "Jiang Hu: The Triad Zone"). It was this genre that gave Hong Kong auteurs John Woo (with "A Better Tomorrow") and Wong Kar-wai (with "As Tears Go By") their big breaks. And outside of Hong Kong, Japanese cinema icon Takeshi Kitano has built a huge international following with his own brand of blood-soaked gangland sagas, such as his recent "Brother".

Like Hong Kong and Japan, South Korean cinema is no stranger to the gangster genre, and one of the best examples from the peninsula would have to be "Friend", which currently holds the country's box office record. A semi-autobiographical look by director Kwak Kyung-taek at how four childhood friends take divergent paths in the criminal underworld as they grow up, "Friend" hits all the notes one would expect from the premise. However, what makes "Friend" a winner is the execution, where beautiful cinematography, a good script, and strong performances go hand-in-hand to create a stirring motion picture.

The story kicks off in 1976, where the main characters are introduced as trouble-making kids in the city of Pusan who spend their days exploring the wonders offered by something called a 'VCR', shoplifting, and making quick cash by selling pages out of Playboy magazines to their fellow students. The film then fast-forwards to 1981, when the kids are attending a local high school. Jeong-suk (Yoo Oh-sung), the son of a gangster, is at the top of the food chain at school, with the pugilistic Dong-su (Jang Dong-gun) as his loyal sidekick. Jeong-ho (Jeong Un-taek) is the clown of the group, while Sang-taek (Seo Tae-hwa) is the most diligent and quiet of the group (and the stand-in for the director).

At this point, it is clear that Jeong-suk places a high value on his friendship with Sang-taek, which leads to a fateful decision to defend Sang-taek from being beaten by a rival gang. As a result of the bloody brawl at a movie theater, Jeong-suk and Dong-su are expelled from school, driving them further into the triad world. Over the next decade, Jeong-ho and Sang-taek go to college

Yoo Oh-sung, Seo Tae-hwa, Jeong Un-taek, and Jang Dong-gun (*image courtesy of Korea Pictures*)

and become career professionals, while Jeong-suk and Dong-su split off into different gangs, eventually finding themselves on opposite ends of a gangland conflict, which leads to the ultimate test of their friendship.

If you have seen an Asian gangland saga before, then on the plot of "Friend" doesn't hold any surprises. However, director Kwak's distinctive visual style, which contrasts the warmth and camaraderie of their youth with the bleakness that greets them in adulthood, makes "Friend" a sumptuous feast for the eyes. From the MTV-school-of-filmmaking sequences (such as when the four friends race to see a movie after school), to the explosive fight sequences (such as the brawl that erupts at the theater), to the film's gravest moments (such as a bloody curbside assassination during the Nineties), "Friend" offers the viewer plenty of stirring and unforgettable images, aided by Choi Man-shik's pensive score.

In addition to the cavalcade of exquisitely shot set pieces, the smart script grounds the male melodrama in gritty reality and raw emotion, such as Jeong-suk's battle with drug addiction or the last meeting between Sang-taek and an imprisoned Jeong-suk, who tries very hard to hide his regret. The dialogue is also well written and injects some welcome humor into the proceedings, such as the four childhood friends conjecturing that VCRs will put television broadcasters out of business, or a stern teacher coming to the realization that the young man he administered corporal punishment to is indeed the son of a mob leader.

Finally, the performances are the last ingredient making "Friend" unforgettable, with Yoo and Jang the clear frontrunners. Those moviegoers only familiar with Yoo's comic turn in "Attack the Gas Station!" will be pleasantly surprised by the intensity and acting chops he displays here, and how well he is able to carry the picture on his own. Another terrific performance is turned in by Jang as the mercurial Dong-su, who ends up being consumed by his own ambition and blind sense of duty. Last, but not least, Seo and Dong are credible as the remaining members of the quartet, who are all but helpless to watch their former friends destroy one another.

Yoo Oh-sung (*image courtesy of Korea Pictures*)

Since its release in the spring of 2001, "Friend" has gone on to beat the box office records of both "Shiri" and "Joint Security Area", bringing in over 8 million admissions nationwide. In other words, it has probably been seen by at least 50% of the adults between the age of 18 and 35 in South Korea. With its nostalgic look back at twenty years of recent Korean history, it is not surprising that the film's biggest supporters have been men over the age of 30. However, with the rich story and handsome leads, "Friend" has also managed to snare the key demographic of female moviegoers below the age of 30, perhaps the largest consumers of cinema in the peninsula. "Friend" may have its roots in the done-to-death gangster genre, but in the capable hands of director Kwak Kyung-taek, the material cannot help but be fresh and compelling.

2009 Lost Memories (2009 Losteu memoreejeu) - 2002

Starring: Jang Dong-gun, Toru Nakamura, Seo Jin-ho
Director: Lee Si-myung
Availability: Korean-import DVD (multi-region)
Rating: •••

2009 Lost Memories poster (*image courtesy of CJ Entertainment*)

What if the Nazis had won the Second World War? What if the Roman Empire had not fallen in the fifth century, and continued flourishing well into the Middle Ages, or even into modern times? What if the Apollo program had never been able to land a man on the moon? These are the questions asked in the niche science fiction genre of 'alternate history', which delves into stories around historical 'what if?' scenarios and the possible political, social, and technological consequences.

Some entrants in the alternate history genre certainly contain overt science-fiction elements, such as Harry Turtledove's "Guns of the South", in which a time traveler returns to the year 1864 to give the Confederate Army a supply of AK-47s, thereby ensuring a Southern victory in the American Civil War. However, many other entrants into the genre contain no science fiction elements whatsoever, other than the story taking place in what could be considered an 'alternate universe', the staple of many a "Star Trek" episode. For example, Robert Sobel's "For Want of a Nail" details an alternate history of North America from 1777 to 1971 if the American Revolution had collapsed instead of succeeding, and Stephen Baxter's "Voyage" depicts the consequences on the American space program had John F. Kennedy not been assassinated in 1963.

Of course, alternate history stories have not been limited to only the printed word. Over the years, there has been a small trickle of films that delve into alternate history scenarios, with the most noteworthy being the chilling British independent production "It Happened Here" and the HBO television movie "Fatherland", both of which detail the ever-popular 'what if?' scenario of Nazi

Germany emerging victorious from the Second World War.

The latest entrant in this select group of films would be the 2002 Korean blockbuster "2009 Lost Memories", a decidedly more action-oriented take on the genre set in an alternate universe where Korea has become a permanent part of Japan. And though the over-the-top John Woo-style action does end up overwhelming the science fiction, this stimulating and slickly produced sci-fi flick is definitely a must-see.

The film's 1909 prologue begins in the Chinese city of Harbin with an attempt on the life of occupied Korea's Japanese governor, Ito Hirobumi. However, before Korean gunman Ahn Jung-geun is able to complete his task, he ends up being shot and killed by a Japanese soldier. As a result of the failed assassination, the next 100 years of history unfolds in a completely different

Jang Dong-gun (*image courtesy of CJ Entertainment*)

direction. Japan becomes an ally of the United States during the Second World War, which ends with the dropping of an atomic bomb on Berlin. As a result of the alliance with Western powers, Japanese expansion in Asia is unhindered, and Korea and Manchuria become permanent parts of a larger Japan.

The story then skips ahead to 2009. After 100 years of Japanese occupation, Seoul has become the third-largest city in Japan and native Koreans have become completely immersed into Japanese society, adopting Japanese surnames and using Japanese as the official language. A group of heavily armed pro-Korean independence terrorists calling themselves the Hureisenjin disrupt an exhibition of Korean antiquities and take hostages. The Japanese Bureau of Investigation (JBI) is called in, with top agents Masayuki Sakamoto (Jang Dong-gun) and Shojiro Saigo (Toru Nakamura) leading the charge. Though Sakamoto is Korean by blood, he follows his duties to the letter and assists his partner in quelling the disturbance.

In the aftermath of the attack, the initial investigation raises a number of questions, including what the true objective of the terrorists was. After some more digging, Sakamoto learns that the Hureisenjin have staged numerous attacks in the past on the historical society that hosted the exhibit, the Inoue Foundation, and that they were likely after an ancient stone artefact. Furthermore, he learns that the last assignment of his father, a disgraced cop who was subsequently killed for treason, was connected to a Hureisenjin attack in 1985.

Meanwhile, the Hureisenjin continue their attacks. While responding to an attack on an Inoue Foundation truck convoy, Sakamoto catches a glimpse of one of the terrorists, a woman named Oh Hye-rin (Seo Jin-ho), whom he recognizes from the recurring dreams that plague his sleep. Unfortunately, Sakamoto's investigation is cut short when his bosses in the JBI prevent him from digging deeper into the Inoue Foundation and its artefacts. In addition, some key data on previous Hureisenjin attacks has been erased, leading Sakamoto to suspect that there is a grand conspiracy at play. However, nothing can prepare him for the astonishing truth underlying the Hureisenjin actions and the JBI's interest in keeping things quiet.

Toru Nakamura and Jang Dong-gun
(*image courtesy of CJ Entertainment*)

It seems that in 2008, after the discovery of an ancient 'doorway through time', a right-wing Japanese group sent a man back into the past to stop Ito's assassination, thereby perverting history into a new timeline. It is the goal of the Hureisenjin to collect the necessary artefacts to reconstruct the time machine and return history to its proper trajectory-- a mission of monumental importance in which Sakamoto plays a key role.

"2009 Lost Memories" actually does spin its story from historical fact. Ito Hirobumi was a real Japanese politician who became the first resident general of Korea. In 1909, he was assassinated by Ahn Jung-geun after stepping off a train in Harbin, and this incident is the subject of the 1972 film "Uisa Ahn Jung-geun". The rest of the film's script, except for the occasional plot hole, also does a decent job of fleshing out its characters and establishing the fascinating setting of a Japan-dominated Korea.

The evolving relationship between Sakamoto and Saigo is well handled, as their friendship becomes increasingly strained by their displaced loyalties. While Sakamoto becomes increasingly disenchanted with his duties to the JBI after he realizes that he is little more than an errand boy for the Japanese, Saigo is increasingly motivated to preserve the history as he knows it-- if the proper timeline is restored, an atomic bomb will have been dropped on Nagasaki and his wife and daughter will have never existed.

Where the script does fall down is in the details about the ancient 'doorway through time'. Little explanation is provided in terms of exactly how it works, and even more distressing is the number of plot holes surrounding its use. Though the Japanese government is very aware of the artefacts and the Hureisenjin's intentions, they still allow them to be moved around the world for public display instead of being kept under high-security lockup. Furthermore, the recurring dreams that Sakamoto has, hinting at a previous involvement with Oh (perhaps 'lost memories' from the other timeline?) make little sense after the story has run its course.

It is also somewhat disappointing that the script did not explore the implications of restoring the proper timeline. Though the altered timeline does have Korea under Japanese rule, the original timeline (i.e., our history) has Korea being divided by war into the communist North and democratic South. It would have been nice to see the characters at least mull over the tradeoffs of their actions.

JBI forces move in on the Hureisenjin headquarters (*image courtesy of CJ Entertainment*)

In terms of action, "2009 Lost Memories" delivers the goods. The film's numerous action sequences are well choreographed, technically proficiently, and artfully directed. Fans of John Woo's 'Heroic Bloodshed' era of Hong Kong filmmaking will delight in how director Lee Si-myung executes the shootouts. One particular stunning sequence, in which JBI officers raid the secret headquarters of the Hureisenjin, uses the old Woo technique of counterpoint, where Sakamoto's witnessing of the JBI's ruthlessness is juxtaposed with Saigo celebrating a Japanese festival with his family. The action is also nicely complemented by Lee Dong-jun's evocative score, which calls to mind the rousing orchestrations of "Shiri" (which Lee also composed for) and Ridley Scott's "Gladiator", with a touch of the melancholy operatic compositions found in "Friend".

However, director Lee does on occasion stretch the credibility of the action sequences. During the film's more heartfelt moments, all of the bad guys shooting at Sakamoto tend to suddenly become bad shots, even if he is standing still out in the open. Another scene has the honor-bound Sakamoto and Saigo facing off in a bamboo forest, and though it may be beautiful to look at, it ends up looking a bit pretentious.

As the film's hero, Jang demonstrates his versatility as an actor. Despite most of the Sakamoto's dialogue being in Japanese, Jang effortlessly handles his lines with only a slight hint of a Korean accent. Furthermore, as he did in Yu Young-shik's "The Anarchists", Jang seems to be channelling Chow Yun-fat during the action sequences, demonstrating both confidence and poise. As Saigo, Nakamura is credible as the film's most balanced Japanese character in the film, a man who is torn between his friendship to Sakamoto, his duty to his homeland, and doing what he must to safeguard the lives of his wife and child. As Sakamoto's potential love interest, Seo acquits herself decently, though the script gives her character little to do. Fans of 1999 horror film "Memento Mori" will also recognize actress Kim Min-sun's cameo in the film's epilogue.

After being released in its native Korea, "2009 Lost Memories" became a big hit in the early part of 2002. It also ushered in the arrival of the 'year of the sci-fi blockbuster' in Korean cinema, paving the way for several other high-profile films (all of which have some sort of time-travel plot), such as Jang Sun-woo's "Resurrection of the Little Match Girl" and Jun Yun-soo's "Yesterday". Despite a few faults along the way, "2009 Lost Memories" ends up being an action-oriented science-fiction thriller with the right combination of visceral and narrative elements from Hong Kong actioners and Hollywood productions à la "The Terminator" and "Aliens". If Lee Si-myung can build on this impressive directorial debut, he may very well become South Korea's answer to James Cameron.

My Wife is a Gangster (Jopog manura) - 2001

Starring: Shin Eun-kyung, Park Sang-myun, Choe Eun-ju, Ahn Jae-mo, Kim In-gweon
Director: Jo Jin-gyu
Availability: Hong Kong-import VCD and DVD (Region 3), Korean-import DVD (multi-region)
Rating: ••••½

My Wife is a Gangster poster (*image courtesy of Korea Pictures*)

In the fall of 2001, as a testament to the growing international recognition of South Korean cinema, a box office hit on the peninsula caught the attention of several major Hollywood studios. Despite only being shown a print without any English subtitles, several studios initiated an intense bidding war for the film's U.S. remake rights. Within a few days, Miramax came out on top, having closed a deal worth almost $1 million U.S. for the remake rights, as well as $150,000 for U.S. distribution rights on the original film. Thus, "My Wife is a Gangster" became the first Korean film to ever be sold to a U.S. studio for a remake. And it is not difficult to see why it got Hollywood's attention: "My Wife is a Gangster" is a laugh-out-loud mix of hyper-kinetic Hong Kong-style martial arts and hilarious 'fish out of water' comedy that is not to be missed.

Meet Cha Eun-jin (Shin Eun-kyung), who is a bit of an anomaly in the Korean criminal underground. This scrappy 26-year old, orphaned and separated from her older sister when she was still a child, has fought her way up the food chain to become the leader of her own gang. Known in mob circles as Mantis, her skills in hand-to-hand and weapons combat are unsurpassed, and anyone who crosses her can expect a beating-- her own men included. Having grown up in such a male-dominated and violence-prone environment, Eun-jin has adopted a tomboy lifestyle, walking, talking, and dressing like a man.

However, this is all turned upside-down when Eun-jin finally is reunited with her long-lost sister (Choe Eun-ju). Unfortunately, she is dying from cancer and asks a favor of Eun-jin: to get married and settle down. So what does the legendary gang leader do? She sends out her men to find a husband for her as quickly as possible. Of course, this is easier said than done. Though they hire a professional to give Eun-jin a makeover and give her dating lessons, this ends up backfiring as she keeps lapsing back into gangster mode.

Finally, Eun-jin settles on Kang Su-il (Park Sang-myun), a civil servant who has no idea what is going on most of the time. Seeing Su-il as the quickest way to fulfill her sister's dying wish, Eun-jin gets hitched, which is when the fun really begins, as she tries to

Shin Eun-kyung and Park Sang-myun (*image courtesy of Korea Pictures*)

play housewife to the clueless Su-il while continuing to run her gangland operations. Unfortunately, matters are complicated as the leader of a rival gang tries to muscle in on Eun-jin's territory. And if that wasn't enough, the dying sister makes one more request: for Eun-jin to become a mother.

Imagine "Miss Congeniality" spliced with "The Godfather", with the fight sequences of "Charlie's Angels" thrown in, and you will have a pretty good idea what to expect in "My Wife is a Gangster". As the eternally stern-faced Eun-jin, Shin carries the film as a tough-as-nails mob boss trying to get in touch with her feminine side. The film's first half is a laugh riot as Eun-jin is faced with things that the mean streets of Seoul never taught her, such as how to wear high heels, how to go on a date, or what to do in bed. The script also pokes fun at the conventions of the male-dominated society in Korea, as Eun-jin is frequently mistaken as a gangster's moll and treated as such-- something that she doesn't take very well. As Eun-jin's unwitting husband, Park is the perfect comic foil for Shin. In addition to sharing some chemistry with his co-star, Park is sympathetic and lovably dumb as a man whose ideas about love and marriage are almost as naive as Eun-jin's.

The film's action sequences are also quite impressive, using flashy cinematography and wire-fu to punch up the fight scenes. Standout set pieces include the film's opening sequence, where Eun-jin takes on an entire gang in the pouring rain, a hillside knife duel laced with humor, and the film's final battle, where Eun-jin takes on an entire warehouse of her rivals.

However, "My Wife is a Gangster" is far from perfect. The film is most engaging when Eun-jin and Su-il are front and center. Unfortunately, director Jo Jin-gyu spends far too much time on the less-interesting antics of Eun-jin's lieutenants, such as Romeo (Ahn Jae-mo) and the dim-witted Boxers (Kim In-gweon), who like to pick fights, and not enough on the more interesting ones,

Hyperkinetic martial arts dominate in My Wife is a Gangster (*image courtesy of Korea Pictures*)

such as a steel-plated thug (Shim Weon-cheol) who secretly holds a flame for his Eun-jin. With this in mind, a tighter script could have easily excised fifteen minutes from the film's somewhat sluggish second half without sacrificing the main story. Also, as in many Hong Kong films, the line between comedy and bloody action is sometimes very thin in this film, such as in the aforementioned final battle, which may make some viewers uncomfortable with how it brutalizes Eun-jin.

It will be interesting to see what Miramax does with the remake ("The Godmother", maybe?), given how the original film is deeply rooted in Korean culture and Asian gangster genre films. However, until that day, assuming that it doesn't fall into development hell, there's always the original "My Wife is a Gangster". Despite a few flaws, this comic gem is a refreshing and thoroughly enjoyable romp from start to finish.

Attack the Gas Station! (Chuyuso supgyuk sa keun) - 1999

Starring: Lee Sung-jae, Yoo Oh-sung, Kang Seong-jin, Yoo Ji-tae, Park Yeong-gyu, Jeong Jun, Lee Yu-won
Director: Kim Sang-jin
Availability: Hong Kong-import VCD and DVD (multi-region), Korean-import DVD (multi-region)
Rating: • • • •

Attack the Gas Station! poster (*image courtesy of Cinema Service*)

Directed by Kim Sang-jin, this wicked comedy went on to become a national phenomenon among South Korean students in 1999, making it the second-highest grossing film at the box office that year (right behind "Shiri"). With its subversive script brought to life by Kim's giddy and exuberant direction, "Attack the Gas Station!" is a wonderfully absurd take on modern life in South Korea.

The story begins with four juvenile delinquents trashing and robbing a gas station, leaving the manager (Park Yeong-gyu, who would later parody this role in 2002's "A.F.R.I.K.A.") and his teenage staff shaken. Out of sheer boredom, they return to the gas station the following night, only to find themselves thwarted by the manager, who has given the money to his wife to deposit in the bank. Without a clue about what to do next, the four youths decide to hold the gas station employees hostage, and under the direction of their leader (Lee Sung-jae), they start running the gas station themselves, collecting the cash from the customers who stop in.

However, over the course of the night, the quartet gradually finds themselves in increasingly absurd situations as the social order of this microcosm is increasingly turned on its ear. The requests by the gas station manager for preferential treatment (simply because of his status as a 'manager') fall on deaf ears with the hostage-takers, and he is quick to accuse his high school employees for instigating the siege. The high schoolers, recognizing that their boss is no longer the voice of authority, subsequently turn on him. Meanwhile, the delinquents have a field day insulting and overcharging the well-heeled customers that drop in through the night-- those who don't pay up are either locked in their trunks or thrown in with the rest of the hostages. When some local toughs come to extort money from one of the gas station employees, they also find themselves taken hostage. And when the would-be hostage-takers refuse to pay for some Chinese take-out, they evoke the ire of a delivery boy who decides to teach them a lesson. This then sets off a chain-reaction that results in a full-scale riot involving local gangsters, a cadre of delivery boys, and the police, a conflagration that threatens to destroy the entire neighborhood.

Filmed with the exuberance of Doug Liman's "Go" and Guy Ritchie's "Lock, Stock, and Two Smoking Barrels", "Attack the Gas Station!" gleefully pokes fun at the social and political mores of contemporary South Korean society. Similar to the point made by Goran Paskaljevic's "Cabaret Balkan",

All hell breaks loose in Attack the Gas Station!
(image courtesy of Cinema Service)

which condensed the dynamics of the Balkan wars into one night in Belgrade, "Attack the Gas Station!" satirizes how the rigid social strata of modern South Korea has contributed to the country's recent turmoil. True to recent history, the most volatile elements in the film are the students and the blue-collar workers (represented by the delivery boys), who have traditionally been the most active and fanatical proponents of reform in Korean society. Another interesting aspect is how the film illustrates the dynamics of power in the country's troubled history, as allegiances and power bases among the hostages and their captors shift as different characters enter and leave the room.

With its surprise-filled script, off-the-wall black humor, terrific production values, and top-notch comic performances from its cast, "Attack the Gas Station!" is a film that will get you pumped.

Christmas in August (Palwol ui Christmas) - 1998

Starring: Han Suk-kyu, Shim Eun-ha, Goo Shin, Oh Ji-hye, Lee Han-wi
Director: Hur Jin-ho
Availability: Hong Kong-import VCD and DVD (multi-region), Korean-import DVD (multi-region)
Rating: ●●●½

Christmas in August poster (*image courtesy of Mirovision*)

Han-Suk-kyu and Shim Eun-ha are probably the most recognized film stars of the latest 'Korean New Wave'. Considered the 'Tom Cruise' and 'Julia Roberts' of South Korean cinema, their films have consistently performed at the box office, and their most recent collaboration, Chang Yoon-hyun's "Tell Me Something", was the third-highest grossing film of 1999 (behind "Shiri" and "Attack the Gas Station!"). However, the film that they are probably best remembered for is Hur Jin-ho's impressive debut from 1998, "Christmas in August".

The plot of "Christmas in August" is simple: photo shop proprietor Jung-won (Han Suk-kyu) is terminally ill, a fact that he has only shared with his father (Goo Shin) and sister (Oh Ji-hye), and none of his closest friends. Preferring to spend his remaining days in his store to bide his time, his life (or more exactly, what is left of it) takes an unexpected turn when Da-rim (Shim Eun-ha), a comely meter maid, becomes a regular customer. Da-rim also finds herself attracted to Jung-won, and she is gradually able to coax the quiet but kind shopkeeper out of his shell. Though Jung-won is appreciative of Da-rim's very forward advances and finds comfort in her company, he never expresses the amorous feelings he has for her. And perhaps out of a misguided desire to spare Da-rim's emotions, Jung-won also does not let Da-rim know about his condition nor what little time he does have left.

While the 'terminal illness' angle in the romance genre has literally been done to death, first-time director Hur Jin-Ho traverses this well-tread territory in a refreshingly understated manner in "Christmas in August". Instead of the heavy-handed and melodramatic schmaltz found in films such as "Autumn in New York" or "Sweet November", Hur uses a low-key approach akin to Wong Kar-wai's "In the Mood for Love", where the film's emotional resonance stems not from what the characters say, but what they do not say. Though Jung-won seems to have accepted the inevitable, he lacks the courage to reveal the truth to his friends and loved ones (especially Da-rim). This internal conflict and the tension it creates, underscores the entire film, giving the ending an uncommon level of poignancy.

In the film's earlier scenes, Han's portrayal of Jung-won as a seemingly happy-go-lucky protagonist may mislead some viewers into questioning the veteran actor's thesping abilities, as it seems that his character in a perpetually good mood, laughing everything off. However, as more is revealed about him, it is apparent that this jovial demeanor is Jung-won's 'defense

Shim Eun-ha and Han Suk-kyu (*image courtesy of Mirovision*)

mechanism', disguising the difficult truth about his condition from others...and himself. Despite his inner turmoil and inability to share his innermost thoughts with others, there is a quiet dignity in how Han portrays Jung-won, from the mundane details of his daily routine to the film's weightier moments. Without the benefit of dialogue, Han is able to speak volumes with the subtlest of facial expressions, such as in what may be the film's most powerful moment, when he expresses his heartfelt affection for Da-rim while watching from afar.

Complementing Han's performance is Shim's award-winning portrayal of Da-rim. There is an earnest quality to her performance, and like her co-star, much of it relies on the subtlety of expression and non-verbal cues. From her initial appearance as a demanding customer, to her growing intimacy with Jung-won, and finally to her heartbreak as Jung-won's lack of courage gets the better of him, Shim is an integral component of the story's emotional core, as well as part of the film's ultimate tragedy.

In addition to developing a strong following at the South Korean box office, "Christmas in August" swept the Korean Film Awards in 1998, landing Best Film, Director, Actress, and Cinematography, all well deserved. This is a singular romance in which no one actually says, "I love you" or displays any other such overt signs of affection, yet the emotional undercurrent is no less stirring.

Failan (Pairan) - 2001

Starring: Choi Min-shik, Cecilia Cheung, Son Byeong-ho, Kong Hyeong-jin
Director: Song Hae-seong
Availability: Hong Kong-import VCD and DVD (multi-region), Korean-import DVD (multi-region)
Rating: ● ● ● ● ●

Failan poster (*image courtesy of Tube Entertainment*)

Whether you are talking about the high art of "Shakespeare in Love" or the banality of "She's All That", the emotional peak in your typical romance comes when the heroes meet face-to-face, declaring their undying love for one another in the shadow of the insurmountable challenges that threaten to tear them apart. However, what happens when you have a romance in which the protagonists never actually meet? Can the same level of emotional intensity be achieved? Well, if the South Korean-Chinese co-production "Failan" from 2001 is any indication, the answer is undoubtedly 'yes'. Not only does "Failan" brilliantly pull off the conceit of crafting a romance between two characters without even a single shared conversation, but it does it so well that it will make even the most cynical of moviegoers weepy-eyed.

The film starts off as what appears to be yet another gangland saga, one that is centered on Kang-jae (played by popular actor Choi Min-shik), a slovenly small-time hoodlum based in Inchon. Though he acts and talks tough, it quickly becomes obvious that his bark is far worse than his bite-- he is easily beaten back by an old lady while trying to collect protection money, and is considered to be a joke by his fellow gang members. Even his long-time 'friend' and boss, ruthless gang leader Yong-shik (Son Byeong-ho) complains that he is 'too soft' to be 'in the business'. Unfortunately, it seems that his only shot at redemption is to take the fall for Yong-shik, who has murdered a rival gang member, by going to jail for ten years. In return, not only will he earn the respect of his peers, but he will also have enough money to buy the fishing boat he has been dreaming about.

With few prospects and even less dignity, Kang-jae decides to do the time.

However, before he can turn himself in, the police notify him that his wife, Kang Failan (Hong Kong actress Cecilia Cheung), has just died, requiring him to head out of town to claim the body. The film then jumps back one year, where we see the arrival of Failan in South Korea from Mainland China. She has come to live with her aunt following the death of her mother, but she soon learns that her aunt had emigrated to Canada two years prior. Penniless and alone in a strange land, Failan heads to a local employment agency, but because of her tourist visa, she is not allowed to work.

Desperate, Failan agrees to a paper marriage to Kang-jae, whom she has never met, which allows her to stay in the country and work. In return, Kang-jae makes some quick cash and the local triads have a new source of revenue. After a close call with Korea's sex trade, Failan eventually settles in a seaside town as a laundress. Despite her long working hours, she remains

Cecilia Cheung (*image courtesy of Tube Entertainment*)

ever appreciative of her marriage to Kang-jae, and eventually falls in love with him because of this singular act of 'kindness'. Meanwhile, in the present, as Kang-jae makes his way to claim Failan's body, he slowly learns about the woman he 'married' and quickly forgot about-- her struggles, her loneliness, her illness, and the feelings she had for him.

Choi Min-shik (*image courtesy of Tube Entertainment*)

"Failan" is the sophomore feature of director Song Hae-seong, who made a splash in 1999 with another time-twisting romance, "Calla". This time around, working with acclaimed Japanese novelist Jiro Asada and his best-selling novel "Love Letter" (which had been previously made into a memorable Japanese film in 1995), Song has created a stirring romantic tragedy with an emotional wallop that is not easily shaken. Executed with the same quiet subtlety seen in other contemporary Korean romances, "Failan" poignantly and convincingly illustrates the tragic missed opportunity between its two star-crossed lovers, while eloquently dissecting what it means, and how it feels, to be in love. Despite having never met, they end up giving each other the dignity and self-respect that their lives had been missing for so long. Unfortunately, the realization of what he meant to Failan comes to Kang-jae comes too late, leading to the film's most heartbreaking scene, which is compounded by the irony of how she treasured what he quickly forgot or cast off.

Cecilia Cheung (*image courtesy of Tube Entertainment*)

As the film's titular character, Cheung easily does the best work of her career. Though her Mandarin is sloppy, and she occasionally lapses into Cantonese for no apparent reason, her sympathetic turn as the quiet Failan is a marvel to watch. Up until now, after having seen her 'act' in Hong Kong films such as "Legend of Zu" and "Shaolin Soccer", I had never considered Cheung a serious actress. But all that changed with "Failan" as she breathed life into the story's tragic heroine, particularly with two of the film's more memorable sequences: Failan using quick-thinking to avoid being sold to a strip club, and her heart-wrenching first night at her new home. It is also easy to see why Choi, as Cheung's love interest, is one of Korea's most popular actors. Despite his character's slovenly appearance and boorish behavior, Choi evokes sympathy for Kang-jae with a measured performance that reveals the man's insecurity and gentle spirit.

Having won the hearts of critics both at home and abroad (including at the 2001 Cannes Film Festival), "Failan" has developed quite a large following in a very short time, having taken a relatively simple story and gently woven an unforgettable emotional experience of unparalleled depth and power.

My Sassy Girl (Yeopgijeogin geunyeo) - 2001

Starring: Jeon Ji-hyun, Cha Tae-hyeon
Director: Kwak Jae-yong
Availability: Hong Kong-import VCD and DVD (Region 3), Korean import DVD (Region 3)
Rating: • • • • •

My Sassy Girl poster (*image courtesy of Mirovision*)

During the summer of 2001, South Korean moviegoers went crazy for the romantic comedy "My Sassy Girl". By year's end, it had become the second-highest grossing film for 2001 (just behind the gangland saga "Friend"), and had earned a place in the record books as the highest grossing homegrown comedy in the country's box office history. In February of 2002, Dreamworks SKG negotiated the U.S. remake rights for the film, joining "My Wife is a Gangster" and "Hi, Dharma" in being the very first Korean films to be picked up by Hollywood for transplantation purposes. With its easy yet unpredictable blend of laugh-out-loud broad comedy, metaphysical romance, and fun characters, "My Sassy Girl" can easily be included among the best that Korean cinema has to offer.

"My Sassy Girl" is based on an on-line serial written by Kim Ho-sik that detailed his relationship with his off-the-wall college girlfriend. This was eventually compiled into a best-selling book and caught the attention of director Kwak Jae-young, who wrote the script for the film. The story kicks off with college student Kyun-woo (Korean pop singer Cha Tae-hyun, in his feature film debut) crossing paths

Cha Tae-hyeon and Jeon Ji-hyun
(*image courtesy of Mirovision*)

with a drunk girl (Jeon Ji-hyun) on a late-night subway. Just before she passes out, the girl looks at Kyun-woo and calls him 'honey'. The other passengers, assuming him to be the hapless girl's boyfriend, demand that Kyun-woo look after her. After carrying her on his back for what seems to be miles, Kyun-woo drops the girl off at a motel. But instead of leaving her and getting on his way, Kyun-woo finds himself intrigued by the nameless girl and vows to do whatever he can to heal her sorrow.

Unfortunately, he gets far more than he bargained as he becomes wrapped around the finger of this strange girl, whose dramatic mood swings are outmatched only by her penchant for sociopathic behavior. When they dine out and Kyung-woo orders anything but coffee, she barks her mantra "Do you wanna die?" and then promptly changes his order to coffee. When her feet begin aching from walking, she forces Kyung-woo to switch his comfortable running shoes for her high heels. And being a budding screenwriter, she demands that Kyung-woo read her wacky treatments, or suffer an ass kicking. However, despite these crazy antics (not to mention landing in jail a few times), Kyun-woo finds himself hopelessly hooked on this 'sassy girl'. And though the girl seems to relish in humiliating and belittling those around her, it becomes clear that underneath the brash exterior is a wounded soul who holds a genuine affection for Kyun-woo.

This cleverly scripted comedy covers a lot of territory in its two-hour running time, containing enough material for at least two movies. The film's first half (a fact that is irreverently highlighted with a big bold pastel-colored title) deals with Kyung-woo's initial misadventures with the 'sassy girl' and the absurdity he faces in her company. In addition to the obvious comic set-pieces revolving around the girl's anti-social tendencies, Kwak has some fun visualizing her female-centered film

Cha Tae-hyeon and Jeon Ji-hyun (*image courtesy of Mirovision*)

treatments, such as "Demolition Terminator", featuring a female warrior from the future gunning down bad guys à la "The Matrix", or a martial arts drama that mocks Wong Kar-wai's "Ashes of Time". Another great gag has Kyung-woo being instructed to drop off her treatment at Shin Cine (the production company behind "My Sassy Girl") and making the suggestion that box office draws Han

Suk-yu and Shim Eun-ha ("Christmas in August", "Tell Me Something") be cast in the lead roles.

However, as the film moves into its second half (declared with more pastel-colored lettering) and even overtime (check), the bottled-up emotions and vulnerable side of the 'sassy girl' start to reveal themselves, and the film moves into more melodramatic territory, reflecting the growing maturity of the two lead characters. The film even takes a riff from the ever-popular 'love across time' genre (which includes "Failan") as the would-be lovers spend some time apart and are reunited by an unexpected and clever plot twist. Despite the more serious mood of this latter half, Kwak manages to avoid the melancholic overkill that permeates the typical Korean romance, while still providing a strong emotional footing for the story.

Cha Tae-hyeon and Jeon Ji-hyun
(*image courtesy of Mirovision*)

If there is one really good reason to watch "My Sassy Girl", it would have to be Jeon Ji-hyun's turn as the film's unnamed heroine. From her unforgettable first appearance as a wasted commuter, to her rambunctious bullying of Kyun-woo, to the heartbreak she wears on her sleeve, Jeon displays an unparalleled level of enthusiasm and dramatic range in portraying a young woman whose domineering exterior is but a smokescreen for her own vulnerability-- it is almost difficult to believe that this same actress who played the quiet and introspective Kim Eun-ju in "Il Mare". As her opposite, the likable Cha Tae-hyeon is the perfect comic foil/underdog for Jeon's bundle of untamed energy, and his 'constipated' facial expression, when faced with one of her 'outbursts', is priceless.

Like the best Korean films, "My Sassy Girl" is a genre-bending exercise that throws in elements of the teen comedy, the traditional melodramatic romance, and even some genre parody and blends them into a unique cinematic experience that defies categorization. The film's original Korean title, Yeopgi, which means 'novelty-seeking', is in reference to the youth craze that was started by Kim Ho-sik's original Internet postings about his eccentric girlfriend. Though the English title for this film doesn't mean quite the same thing, it certainly does convey what to expect.

Peppermint Candy (Bakha satang) - 2000

Starring: Sol Kyung-gu, Mun So-ri, Kim Yeo-jin, Jung suh
Director: Lee Chang-dong
Availability: Korean-import DVD (multi-region)
Rating: ●●●●½

Peppermint Candy poster (*image courtesy of Shindo*)

Similar to Christopher Nolan's mind-bending indie hit "Memento", the 2000 South Korean film "Peppermint Candy" starts at the end of the story, and gradually works its way back to the beginning. However, whereas "Memento" was a revenge thriller spanning a mere two weeks, the ambitious canvas of "Peppermint Candy" covers two decades of recent South Korean history, with its contemplative and poignant tale of innocence lost, echoing the social, political, and economic turmoil of a nation's arduous climb to democracy. Of all the films to have sprung from the recent renaissance in Korean cinema, "Peppermint Candy" is perhaps one of the more substantial ones, easily making this South Korean-Japanese co-production a modern classic.

The 'ending' of the story begins in the spring of 1999, where a group of former high school friends gather at a riverbank for a 20-year reunion picnic. A well-dressed but emotionally erratic man wanders into the sedate setting, whom the picnickers recognize as Yongho (Sol Kyung-gu), a member that they had lost contact with long ago. Unfortunately, before they can catch up on old times, Yongho climbs onto a railroad bridge, seemingly with the intention to jump. In the last few seconds of his life, just before he is hit by an approaching train, Yongho defiantly declares, "I'm going back!"...

... which he does, in a way, as the story jumps back three days before, filling in the holes as to who Yongho is and why he ends up killing himself. Unfortunately, Yongho is not in much better shape-- he has lost all his money to a stockbroker, he is heavily in debt with a loan shark, and his wife has left him. With his last bit of savings, he has purchased a handgun to put himself out of his own misery. However, before he can do so, he learns that his first true love, Sunim (Mun So-ri), is on her deathbed, and he has been asked to see her one last time.

The story then continues to jump back through time, gradually revealing more about Yongho, his relationship with Sunim, and the circumstances that end up unraveling the tapestry of his life. As the story moves back through Yongho's life, director Lee Chang-dong segues each segment with footage of a train moving backwards. In addition, the action of each segment prominently features railroad tracks and a passing train in the background, emphasizing that each of these vignettes comprise the same thread of history, permanently linking Yongho's past with his destiny.

The next stop is 1994, where we find Yongho juggling his small business, his unhappy marriage to Hongja (Kim Yejin), and an affair with his one of his employees. A chance meeting in a restaurant, where Yongho runs into a figure from his past, then leads into the film's next sequence, set in 1987. In this time period, Yongho is a policeman who is willing to use any means necessary, including

Sol Kyung-gu (*image courtesy of Shindo*)

torture, to extract confessions from government dissidents. In addition, Hongja is pregnant with their daughter, and it is already apparent that the seeds for the marriage's dissolution have already been sown. When we catch up with Yongho in 1984, he is a rookie cop who ends up being traumatized when he beats his first confession out of a suspect. But the defining moment for Yongho comes in 1980, when as a soldier, his unit is called on to quell a civil disturbance and he ends up accidentally shooting an innocent bystander.

When the film reaches its end at the beginning of the story, the year is 1979 and the setting is the same riverbank seen at the beginning of the film. The picnickers are twenty years younger, and among them are Yongho, a young man full of hope and innocence who aspires to be a photographer one day, and the love of his life Sunim. Unfortunately, because of what has come before this, we know that none of his dreams will come true, the love of his life will slip through his fingers, and he will end up a tragic figure, lonely and heartbroken on the same riverbank twenty years later.

In many respects, "Peppermint Candy" has much in common with "Forrest Gump". Similar to how the titular protagonist of the 1994 Robert Zemeckis film was a stand-in for the American people and his adventures through history reflecting the experiences of the Baby Boomer generation, Yongho is a stand-in for the South Korean people, with his degradation and despair a reflection of the country's long uphill climb towards democracy.

The most important turning point in the development of Yongho's character, when he accidentally shoots a student on her way home, is set against the backdrop of the Kwangju Massacre. This important landmark in the South Korean democratic movement, in which a clash between government troops and student pro-democracy demonstrators resulted in 200 dead (mostly civilians), was a specter that would haunt Korean politics for the next two decades.

During much of the Eighties, we see Yongho's character being hardened by the brutal tactics employed by the police. Similarly, the Eighties were a turbulent period for South Korea under the leadership of General Chun Doo Hwan, whose iron-fisted regime kept the country in a state of martial law and blocked all efforts towards constitutional reform.

Finally, in the Nineties, we see a battle-scarred Yongho initially riding the wave of economic expansion brought about by the new constitution of 1988, only to come crashing down during the economic crisis of 1997, when investors abandoned the debt-ridden South Korean economy, the currency rapidly depreciated, and the country was ravaged by soaring unemployment and bankruptcies.

However, even if one does not have a passing knowledge of South Korean politics, "Peppermint Candy" is still a compelling film with its stirring portrayal of a man's disintegration. With his moving portrayal of Yongho, Sol exhibits tremendous dramatic range, from the film's opening scenes, as an unsympathetic and volatile boor, to the very end, as a poignant and tragic figure whose dreams will never come true. Given his unsavory introduction, as well as a number of scenes that underscore his volatility (such as how his temper ruins a celebratory get-together with friends), there is a constant threat of Yongho exploding in violence at any time, which brings an added level of tension to the film.

Regardless of whether "Peppermint Candy" is viewed from a personal or political angle, there is little doubt that director Lee Chang Dong has created a modern masterpiece. With a well-crafted narrative structure and the brooding performance of Sol Kyung-gu, "Peppermint Candy" is a bittersweet confection that illustrates how the innocence and optimism of youth can end up crushed under the relentless march of time, the travails of happenstance, and the frailties of the human heart.

Chapter 5: Gangsters, Guns, and Girls – Action Films

Elements of Hong Kong action cinema are quite prevalent in Korean action films, such as the dominance of films involving gangsters, the artistic use of gunplay, and acrobatic martial arts sequences. However, instead of South Korea's actioners merely being 'best of Hong Kong cinema' film clips, Korean directors take these traditional elements and 'genrebend' them into new directions. For example, "Guns & Talks" takes the 'hired killers' subgenre and spins a humorous tale about a band of four assassins with a soft side, "No Blood No Tears" is a Guy Ritchie-style caper flick with two women knee-deep in double-crosses, while "Volcano High" takes "Crouching Tiger, Hidden Dragon"-style martial arts and sets it in a high school. And then there is the mother-of-all-genrebenders, "Nowhere to Hide", which combines the visual sensibilities of anime, police-procedural plotting, John Woo-inspired action sequences, and "Three Stooges" antics into an exhilirating arthouse actioner.

But regardless of what your action preferences are, the diverse range of Korean action films will likely suit any taste. Whether you prefer the swordplay of *wu shu* epics à la "Musa" and "Bichunmoo", enjoy firefighting epics such as "Libera Me" or "The Siren", or like to kick back with the mindless destruction of monster movies as in "Yonggary", there are plenty of films to appease the action maven in the latest 'Korean New Wave'.

Guns & Talks (Killerdeului suda) - 2001

Starring: Shin Hyun-june, Shin Ha-kyun, Chung Jae-young, Won Bin, Jeong Jin-young
Director: Jang Jin
Availability: Hong Kong-import VCD and DVD (multi-region), Korean-import DVD (Region 3 only)
Rating: ●●●●½

Guns & Talks poster (*image courtesy of Cinema Service*)

Since the departure of John Woo from Hong Kong in the early Nineties, there has been a dearth of interesting (let alone intelligent) films in the 'hired killers' subgenre of Hong Kong action films. True, there have been a few interesting entries over the years, such as Patrick Leung's "Beyond Hypothermia" from 1996 or Wong Kar-wai's 1995 arthouse favorite "Fallen Angels". However, similar to the overall decline in quality that has afflicted Hong Kong filmmaking over the past decade, the 'hired killers' sub-genre has literally been done to death, particularly by the producing team of Johnny To and Wai Ka-fai, who were responsible for 2001's unforgivable "Full-time Killer", an incomprehensibly pretentious blend of "Assassins" and "Moulin Rouge" (yes, really). That said, it should be of little surprise that perhaps one of the most refreshing entries in this long-standing Hong Kong action subgenre ends up being a film from South Korea. Though "Guns & Talks" from 2001 is far from perfect (particularly with its unbelievably cheerful conclusion), it possesses enough wit and charm to make it a must-have for any Hong Kong action fan.

"Guns & Talks" revolves around four young professional killers. Sang-yeon (Shin Hyun-june) is the leader, Jung-woo (Shin Ha-kyun) is the demolitions expert, Jae-young (Chung Jae-young) is the resident sniper, while Sang-yeon's younger brother Ha-yeon (Won Bin) eagerly awaits the day when he is allowed to carry a gun. The foursome work out of their shared house, and their claim to fame is following the wishes of their clients down to the very last detail-- if the client only wants someone's left hand blown off, they will do it, no questions asked.

Despite their cold-blooded work, they are actually quite harmless and congenial when they are not being assassins. In addition, for all things not work-related, they are pretty dense (one telltale scene has the quartet misinterpreting the English warning "I will never miss you" as "I am never Miss Yu"). This, of course, in addition to contributing to their charm, leads to some absurd situations. They find themselves harassed by a high-school girl who knows their true identity and insists that they kill someone who broke her heart-- Ha-yeon eventually falls for her. Jae-young is given the distasteful task of killing a pregnant woman, though he finds himself incapable of going through with it when he begins falling in love with his intended target. Meanwhile, Sang-yeon accepts a risky job from a pretty television anchorwoman (Ko Eun-mi) whom they all worship. And if things weren't complicated enough, a public prosecutor named Cho (Jeong Jin-young) is hot on their trail for the assassination of a witness.

"Guns & Talks" offers a cynic's point of view on the sub-genre. Ha-yeon, the film's narrator, ponders deeply about the morality of the work they do in his incessant voice-overs, though it is obviously a joke when he begins tripping over words during his internal monologue. Another absurd moment occurs when Ha-yeon is overcome with emotion over Jae-young's refusal to carry out a hit and begins to wax philosophically about the wonders of true love (artsy-fartsy hand

Chung Jae-young, Shin Hyun-june, Shin Ha-kyun, and Won Bin (*image courtesy of Cinema Service*)

gestures included). Though this scene reeks of the same pretentiousness of lesser films (e.g., "Full-time Killer"), it is eventually revealed to be part of an elaborate jab at audience expectations.

Fans of Hong Kong actioners will also find plenty to like in the visual dynamic that iconoclastic director Jang Jin injects into the proceedings. In addition to the usual blend of John Woo-inspired slo-mo and 'bullet-time' action sequences, Jang shows that he has a few tricks of his own. In one sequence, which features Cho searching the quartet's home for evidence, the screen is divided into three, with each third showing a different camera angle on Cho. However, as Cho begins his walkaround, it quickly becomes clear that each 'angle' is an entirely different scene, with each 'Cho' investigating a different part of the house. Jang also constructs an elaborate and well-shot assassination set piece that takes place during a performance of Hamlet at an opera house (with the Korean dialogue remarkably faithful to the original text).

Unfortunately, where "Guns & Talks" could have used some work is in the ending, in which the character motivations, plot mechanics, and plain-old logic must jump through hoops in order to achieve the film's impossibly happy ending. It seems as though Jang (who also wrote the script), having painted himself into a corner during the last act while still having too many balls in the air, tried to tie up all the loose ends as quickly as possible-- too bad it all seems so contrived.

Shin Hyun-june (*image courtesy of Cinema Service*)

Despite a weak ending, "Guns & Talks" is still a lot of fun to watch, due in part to the performances of the talented cast. Shin Hyun-june abandons his usual 'bad guy' persona (cultivated in films such as "Bichunmoo" and "The Gingko Bed") to portray Sang-yeon as the quartet's kind-hearted and well-intentioned leader, while Chung and Won are both up to the task with sympathetic portrayals of their love-struck characters. Jeong Jin-young also acquits himself nicely as the dedicated public prosecutor on their trail, though his character's motivation gets a little fuzzy near the end.

Slick, humorous, and fun, "Guns & Talks" takes the cinematic stylings of John Woo, Guy Ritchie, and Quentin Tarantino and whips them into one neat package. This is a film that truly speaks to the innovation and surprise awaiting moviegoers in today's cutting-edge Korean cinema.

Volcano High (Whasango) - 2001

Starring: Jang Hyuk, Shin Min-ah, Kim Su-ro, Huh Jin-ho
Director: Kim Tae-gyun
Availability: Hong Kong-import VCD (multi-region) and DVD (multi-region), Korean-import DVD (Region 3)
Rating: ● ● ● ●

Volcano High poster (*image courtesy of Cinema Service*)

If "Harry Potter and the Sorcerer's Stone" had been directed by the Wachowski brothers ("The Matrix"), with a smidgen of "Crouching Tiger, Hidden Dragon" thrown in, you would probably end up with something like "Volcano High". Taking place in a high school where the 'gifted class' possesses supernatural powers, this 2001 action-comedy blends martial arts fantasy, wire-fu acrobatics, and dazzling computer graphics to create unforgettable visuals that more than compensate for a lackluster script.

Based on the winning submission from a 1997 Korean screenwriting contest, "Volcano High" revolves around troubled teenager Kim Kyung-soo (Jang Hyuk), who is blessed (or cursed, depending on how you see it) with special powers, including the ability to levitate and hurl energy projectiles at his foes. The story kicks off with Kyung-soo arriving at the titular high school after having been expelled from eight previous schools for assaulting teachers and fellow students. With this being his 'last strike', Kyung-soo tries very hard to fit in with his new classmates, control his temper, and avoid the type of supernatural displays that result in expulsion.

Unfortunately, Volcano High is unlike any high school that Kyung-soo has been to, as many of his fellow students also possess mystical powers. Furthermore, Kyung-soo finds himself caught in the middle of a power struggle between the school's principal, vice-principal, and rival student clubs over the 'Secret Manuscript', a tome which grants its bearer absolute control over the school. When Principal Jang Oh-ja (Kim Il-wu) suddenly falls into a deep trance, Vice-principal Jang Hak-sa accuses the school's top student Song Hak-rim (Kwong Sang-woo) of trying to steal the Secret Manuscript and has him jailed. In actual fact, the vice-principal is after the book himself, and he enlists the help of school bully 'Dark Oxen' Jang Ryang (Kim Su-ro) to get the rest of the students in line.

Meanwhile, because of the power vacuum created by Hak-rim's imprisonment, the leaders of the various student clubs try to consolidate their power by enlisting Kyung-soo's support, such as the aggressive captain of the rugby team, Shimma (Kim Hyung-jong), who even enlists the charms of his pretty fraternal twin sister Yoma (Chae Shi-ah). However, Kyung-soo's attention is focused on 'Icy Jade' Yoo Chae-yi (Shin Min-ah), the beautiful and chaste captain of the all-female kendo team. And to make matters worse, the vice-principal brings in five new teachers, led by Ma Bang-jin (Huh Jun-ho), who specialize in reigning in wayward students with their seemingly unbeatable powers. Let the games begin!

If you are a fan of wire-fu flicks, such as "Crouching Tiger, Hidden Dragon", or are looking for something to fill the time until the next "Shaolin Soccer", then you will probably think that you have died and gone to

Jang Hyuk (*image courtesy of Cinema Service*)

heaven when you watch "Volcano High", which is wall-to-wall with characters that fly, do impossible backflips, and do battle with stylish cartoon violence. As per the film's central conceit, 'martial arts set in a high school', "Volcano High" takes the conventions of *wu shu* martial arts epics and transposes them into a high school setting. For example, characters are introduced with subtitles bearing their names and descriptions (reminiscent of the Hong Kong film "Stormriders"), rival warlords and clans become student associations that don't get along, and dramatic camera angles are used to give the on-screen action an anime feel.

However, despite the emphasis on martial arts, the tone of the film is mostly jokey and irreverent. For example, Kyung-soo's dramatic arrival at Volcano High is punctuated by the image of a student falling out of a window, to which Kyung-soo is completely oblivious. One brief digression relays Kyung-soo's backstory as a sepia-toned educational training film. And despite his super powers, Kyung-soo is a bit of a klutz, especially in the presence of Chae-yi, for whom he can only muster a meek wave and a goofy smile.

If there is a complaint to be made about "Volcano High", it would have to be levelled against the script, which trades in comic book characterizations and cliché-ridden plotting as it swings wildly from one action sequence to the next.

The film also touches briefly on the stifling authoritarian environment of the Korean high-school system, though it is more of a scratch on the surface, as opposed to the more thoughtful examinations mined by "Whispering Corridors" or even "My Boss, My Hero". And because the script introduces a flurry of characters, their allegiances, and numerous plot points within the first half, some viewers may find the story a bit confusing and difficult to follow (hint: the story is not too dissimilar from "Harry Potter and the Sorcerer's Stone").

Kwong Sang-woo and Jang Hyuk (*image courtesy of Cinema Service*)

Performances are also as expected for such a spectacle-laden film. Top nod goes to Jang, whose charismatic and comic performance as the story's unwilling hero is second only to the outrageous special effects. As Kyung-soo's love interest, Shin is perfectly cast as the cool Chae-yi, and she warms up nicely as the story unfolds. Kim, with his long locks and over-the-top facial expressions, is no stranger to playing bad guys (such as in "Attack the Gas Station!" and "The Foul King"), and in "Volcano High", he lends credence to the moniker 'Dark Oxen' with another fearsome performance.

It may lack brains, but "Volcano High" more than makes up for this shortcoming with its brawn. In addition to its light-hearted tone and the way it recontexualizes the *wu shu* epic into the confines of a high school, "Volcano High" benefits from imaginative fight sequences and dazzling special effects. Indeed, "Volcano High" is a wildly entertaining romp... exactly the type of film that fans of Asian action have been craving for a very long time.

No Blood No Tears (Pido nunmuldo eobshi) - 2002

Starring: Jeon Do-yeon, Lee Hye-yeong, Jeong Jae-yeong
Director: Ryu Seung-wan
Availability: Korean-import DVD (Region 3)
Rating: ●●●●

No Blood No Tears poster
(*image courtesy of Cinema Service*)

If "Lock, Stock, and Two Smoking Barrels" and "Snatch" director Guy Ritchie ever made a Korean flick, it would probably look something like "No Blood No Tears". This so-called 'pulp noir' sophomore feature from director Ryu Seung-wan, who made a name for himself in 2000 with "Die Bad", follows the Ritchie formula from start to finish, as it details the brutal violence, double-crosses, head-turning twists, and absurd situations that surround a bag of money and the people who want it.

At the center of the mayhem are two women, Su-jin (Jeon Do-yeon) and Gyeong-seon (veteran actress Lee Hye-yeong). Su-jin is the long-suffering moll of a pugilistic middle-middle management thug named Bulldog (Jeong Jae-yeong), while Gyeong-seon is a former-thief-turned-legitimate cab driver working around the clock to make a living. Despite their differing backgrounds, they both desperately want to break free from their miserable lives-- Su-jin wants to get away from Bulldog, undergo surgery to correct a scar on her face, and make it big as a singer in Japan; Gyeong-seon wants to get out from under the crushing debt she owes to some loan sharks and be reunited with her estranged daughter.

The story gets in gear after Su-jin crashes her car into Gyeong-seon's taxi. Despite such a rocky start, Su-jin senses an opportunity to work with Gyeong-seon, and proposes a bold plan to rip off the proceeds from the dogfights that her boyfriend runs for crime boss Kim Geum-bok (Shin gu), also known as 'KGB'. At first, Gyeong-seon balks at the idea, as Su-jin's trustworthiness and brains are both suspect. However, when the loan sharks threaten to harm her daughter if she doesn't pay off her debts, Gyeong-seon decides to take part in the scheme.

Of course, nothing goes as planned when it comes to actually pulling off the heist. And if that wasn't bad enough, a number of additional players show up to complicate matters further, including a veteran detective (Lee Yeong-hu) who has made it his life's work to bring down KGB, three dim-witted teenagers out for an easy score, and reminiscent of Vinnie Jones' characters from Ritchie's films, KGB's strong-but-silent enforcer (Jeong Du-hong, who also served as martial arts choreographer on this film) who doesn't take 'no' for an answer.

For the most part, "No Blood No Tears" is a tautly paced and fun film to watch, as Ryu masterfully keeps all the various subplots and characters humming along until they converge into one big conflagration around the bag of money that everyone is after. The screenplay by Ryu and collaborator Jeong Jin-wan has a lot of fun with the characters, who effortlessly move from one absurd situation to the next, brought on either by (a) their own stupidity, (b) the stupidity of others, or (c) plain bad luck, or (d) varying combinations of the above. Fans of Guy Ritchie will also appreciate the sparkling technical credits of the film, where inventive lighting, varying camera speeds, and unconventional shot compositions make the film a feast for the eyes as well. Furthermore, the hyperkinetic fight sequences choreographed by Jeong Du-hong (who also choreographed the action in "Musa" and "Public Enemy") are dazzling to watch, with the characters pummelling each other with both acrobatic grace and lightning speed.

Unfortunately, the proceedings also have a very dark and mean-spirited undercurrent, which becomes increasingly apparent as the film moves into its second half. Despite the apparent light-hearted tone of the story, the violence in the fight scenes become increasingly distasteful and go on far longer than necessary, such as Bulldog's pounding by KGB's enforcer, or his stomach-turning manhandling of Su-jin and Gyeong-seon during the film's bloody climax.

Cast-wise, Jeon and Lee lead the pack playing roles that they usually aren't associated with. Jeon once again demonstrates her chameleon-like thesping skills (seen previously in films such as "The Harmonium in My Memory" and "I Wish I Had a Wife") in her unforgettable portrayal of the ditzy, sassy, and trashy Su-jin, while Lee is credible as the tough-talking and butch Gyeong-seon. Jeong is also effectively creepy as the borderline psychotic Bulldog, a bully with no discernible redeeming qualities whatsoever. Shin, whom audiences may recognize from "Christmas in August", where he played Han Suk-kyu's father, also acquits himself nicely as the polite but cruel KGB.

Despite being smartly scripted, well shot, and well acted, Ryu's much-ballyhooed "No Blood No Tears" ended up being a dismal failure at the Korean box office when it was released in the spring of 2002, and audiences were likely turned off by the film's increasingly pessimistic and dark tone and ultra-violence, both of which are genuine complaints. But with its release on DVD, hopefully this remarkable film will find its audience and receive a second lease on life, providing moviegoers a chance to better appreciate the handiwork of one of South Korea's fast-rising stars.

Nowhere to Hide (Injong sajong bolgeot eobda) - 1999

Starring: Park Joong-hoon, Jang Dong-gun, Ahn Sung-ki, Park Sang-myun
Director: Lee Myeong-se
Availability: Hong Kong-import VCD and DVD (multi-region), Korean-import DVD (multi-region), North American DVD
Rating: ●●●½

Nowhere to Hide poster (*image courtesy of Cinema Service*)

With its police-procedural plotting, martial arts choreography, anime-inspired cinematography, and "Three Stooges"-style antics, "Nowhere to Hide" is Korean genre-bending taken to the nth degree. Veteran director Lee Myeong-se takes a simple story about two maverick cops tracking down an elusive killer, and executes it with an 'anything goes' attitude that utilizes every trick in the book, along with some new ones-- appropriately enough, the film's original Korean title translates into something like "I Don't Give a Shit About Anything". And though the narrative feels disjointed at times with all the fast-and-furious experimentation, there is no doubt that this exercise in style is one of the most unique films to come out of the latest 'Korean New Wave'.

The action is kicked off when a murder is committed at the '40 Steps' in downtown Inchon. The renegade Detective Woo (Park Joong-hoon) and his clean-cut partner Kim (Jang Dong-gun) are put on the case. Using their traditional investigative methods, which include roughing up informants and beating up potential accomplices, their search for the killer homes in on master criminal Chang Sung-min (Ahn Sung-ki). But Chang turns out to be a slippery master of disguise, turning his capture into an extended game of cat-and-mouse that stretches from autumn into winter.

The film's most glaring weakness is its plot. The film is essentially being one big chase from beginning to end, and very few details are given about its characters, particularly Chang, whose motives and background are kept in the dark. Indeed, the plot serves only as a clothesline from which to stage the numerous action sequences and visual experimentation techniques that Lee has up his sleeve.

Regardless of narrative issues, director Lee certainly gives the audience plenty of eye candy to chew on. The most obvious are 'the scenes'-- unforgettable images, set pieces, and gorgeous cinematography that remain with the viewer long after the closing credits have rolled. For example, there is the iconic rain-drenched '40 Steps' murder framed by the orange and golden hues of autumn and set to the tune of the Bee Gees' "Holiday" (which was later parodied in "Funny Movie"). A tense moment during a stakeout includes the camera following a bead of sweat as it falls and splashes on the ground. Another action sequence has Chang cornered by Woo and Kim on a passenger train, which Lee executes in John Woo-style slow motion. And few could forget the climactic anime-inspired showdown between Woo and Chang in the middle of a torrential downpour-- a scene that has been emulated in more recent films such as "My Wife is a Gangster" and "My Boss, My Hero".

Thankfully, Lee is not content to let his film be merely wall-to-wall action sequences, and injects some much needed, albeit offbeat, humor. Some viewers may find it difficult to sympathize with Woo and his colleagues, especially with their habit of beating up suspects or the ineptness they demonstrate as they go about their work. However, it is in their rough-and-tumble approach to police work that most of the comedy arises. For example, shades of "The Three Stooges" are seen while Woo is staking out the house of Chang's girlfriend-- an unexpected knock at the door leaves Woo's team in disarray as they madly scramble for a suitable hiding place. A fistfight with one of Chang's accomplices transforms into shadow puppetry and then into a tango (complete with music). Woo's penchant for pursuing suspects on foot leads to some unexpected laughs, such as a chase

Ahn Sung-ki (*image courtesy of Cinema Service*)

after an informant that turns into an absurd race. And if the addition of comedy wasn't enough, Lee also has time to pack in that age-old staple of Korean cinema, romantic melodrama, through Woo's growing attraction to Chang's girlfriend (Choi Ji-woo).

Park Joong-hoon and Ahn Sung-ki
(*image courtesy of Cinema Service*)

Despite the limitations of the script, the performances in "Nowhere to Hide" hit the right notes. Park, with his brutish and dishevelled looks, is perfect as the dim-witted but determined Woo. He is complemented nicely by Jang as his fiercely loyal, not to mention good-looking, sidekick. Ahn is given very few lines of dialogue in the film, though he manages to speak volumes with his impressive screen presence. Finally, Park Sang-myun, who would later find fame in "My Wife is a Gangster" and "Hi, Dharma!", has a memorable turn as one of Chang's accomplices, while Choi is somewhat affecting as the film's resident love interest.

In addition to being a big hit in its native Korea when it was released in 1999, "Nowhere to Hide" was also one of the first films of the latest 'Korean New Wave' to find a theatrical and DVD release in North America (the North American version runs twenty minutes shorter), and for good reason. The unconventional and dazzling sights of this gutsy genre-bending film transcend all languages and cultures. And though it may be criticized as an emotionally cool example of 'form over function', it is doubtful that you will ever find another film quite as inventive, risk-taking, and visually arresting.

Public Enemy (Gongongeui jeok) - 2002

Starring: Sol Kyung-gu, Lee Sung-jae
Director: Kang Woo-suk
Availability: Korean-import DVD (Region 3)
Rating: ●●●½

Sol Kyung-gu and Lee Sung-jae (*image courtesy of Cinema Service*)

If Harvey Keitel's corrupt cop character from "Bad Lieutenant" ever went after Christian Bale's "American Psycho", you would probably end up with something like the 2002 South Korean thriller "Public Enemy". Smartly directed by veteran Kang Woo-suk, "Public Enemy" features the cinematic pairing of Sol Kyung-gu and Lee Sung-jae, who play a bad cop and yuppie serial killer, respectively.

The film opens up with Detective Kang Cheol-jung (Sol) extolling the virtues of Korea's law enforcement in a voice-over, men and women who tirelessly defend the public against the corruptive influence of criminal elements. However, as the opening scene draws to a close, Kang cynically declares that he doesn't do any of that. Then the audience is introduced to the slovenly Kang, whose moral compass is just as dishevelled as his appearance. Despite having been bribed with a large bag of cocaine and witnessed the suicide of his long-time partner, the Internal Affairs department is unable to pin anything on the veteran homicide detective. Meanwhile, across town, in a scene reminiscent of "American Beauty", we catch investment fund manager Jo Gyu-hwan (Lee) in the shower. However, despite his sharp appearance, it quickly becomes clear that Jo is a very depraved individual.

For the bulk of the film's first hour, the action jumps back and forth contrasting the daily routines of these two disparate characters. As Kang uses dubious investigative methods to ensure that criminals are punished for their crimes, Jo orchestrates an investment scheme that will land him $37 billion won. However, the trajectory of the story does not become apparent until Jo commits the bloody murders of his parents in a fit of rage. While leaving the scene of the crime, Jo has an accidental run-in with Kang, though a heavy rainfall prevents either man from identifying the other.

Later on, when the bodies of Jo's parents are discovered nearby, Kang figures that the mystery man on the street was the murderer. And after meeting the victims' only surviving relative, Jo, Kang is convinced that he is the murderer. Unfortunately, Kang ends up being yet another cop with a theory that no one believes in. Meanwhile, Jo does his best playing the grieving son, and watches with smug delight as Kang struggles to pin the murder on him. Thus begins a cat-and-mouse game between the cop and the criminal that only gets uglier as the chase drags on.

Similar to its unappealing main characters, "Public Enemy" is a gritty picture, rife with violence, wall-to-wall expletives, and stomach-churning gore. However, despite such heavy material, director Kang lightens the load with some unexpected but welcome comic relief. The detective's wanton disregard for the very laws he is charged with protecting is hilariously reflected in his half-assed police work. For example, one early scene has Kang coercing a gangster (Lee Mun-shik) he has just arrested to confess to a series of unrelated break-ins, thereby earning Kang some much-needed recognition. Another scene has Kang recruiting two dim-witted thugs (Sung Ji-ru and Yu Hae-jin) to help him 'conduct' an autopsy on the murder victims, leading to a major break in the case.

Despite his appearances, Kang gradually becomes a more sympathetic character as the story unfolds, particularly as his dogged persistence in pinning the crime on Jo ends up busting him down to traffic-cop status. And even though he conducts himself with callous disregard for following proper procedure, in his heart he is committed to protecting the public trust, and the way he goes about his work betrays an unshakeable sense of honor.

To his credit, Sol is able to effectively convey the two contradictory sides of his character, showing off the acting chops that he honed in the depressing "Peppermint Candy" and the uplifting "I Wish I Had a Wife". As his opposite, Lee takes his usual clean-cut on-screen persona, such as in "Kick the Moon", and stands it on its head with his malicious and delicious portrayal of the psychopathic Jo, a villain who audiences love to hate.

With this character study dressed up as a thriller, director Kang Woo-suk has created a remarkable entry into the serial killer genre. Laced with humor (albeit dark), while featuring two outstanding performances and a suspenseful story, "Public Enemy" will easily make a home on the 'most wanted' list of any Korean cinema aficionado.

Musa - 2001

Starring: Joo Jin-mo, Ahn Sung-ki, Jung Woo-sung, Zhang Ziyi, Yu Ronguang
Director: Kim Sung-su
Availability: Korean-import DVD (Region 3 only)
Rating: ●●●½

Musa poster (*image courtesy of CJ Entertainment*)

In the year 1375, after the Yuan (Mongolian) Dynasty had fallen in what is now modern China, a number of peace envoys were sent by Koryu (Korea) to improve relations with the newly established Ming Dynasty. Unfortunately, the diplomatic mission failed, and all four delegations were captured and imprisoned. Two years later, three out of the four envoys made it back to Koryu, while the fourth was never heard from again. With this bit of historical fact, veteran South Korean director Kim Sung-su has fashioned the historical epic "Musa" (also known as "Wu shi" in China), a Korean-Chinese co-production that conjectures what might have happened to the missing envoy. With a budget of $8 million US, "Musa" is probably the most expensive Korean movie in history. Unfortunately, as is the case with some Hollywood blockbusters, bigger and more expensive do not always necessarily mean better, as "Musa" ends up being a technically proficient yet long-winded costume drama that could have used a tighter script.

The film's first hour is the most dense, as characters and conflicts are thrown at the audience in rapid-fire succession. The film opens with the peace delegation, having been captured and disarmed by the Mings, being marched through the desert. However, a surprise attack by the remnants of the Yuan army defeats their captors, and they are left to the mercy of the heat and sand. With the group's diplomats dying left and right, the young General Choi (Joo Jin-mo) takes command of the survivors, a mish-mash group of civilians, Choi's loyal contingent of professional soldiers, and the poorly equipped troops of the people's army, led by the wise Sgt. Jin-lib (Ahn Sung-ki). Together, they continue through the desert with the objective of reaching Shandong province, where they can catch a boat home back to Koryu.

During a brief stop in a village, where they find a Ming princess, Furong (Zhang Ziyi of "Crouching Tiger, Hidden Dragon" fame), being held hostage by a Yuan general (Hong Kong actor Yu Ronguang). In return for helping her escape and bringing her back to Ming territory, Furong promises to reward the Koreans handsomely, an offer which Choi accepts with the hope that it will also restore Koryu-Ming relations. Unfortunately, the princess' liberation does not go unnoticed, and the Yuan army gives pursuit.

At this point, tensions are already building between the rag-tag coalition, especially between Jin-lib's men and Choi, with the former feeling as if they are being sacrificed needlessly while Choi's own men are held back. In addition, former servant Yeo-sol (Jung Woo-sung), who has been made a free man by his dying master, is angered by his continued treatment as a slave by Choi. However, with the princess in tow, the conflicts escalate further and threaten to tear them apart. Choi's followers see the honor and political upside of returning Furong to her kingdom, while Jin-lib's men would rather surrender the princess than have their already sparse numbers whittled down trying to protect her. In addition, a love

Zhang Ziyi (*image courtesy of CJ Entertainment*)

triangle develops between Yeo-sol, Choi, and Furong-- Furong has an eye for Yeo-sol, while Choi finds himself attracted to Furong.

Running at three hours, "Musa" is a very long film to sit through. True, the production values are top-notch, such as how the film's vast desert landscapes are captured beautifully by Kim Hyung-ku's brilliant lensing. Unfortunately, the light story does not live up to the impressive collection of images that Kim has captured on film, and "Musa" quickly becomes repetitive and tiresome. For example, the film's numerous battle scenes, often involving hundreds of extras and edits, are certainly impressive to watch, reminiscent of the opening scene of "Gladiator", or the grand battle scenes in Chen Kaige's "The Emperor and the Assassin". However, as technically proficient as Kim is in recreating battles from the 14th Century, how many times does the audience need to see people being shot in the neck by arrows, decapitated, dismembered, or cut down from behind? Even the film's somewhat engaging final act, which kicks into "Assault on Precinct 13" mode as the Koreans barricade themselves inside an abandoned fortress, is needlessly drawn out as Kim fails to reign in such indulgences.

Another disappointing aspect of "Musa" is how it shamelessly trades in clichés, dropping in every stock character and well-tread convention it could get its hands on. The ineffectual yet headstrong leader. The ever-loyal sidekick who never questions orders... until the leader totally screws up. The strong and silent loner who can kick ass and look cool at the same time. The pampered princess who gradually learns to shoulder some responsibility. The coward who runs away at the first sign of danger, only to find courage when it really counts. The grizzled veteran who has the skills and the smarts to survive. The swapping of stories around the campfire about wives and babies waiting at home. The young novice who pays the ultimate price for his bravery. Even Yeo-sol's initial encounter with Furong seems to have been plucked from "Crouching Tiger, Hidden Dragon".

Despite the superficial characterizations, the performances in "Musa" are decent. The most high-profile member of the cast, Chinese 'It' girl Zhang Ziyi, starts off as a little one-dimensional in her portrayal of Furong, though as her character matures, the dramatic range of her performance improves greatly. As Yeo-sol, Jung is given very little to do other than look cool during the fight scenes and speak tersely. Joo, as the similarly one-dimensional Choi, shows off a little more range, while Ahn injects his portrayal of Jin-lip with a level of dignity befitting such a wise and battle-scarred veteran.

Other than film festivals (such as the 2001 Toronto International Film Festival), the only way to catch "Musa" currently is through the Region 3 (Asia only) DVD. However, with its lightweight script, repetitive battle sequences, and unnecessarily long running time, it is difficult to give "Musa" a strong recommendation and justify the effort. However, if you like historical epics with lots of big battle scenes, then "Musa" is certainly worth a look, and maybe even the effort to track it down.

Last Witness (Heuksuseon) - 2001

Starring: Lee Jung-jae, Ahn Sung-ki, Lee Mi-yeon, Jeong Jun-ho
Director: Bae Chang-ho
Availability: Korean-import DVD (Region 3)
Rating: ●●●½

Lee Jung-jae (*image courtesy of Cinema Service*)

South Korean blockbuster "Last Witness" belongs to that select group of films that work far better as a beautifully shot and alluring trailer than as an unimaginative and cliché-ridden two-hour movie. Based on the best-selling novel by Kim Seong-jong and the handiwork of prominent Eighties director Bae Chang-ho, this politically minded feature dabbles in the territory previously explored by "Shiri" and "Joint Security Area", that is, the scars left by the Korean War and the subsequent division of the country into the communist North and democratic South. Unfortunately, "Last Witness" ends up being a disappointing mess where the emotional weight and political subtext play second fiddle to gratuitously overblown action sequences, amateur melodrama, and tired murder-mystery conventions.

The film's opening scene contrasts the release of political prisoner Hwang-seok (Ahn Sung-ki) after fifty years in solitary confinement and the discovery of a stabbing victim in a harbor, who is later identified as Yang Dal-su (Lee Ki-yeong). Renegade cop (is there any other type?) Oh (Lee Jung-jae), who has a penchant for using excessive force, is put in charge of identifying who killed Yang and why. His investigation, which includes visiting a trendy nightclub (thereby allowing lenser Kim Yun-su to film skimpily attired young women getting jiggy with it in slow motion), eventually leads him to Geoje Island, which once housed Korea's infamous Geoje Camp where North Korean POWs and South Korean communists were once incarcerated (this is the same camp that is briefly mentioned in "Joint Security Area").

However, the pieces of the puzzle start coming together when Oh comes across a fifty-year old diary written by Sohn Ji-hye (Lee Mi-yeon), who is now blind and running an antique shop. The diary reveals Ji-hye's involvement in an escape attempt at Geoje, which was aimed at liberating her family's wrongly imprisoned former servant, Hwang-seok-- the man she loves. Also mentioned in the diary are the leader of the escape attempt Han Dong-ju (Jeong Jun-ho) and the man who was sent to track them down, murder victim Yang. Thus, the recently released Hwang-seok immediately becomes the police's number one suspect. However, a few things still don't add up, and so Oh takes a detour to Japan to track down who he thinks may be the real killer...

If there is one thing that director Bae does right in "Last Witness", it is committing to film some of the most beautiful and eye-catching images. The film is almost wall-to-wall with stunning cinematography, with some of the more impressive set pieces being the slo-mo rain, mud, and blood-soaked escape from Geoje Camp, Hwang-seok being given chase by South Korean soldiers in a forest, Oh's gun battle with an assassin amidst bamboo just as it begins to rain, and the film's finale in a train station. And with the judicious use of classic opera pieces in the soundtrack (such as Puccini's "Madame Butterfly"), "Last Witness" is a feast for both the eyes and the ears.

However, all this visual and aural eloquence ends up being wasted with a threadbare script that seems more concerned with pumping out an action sequence every ten minutes as opposed to providing more background on the characters or telling an emotionally meaningful story. As a result, the doomed romance between Hwang-seok and Ji-hye, which is supposed to give the film its emotional weight, ends up being little more than a signpost along the way. The same goes with Detective Oh, who is given little to do other than following the clues and beating up the bad guys.

Among the cast, veteran actor Ahn is easily the most interesting person on the screen, who adroitly conveys the innocence and earnestness of Hwang-seok's youth, as well as his heartbreak of the present. On the other hand, the performance of his co-star Lee Mi-yeon is bland and unconvincing, particularly in the scenes that take place in the present, where she is supposed to be playing a seventy-year old woman-- not only is her wrinkle-free makeup unconvincing, but so is her acting. Finally, Lee Jung-jae, playing the Korean equivalent of Dirty Harry, is passable as Oh, with his performance constrained by the limitations of the material.

Within its two hour running time, "Last Witness" dishes out Hong Kong style action, hard-boiled police procedural, historical and political drama, and romantic melodrama. Unfortunately, other than the stunning eye and ear candy that director Bae deliberately injects to the proceedings, very little in this slick production registers. Unfortunately, it seems that Hollywood and today's Hong Kong don't have the market completely cornered when it comes to combining the visceral with the vacuous.

Jakarta - 2000

Starring: Kim Sang-jung, Yun Da-hun, Lee Jae-un, Lim Chang-jung, Jin Hee-kyung, Kim Se-jun
Director: Jung Cho-shin
Availability: Korean-import DVD (multi-region)
Rating: ●●●½

Jakarta poster (*image courtesy of CJ Entertainment*)

The title of "Jakarta" does not refer to where the story takes place, but with what each of the film's characters hope to achieve. You see, to pull a 'Jakarta' means to commit the perfect crime, which is what three distinct groups of would-be bank robbers try to do for a $3 million prize. And though the film starts off weakly, as though it were some pale imitation of a Quentin Tarantino-inspired caper flick, the fast-and-furious revelations made in the second and third acts make "Jakarta" worth a look.

The film starts off with the three groups converging on a bank, where $3 million lies waiting in a vault. The first group is a trio of high-tech criminals that try to enter the bank's vault from underneath-- drill man Blue (Lim Chang-jung), resident loudmouth White (Kim Se-jun), and the beautiful and brainy Red (Jin Hee-kyung). Meanwhile, the Vice President of the bank, Sa-hyun (Yun Da-hun), with the help of his teller lover Eun-ah (Lee Jae-un), plans to waltz into the vault and grab the cash for himself.

Upon entering the vault, Sa-hyun sees Blue stuffing the cash into a bag and apprehends him. The police are called and two officers, Hae-ryong (Kim Sang-jung) and Doo-san (Park Jun-gyu), respond almost immediately and take both Sa-hyun and Blue into custody for further questioning. However, it seems that the two policemen are actually another group of bank robbers with their eyes on the cash. They then take Sa-hyun and Blue to a remote location and hold them for ransom. Unfortunately, the plan doesn't go off as expected, and plenty of blood is spilled... or does it?

Up until the end of the first act, "Jakarta" appears to be a monumental waste of time. The plot seems a little too simplistic, such as how the Red/White/Blue team is dumb enough to break into the vault just as the bank is about to open for business. Furthermore, the dialogue is hardly witty and the story appears to lack the complexity one would expect from the coincidental convergence of the would-be bank robbers.

Thankfully, director Jung Cho-shin redeems himself in the subsequent acts, in which the story rewinds back a few days and reveals the behind-the-scenes goings-on of what led up to and transpired during the supposedly botched caper. The hidden agendas of the various characters are revealed, as are the multiple layers of double-crosses between them. Characters deemed to be innocent in the first act are revealed to be conniving master criminals, while the more ruthless characters actually end up being the most sympathetic. Even telephone calls from the first act that are assumed to be between two characters are revealed to be components of two completely different conversations. And most important of all, the otherwise grim proceedings of the first act are lightened up with some much-needed humor.

Among the performances, Lee ends up being the most memorable, whose wallflower-ish portrayal of Eun-ah gradually gives way to reveal that she is actually the smartest of all the characters. Lim is also good as the charismatic and blond-haired Blue, as is Kim Sang-jung, who is not the cold-blooded killer that he first appears to be. Unfortunately, the same cannot be said for the rest of the cast, who turn in dismal performances, particularly Kim Se-jun, a Tony Leung-look-alike who seems to serve no purpose.

As an action-comedy caper flick, "Jakarta" is a pleasant timewaster that does end up having more than a few surprises up its sleeve. Tarantino-buffs will probably enjoy its non-chronological and multiple-perspective narrative structure à la "Pulp Fiction" and "Jackie Brown", even if the film ends up being plagued by some so-so performances. It may not be perfect, but it certainly isn't a crime.

Bichunmoo - 2000

Starring: Shin Hyun-june, Kim Hee-sun, Jeong Jin-young
Director: Kim Yeong-jun
Availability: Hong Kong-import DVD (multi-region), Hong Kong-import VCD (no English subtitles), Korean-import DVD (Region 3)
Rating: ●●●

Shin Hyun-june and Kim Hee-sun (*image courtesy of Cinema Service*)

With the runaway international success of Ang Lee's "Crouching Tiger, Hidden Dragon" in 2000 and 2001, the *wu shu* ('fantasy swordplay') genre has become increasingly crowded with filmmakers and studios trying to cash in on the craze. Miramax, having acquired a sizable catalog of Hong Kong films, dusted off 1993's "Iron Monkey" for theatrical release in the fall of 2001, and currently has plans to release Tsui Hark's "Legend of Zu" (re-edited and renamed as "Zu Warriors") directly to video soon. Meanwhile, Chinese director Zhang Yimou is in the midst of shooting "Hero", an all-star martial arts epic that brings together Jet Li, Maggie Cheung, Tony Leung, and Zhang Ziyi. And Jackie Chan buddy Sammo Hung is in the process of releasing his own "Flying Dragon, Leaping Tiger".

However, one of the first films to jump on the "Crouching Tiger, Hidden Dragon" bandwagon was the South Korean film "Bichunmoo" from 2000. Billed at the time as the 'most expensive Korean movie ever made' (a claim which has now been eclipsed by other films, such as "Joint Security Area" and "Resurrection of the Little Match Girl"), first-time director Kim Yeong-jun has created a technically proficient and decidedly Korean take on Hong Kong fantasy swordplay films. Unfortunately, "Bichunmoo" never becomes more than a sum of its parts with its lackluster story, manipulative melodrama, and unimpressive action sequences.

Based on a very popular Korean comic book from the Eighties, "Bichunmoo" opens up in 1343 (about three decades before the events depicted in "Musa"), when China was under the rule of the Mongol Yuan Dynasty, and tells the story of two star-crossed lovers, orphan Jin-ha (Shin Hyun-june) and Sullie (Kim Hee-sun), the daughter of a Mongol general Taruga (Kim Hak-cheol). Taruga, wishing to form an alliance, gives his daughter's hand to Mongol nobleman Namgung Jun-kwang (Jeong Jin-young, who would once again spar off against Shin Hyun-june in "Guns & Talks"). However, when Jin-ha tries to stop Sullie's betrothal, he is apparently killed by Taruga's bodyguards. Thinking that her childhood sweetheart is now dead, Sullie agrees to the marriage.

Unknown to Sullie, Jin-ha survives the scuffle and learns a secret about his past-- he is the long-lost heir of a famous Korean nobleman who was slain by Taruga many years ago. In addition, Jin-ha possesses the secrets to the most powerful martial arts of them all, the Bichun arts of Koryu (ancient Korea). Determined to exact his revenge, Jin-ha changes his name to Jahalang and raises his own band of warriors, who like him, have the ability to glide through the air or make enemies explode.

Meanwhile, ten years have gone by, and Sullie and Namgung now have a son named Sung (Bang Hyoup). With the help of Chinese allies, Jin-ha invades the Taruga stronghold and slays Sullie's father. Despite completing this act of vengeance and being reunited with his long-lost love, there is no rest for Jin-ha. In addition to

Shin Hyun-june (*image courtesy of Cinema Service*)

the imminent return of Namgung, who is off fighting a distant war, there are many who wish to steal the Bichun secrets, some of whom are among Jin-ha's allies...

The production values of "Bichunmoo" are top notch, with director Kim instilling a cinematic look to the film with the effective use of lighting and lensing. Kim also makes use of CGI in a particularly stunning sequence where Jin-ha and Sullie grow from childhood to adulthood as the seasons change around them. And to successfully emulate the swordplay films of Hong Kong, Joe Ma (best known for his work in "A Chinese Ghost Story") was brought on board to choreograph the martial arts sequences. Indeed, some of the fight sequences are impressive (even by Hong Kong standards), such as a nocturnal assault on the Taruga stronghold that has Jin-ha and his black-clad warriors swooping over pagoda rooftops. Unfortunately, most of the film's fights quickly degenerate into the opponents jumping around and doing spin kicks ad nauseum, or Jin-ha merely blowing everyone up, eschewing any of the grace (not to mention sense of purpose) that Ang Lee meticulously worked into "Crouching Tiger, Hidden

Dragon".

However, the biggest disappointment with "Bichunmoo" is the silly script, particularly in the film's latter half when Jin-ha becomes Jahalang, with main characters appearing from out of nowhere and plot points not clearly explained. The film's uninspired dialogue is another sore point, leaving it up to the film's melodramatic score to highlight the story's emotional cues for the audience. However, even more troubling is how emotionally manipulative the story becomes as it tries to create a big tear-jerking scene every so often. Jin-ha must have more lives than a cat, given how many times he 'dies' in "Bichunmoo", only to be miraculously brought back to life a few minutes later. Not to be outdone, the script toys with the audience by apparently killing off Sullie, only to retract it later on.

As Jin-ha/Jahalang, Shin is the typical lone wolf warrior, whose face betrays no emotion, says little, and spends most of his time trying to look cool, as that is about all the script lets him do. Kim Hee-sun, who is considered one of Korea's most beautiful women, is not entirely convincing as the heroine conflicted between her marriage vows to Namgung and her undying love for Jin-ha. As the third player in the love triangle, Jeong Jin-yeong jettisons the cynical demeanor that served him so well in "Ring Virus" and "Guns & Talks" and essentially plays it straight as the honor-bound Namgung, leaving little of an impression.

Fans of the Hong Kong *wu shu* genre will probably find "Bichunmoo" somewhat enjoyable, as it tries very hard to emulate it. Unfortunately, this ambitious production will likely trigger unintentional bouts of head scratching, hilarity, and yawning with its confusing plot, hackneyed script, flat acting, and monotonous fight sequences. One particularly harsh Internet film critic likens watching the film to 'the same feeling one would have when he runs out of a burning house with his hair on fire'. "Bichunmoo" is not quite that bad... at least not with the part about the hair being on fire.

Anarchists (Anakiseuteu) - 2000

Starring: Jang Dong-gun, Jung Joon-ho, Kim Sang-joong, Kim Im-kwon, Ye Ji-won
Director: Yu Young-shik
Availability: Hong Kong-import VCD and DVD (multi-region)
Rating: • • •

Anarchists DVD box art (*image courtesy of Fortex*)

Now here is another film that works far better as a two-minute trailer than as a full-length feature film. At first glance, the 2000 Chinese-Korean co-production "Anarchists" appears to be something straight out of the Hong Kong movie factory, with a historical setting evocative of Tsui Hark's "Shanghai Grand" and action sequences that channel John Woo's 'heroic bloodshed' years. Unfortunately, upon actual viewing, such initial enthusiasm quickly wanes as the film's weak script, barely engaging characters, and slow pacing take over.

The film is loosely based on actual historical events relayed by the grandfather of director Yu Young-shik. The title refers to five Shanghai-based Korean men who carry out guerrilla attacks against local Japanese Imperialist forces, as part of a larger campaign to win freedom for Korea, which has been annexed by Japan since 1910. Han (Kim Sang-joong) is the brains of the operation, Seregay (Jang Dong-gun) is the suave and daring Chow Yun-fat stand-in, Lee (Jung Joon-ho) is his levelheaded best friend, Dol-suk (Lee Bum-soo) is the obligatory volatile hothead, while Sang-gu (Kim In-kwon) is the naïve rookie, who joins the team after being saved from the hangman's noose.

In the beginning, their anti-Japanese campaign achieves a string of successes, and a steady stream of contributions to their war fund allows these self-proclaimed anarchists to dress in the fanciest attire and hang out in the swankiest nightclubs. However, their aggressive tactics soon run them afoul of socialist elements in the provisional Korean government (e.g., those would eventually flee to North Korea twenty years later), who would prefer to stabilize relations with the Japanese.

After their funding dries up, Seregay winds up dead, and Han begins to fall ill from tuberculosis, the rest of the team has little choice but to go into hiding. For a while, they subsist hand-to-mouth on whatever odd jobs they can find, while eluding the watchful eye of Japanese authorities. However, when they receive news of an important meeting of Japanese officials on a cruise ship, they decide to climb back into the saddle for one last shot at glory.

The good news is that "Anarchists" delivers on the action sequences seen in the impressive trailer. The bad news is, if you have seen the trailer, you pretty well have seen almost all of the double-fisted slo-mo shoot-outs in their entirety-- spectacular as they are (particularly with Seregay flying through the air as he fires away), the action scenes are also frustratingly short.

Furthermore, the film is rather talky, and not in an interesting-like-"The Godfather" kind of talky either, as the behind-the-scenes political intrigue lacks substance and subtlety (i.e., the anarchists simply don't agree with the future leaders of North Korea), the character development is spotty, and the story seems to lose its momentum. This is most noticeable in the second-half, where plenty of long and unexciting stretches pretty well kill any desire to continue watching.

Cast-wise, the five principal male leads look great in black, which seems to be all that is asked of them. Heartthrob Jang does quite a good job as the Korean equivalent of Chow Yun-fat, with the requisite good looks and athleticism to make his semi-automatic derring-do look credible and cool. Jung, on the other hand, is saddled with a bland character that isn't really given much to do other than try to keep the peace between his comrades-in-arms. Kim, who played a similar role in "My Wife is a Gangster", is passable as Sang-gu, though his character's comic-relief trappings end up being a continuing distraction. Finally, as the only prominent female members of the cast, Ye Ji-won, seen recently in "On the Occasion of Remembering the Turning Gate", has beauty to spare as the nightclub-singing femme fatale who becomes romantically entangled between Seregay and Lee, while Zhu Ying shows up as a bubbly photo shop girl who becomes the object of Sang-gu's affection.

On a final note, given current events, "Anarchists" does have one more troubling aspect. For all intents and purposes, the so-called "Anarchists" are terrorists, and though it is not explicitly stated in the film, it is conceivable that their attacks could bring harm to innocent civilians. True, they are fighting Japanese Imperialist forces for the liberation of their homeland, but then again, that also has an all-too familiar ring to it. If the script could have woven in this angle, instead of superficially glorifying their terrorist activities, perhaps "Anarchists" would have been a more meaningful and thought-provoking film, and the heroes would have been more sympathetic for wrestling with such a moral dilemma. Unfortunately, as is, "Anarchists" is little more than a long-winded and emotionally cold piece of cinematic fluff.

Libera Me - 2000

Starring: Choi Min-su, Yoo Ji-tae, Cha Seung-won, Park Sang-myun, Kim Kyu-ri
Director: Yang Yun-ho
Availability: Korean-import DVD (multi-region)
Rating: ● ● ●

Libera Me DVD box art (*image courtesy of Dream Search*)

It seems as though every year, through some odd chance, two or more rival Hollywood studios will come up similarly themed films within the same year. 1997 saw the release of two competing volcano movies ("Dante's Peak" and "Volcano"), 1998 saw the release of three meteor movies ("Deep Impact", "Armageddon", and the straight-to-video cheapie "Tycus"), while 1999 saw a wave of virtual reality movies, ("The Matrix", "eXistenZ", "The Thirteenth Floor", and "Open Your Eyes"). This phenomenon is not limited only to Tinseltown, as witnessed by two "Backdraft"-inspired firefighter movies that duked it out at the South Korean box office in 2000, "Libera Me" and "Siren".

"Libera Me" was clearly the better of the two, amping up the thrills and pyrotechnics that spark when Pusan firefighters Sang-woo (Choi Min-su) and Hyun-tae (Yoo Ji-tae) go up against a psychotic arsonist Hee-su (Cha Seung-weon). The escalating battle between these men begins after Sang-woo loses a firefighter friend while battling a blaze in an apartment building. Unknown to him, the blaze is the handiwork of recently paroled firebug Hee-su. As the films drags on, the stakes escalate to dizzying heights, with Hee-su setting bigger and more elaborate blazes that engulf gas stations and hospitals.

Similar to "Backdraft", the film that inspired it, "Libera Me" relied on purely physical flame effects to create the large on-screen blazes. Working with a hefty budget of $4 million US, director Yang Yun-ho used actual buildings for the film's key action set pieces, such as spending $250K US to build a life-size set of a gas station and then setting it alight. And when you see characters run into the burning buildings, it is the actual actors risking life and limb for the film's moments of cinema verité, as the cast insisted on doing their own stunts. The net result of all this is probably some of the most exciting firefighting footage ever committed to film.

Unfortunately, the film's scatterbrained script is not on par with the special effects. The central story of tracking down the serial arsonist is certainly suspenseful. Unfortunately, the script also throws in a number of cliché-ridden and melodramatic subplots that are hardly interesting and end up grinding the main story to a halt on more than one occasion. In addition, the villain Hee-su seems to suffer from the same affliction of most movie serial killers-- a lack of credible motivation for the things he does, other than being 'crazy', and relying on overly elaborate, deviously entertaining, yet completely implausible schemes to thwart the heroes.

On the acting side, the ensemble that Yang has gathered together is good. The photogenic leading triumvirate of Choi, Cha, and Yoo are all good in their respective roles, and they are ably supported by a Park Sang-myun as a dedicated firefighter who lets nothing get in the way of doing his job, and Kim Kyu-ri as the obligatory love interest and damsel in distress.

Despite being saddled with a meandering script and hackneyed plotting, "Libera Me" still manages to be an incendiary thrill machine that honors the brave exploits of firefighters. With top-notch production values and special effects that push the limits of South Korean moviemaking, "Libera Me" is a respectable entry in the field of Korean blockbusters.

Siren - 2000

Starring: Shin Hyun-june, Jung Joon-ho, Chang Jin-young
Director: Lee Ju-Yeop
Availability: Hong Kong-import VCD and DVD (multi-region), Korean-import DVD (multi-region)
Rating: ●●½

Siren DVD box art (*image courtesy of Seonwu Entertainment*)

"Siren" was the 'other' firefighter movie to grace Korean movie screens in 2000, beating "Libera Me" to the punch by two weeks. The story of this film revolves around two firefighters, Joon-woo (Shin Hyun-june) and Kang-hyun (Jung Joon-ho) who don't see eye-to-eye when it comes to firefighting strategy. Joon-woo prefers to act selflessly, flinging himself at every dangerous situation that comes along, motivated by childhood trauma from a car accident that claimed the life of his father. In contrast, Kang-hyun is a far more cautious man, who prefers to think things through first and places the safety of himself and his team above cowboy heroics.

Unfortunately, their differing philosophies come to a head while putting out a blaze in a burning restaurant. Joon-woo is pulled back by Kang-hyun during the rescue operation, resulting in some minor fisticuffs. In addition, a mother and her young daughter perish in the fire. Because of their unprofessional behavior, Joon-woo and Kang-hyun are suspended from regular duties, which eventually leads to Joon-woo quitting in disgust.

However, Joon-woo doesn't end up staying away from firefighting for long as a rash of arsons start plaguing the city. Unknown to both Joon-woo and Kang-hyun, the fires are being set by the husband and father of the restaurant fire victims, who has been driven mad by grief. Determined to exact revenge on the firefighters who let his family perish, he begins targeting friends and loved ones, with a particular focus on Joon-woo's girlfriend Ye-rin (Chang Jin-young).

In comparison to "Libera Me", "Siren" is rather disappointing. Instead of the over-the-top pyrotechnics of the $4 million US blockbuster, the special effects of "Siren" are decidedly smaller, with the use of computer graphics substituting for actual physical fire effects. The story is also rather lightweight, with sketchy characterizations assigned to the two leads. It also doesn't help that Joon-woo, who is supposed to be the one that the audience identifies with most, is portrayed in a rather flat manner by Shin, who uses the same old terse 'lone wolf' shtick that allowed him to sleepwalk through "Bichunmoo" and "The Gingko Bed". As Joon-woo's girlfriend, Chang is okay, though she isn't given much to do, other than to act as a sounding board for Joon-woo and Hang-kyun, as well as (you guessed it) ending up in dire need of rescuing in the last act-- a disappointing turn for those moviegoers who recall her memorable work in "The Foul King".

Overall, "Siren" is a disappointing effort, combining a lightweight script with so-so visual effects. Without the suspense or eye-popping 'gee, how did they do that?' visuals of "Libera Me", this slow-burning actioner quickly burns itself out.

A.F.R.I.K.A. - 2002

Starring: Lee Yu-won, Kim Min-sun, Jo Eun-ji, Lee Young-jin
Director: Shin Seung-soo
Availability: Korean-import DVD (multi-region)
Rating: ●●½

Jo Eun-ji, Lee Yu-won, Kim Min-sun, and Lee Young-jin (*image courtesy of IM Pictures*)

A PG-rated mixture of "Thelma & Louise" and "Natural Born Killers", "A.F.R.I.K.A." is a road movie that combines stupid gangsters, big guns, and giggling girls on the lam. Unfortunately, this action/comedy has more misses than hits in both categories, and is only memorable for its jokey reference to a much superior film.

The story starts off with two twenty-something young women, the sullen Ji-won (Lee Yu-won) and the bubbly So-hyun (Kim Min-sun), hitting the road for their summer vacation. They have borrowed a car from So-hyun's boyfriend, but unknown to them, the car is actually stolen and contains a case with guns belonging to a corrupt cop and a gangster. So-hyun discovers the case and plays with the guns, thinking that they are fakes, and accidentally shoots out the car's back window. The commotion catches the attention of the local police, and they are forced to continue their trip on foot.

Unfortunately, they quickly learn that life on the road is very dangerous for two young women, and resort to using the guns when they are trapped by two would-be rapists in the middle of nowhere and accosted by two dirty old men in a restaurant. They also find themselves joined by Young-mi (Jo Eun-ji), a flippant coffee shop prostitute (yes, they have those in Korea), and Jin-ah (Lee Young-jin, who starred alongside Kim Min-sun in cult horror hit "Memento Mori"), a dour clothing store sales clerk, both of whom are attracted by the guns. With the guns being seen as an easy way out of any problem, particularly by their newest members, they quickly find themselves being pursued by both the police and the gangsters who want their guns back.

At the same time, with news reports of their activities spreading across the country, these four women become media superstars, with their own fan club and web site-- Adoring Four Revolutionary Idols in Korean Area, or A.F.R.I.K.A. for short. This is then followed by an epidemic of wannabe copycat crimes perpetrated by their fans.

"A.F.R.I.K.A." is billed as an action comedy, but it is unsuccessful in both respects. The film's action sequences are unremarkable, as the gunplay is limited to the four protagonists shooting every which way but on target, fight sequences are essentially the gangsters slapping each other around, and the film's major car chase is disappointingly pedestrian. The same goes with the comedy, with one comic misfire coming after another, such as some lame humor about their criminal activities being conjectured to be the work of North Korean spies, uninteresting slapstick between the gangsters, or a bungled sequence where a heavily armed and unimpressed shop clerk pegs the four women as mere wannabes, instead of the real deal. Veteran writer/director Shin Seung-soo even tries his hand at injecting some social commentary into the proceedings, such as how the sense of empowerment offered by the gun quickly becomes a rift between them, the second-class status of women in Korea, or the role of the media in glorifying antisocial behavior in society-- unfortunately, none of these intriguing ideas are done the proper justice.

In fact, about the only memorable aspect of "A.F.R.I.K.A." is a gag about "Attack the Gas Station!" During their travels, the four women come across a gas station where the manager (Park Yeong-gyu) recognizes Ji-won and asks her if she used to work there, with the joke being that both Park and Lee Yu-won starred in "Attack the Gas Station!". The gag then continues with the manager complaining about fixing telephones, breaking into song, and other miscellaneous references to the 1999 film.

Another problem with "A.F.R.I.K.A." are the one-dimensional characters and the performances that back them up. Lee Yu-won and Kim are the best of the bunch, with the two actresses sharing good chemistry. Unfortunately, the limitations of the script give them very little to do beyond the confines of their characters. Lee Young-jin is okay as sourpuss Jin-ah, while Jo is easily the most annoying person in the cast, as all her character does is act like a mindless and low-class version of "My Sassy Girl", which is further exacerbated by her lack of talent.

After it was released in South Korea at the beginning of 2002, "A.F.R.I.K.A." quickly disappeared from theaters and wound up on DVD not long after, indicative of the quality found in this unremarkable 'girls with guns' action comedy. Other than the "Attack the Gas Station!" gag and the casting of some of Korea's popular young actresses, there is little worth exploring in "A.F.R.I.K.A.".

The Legend of Gingko (Danjeogbiyeonsu) - 2000

Starring: Sol Kyung-gu, Kim Yoon-jin, Lee Mi-sook, Choi Jin-shil, Kim Seok-hun
Director: Park Je-hyeon
Availability: Korean-import DVD (Region 3)
Rating: • •

Legend of Gingko DVD box art
(*image courtesy of KTB Networks*)

Billed as "Gingko Bed 2", a follow-up to Kang Je-gyu's "Gingko Bed", "The Legend of Gingko " actually has very little in common with the 1996 fantasy romance. Produced under Kang's newly minted production company and directed by "Shiri" writer Park Je-hyeon, "The Legend of Gingko" is a disappointing sword-and-sorcery adventure that wastes a talented cast with its incoherent script, jumpy editing, uninteresting characters, and unimpressive fight choreography.

The story revolves around a multi-generational war between the Hwasan tribe and the evil Mae tribe. With the Hwasan having emerged victorious from the latest round of fighting, the matriarch of the Mae tribe, Su (Lee Mi-sook), constructs a holy sword from the blood and bones of a thousand human sacrifices. However, to complete this mighty weapon, Su must sacrifice her newborn daughter Vee. This does not go over well with the girl's father, who abducts her and heads to Hwasan territory, where she can live her life to the fullest.

Several years later, Vee (Choi Jin-shil) has grown up into a young woman and become friends with the Hwasan tribe's two top warriors, Juk (Sol Kyung-gu) and Dahn (Kim Seok-hun). Unfortunately, a love quadrangle has developed between Vee, Juk, Dahn, and Princess Yeon (Kim Yoon-jin)-- Vee and Dahn have mutual affection for one another, Juk is in love with Vee, while Princess Yeon is in love with Juk, whom she intends to marry once Juk becomes leader of the tribe. Meanwhile, as the world turns, Su is still after her daughter. An upcoming lunar eclipse will create the necessary conditions to complete the holy sword, and so Su sends out her troops to capture Vee.

Those expecting "Crouching Tiger, Hidden Dragon", or even another "Musa" will come away from "Legend of Gingko" sorely disappointed. The formulaic soap-opera-like script offers no surprises, the production values are on par with "Xena: Warrior Princess", the furrowing of brows substitutes for acting, and the helter-skelter storytelling is both distancing and perplexing. Even pure-action mavens will be bored by the rote and repetitive swordplay. It is also disappointing how the film wastes the acting talents of three top actors: Sol of "Peppermint Candy" fame, Kim who shined in "Shiri" in 1999, and veteran actress Lee, who made an impressive comeback in 1998's "An Affair".

It also doesn't help that the DVD subtitles appear to have been hastily thrown together, with odd grammar and spelling mistakes in abundance, leading to some interesting dialogue, such as Juk being told that the 'density' of the tribe is in his hands. Unfortunately, about the only time I felt any sort of connection to the on-screen action was when

Kim Yoon-jin and Kim Seok-hun (*image courtesy of KTB Networks*)

Dahn tells Vee that 'everything is confusing', which was exactly how I felt.

Despite its flaws, "The Legend of Gingko" actually managed to make its way into the top-ten Korean films of 2000, just behind the similarly narratively challenged "Bichunmoo". But aside from its financial success, it is likely that this 'Legend' will be quickly forgotten.

This is Law (Igeoshi beobida) - 2001

Starring: Kim Min-jong, Shin Eun-kyung, Im Won-hee
Director: Min Byeong-jin
Availability: Korean-import DVD (multi-region)
Rating: •

This is Law DVD box art (*image courtesy of AFDF*)

Given the presence of Shin Eun-kyung of "My Wife is a Gangster" and slick marketing, I'm sure many Korean moviegoers (not to mention gullible DVD buyers such as myself) thought that "This is Law", also known as "Out of Justice", would have been another double-lightning strike of action and comedy. Alas, this film should have been named "This is Crap" or "Out of Ideas".

The story (and I am using this term very loosely here) revolves around an elite police task force named STF, who are on the trail of a mysterious vigilante known only as 'Dr. Q', who mercilessly kills criminals that have eluded justice and then uploads the snuff-film videos to his web site. When Dr. Q's latest victim turns out to be the head of STF, Detective Pyo (Kim Min-jong) is put on the case. Unfortunately, Pyo's investigation of Dr. Q leads him into a jurisdictional conflict with lowly homicide cop Bong (Im Won-hee), who, in addition to having his own ideas on how to catch the killer, has the hots for a female computer expert named Kang (Shin) on Pyo's team.

"This is Law" is already in trouble within the first fifteen minutes. In addition to blatantly inserted scenes of gratuitous nudity and violence, it is a nightmare trying to understand exactly what is going on and who all the characters are. First-time director Min Byeong-jin directs the story with the steadiness of a crack addict in search of his next hit, jumping from one abrupt scene to the next without any sense of direction or purpose. Even more annoying are the characterizations, which run the gamut from none (such as the cardboard-thin Pyo) to annoying comic relief (such as Bong, who is so stupid and immature that it quickly ceases to be funny). And if this level of incompetence wasn't enough, "This is Law" even fails on the most basic level of visceral thrills with its tired and uninspired action sequences.

However, the most frustrating aspect of "This is Law" has to do with what may be the prime reason for seeing such a lackluster film-- seeing Shin Eun-kyung in action again after the fantastic "My Wife is a Gangster". Unfortunately, despite her top billing in this travesty, Shin is actually given very little to do in this film, other than look terse, surf the Internet, be sexually harassed by Bong, and then surf the Internet some more. Whereas "My Wife is a Gangster" was fun to watch with Shin as a strong and empowered woman, "This is Law" ends up relegating her to being a piece of scenery.

Shin Eun-kyung andKim Min-jong (*image courtesy of AFDF*)

After the comic brilliance of "My Wife is a Gangster", it is difficult to fathom exactly what was going through actress Shin Eun-kyung's head when she joined this cinematic train wreck (actually, that is unfair statement-- train wrecks are far more interesting than this). Despite a cool-looking poster and an intriguing trailer, upon viewing "This is Law", it quickly becomes painfully obvious that this could easily be the worst film of the latest 'Korean New Wave'.

Dream of a Warrior - 2001

Starring: Leon Lai, Park Eun-hye, Lee Na-young
Director: Park Hee-joon
Availability: Hong Kong-import VCD and DVD (multi-region)
Rating: •

Dream of a Warrior poster (*image courtesy of Hanmac Films*)

When it was released in 2001, "Dream of a Warrior" was billed as South Korea's first serious attempt at creating a science-fiction blockbuster, with a big (by Korean standards) budget of $3.2 million US and state-of-the-art special effects. Unfortunately, it has subsequently earned the dubious distinction of being one of the most spectacular box office failures of the latest 'Korean New Wave', as "Dream of a Warrior" managed to disappear from theatres after only one week and was declared by some critics as the worst film of the year.

Hong Kong heartthrob Leon Lai stars as a Korean cop named Dean, whose dreams are haunted by a beautiful woman asking for his help (no, he doesn't actually speak Korean as all of his lines are dubbed). He then learns that the woman is Nam-hong (Park Eun-hye), the daughter of scientist Dr. Jang. Apparently, Dr. Jang used his daughter as a guinea pig to test his time machine invention two years ago, and she never returned. Coincidentally enough, Dean has the correct brainwave pattern that will allow him to go back in time and bring back Nam-hong. And so off he goes into the time machine...

... and ends up in a long-lost technological society known as Dilmoon. Similar to the old television series "Quantum Leap", Dean occupies the body of a warrior/football player who has been chosen to help prevent an evil force named Paxtus from taking over the world. However, on his off-hours, he is secretly in love with Princess Rose, who is Nam-hong's incarnation in this world. Unfortunately, Princess Rose is already betrothed to the ambitious General Shanril (Yoon Tae-young).

If all of this sounds cheesy, that's because it is. In fact, it seems as though the plot and production design of "Dream of a Warrior" was completely lifted from the Playstation 2 videogame "Final Fantasy X", which also featured a star athlete cum warrior being propelled through time to fight a great evil, while navigating a love triangle between a woman of the ruling class and the ruthless military leader she is obligated to marry. Unfortunately, whereas "Final Fantasy X" benefited from strong writing and

Park Eun-hye (*image courtesy of Hanmac Films*)

decent voice acting, "Dream of a Warrior" offers its audience bad writing and even worse acting. The dialogue, which is dominated by embarrassingly incoherent technobabble, lacks any sort of depth, whether it be narrative or emotional. The production design and special effects are a mix of poorly done CGI and rejects from old "Dr. Who" episodes. And if these deficiencies weren't enough, director Park Hee-joon directs and edits this monstrosity with the attention and care of a drunk driver, with complete disregard to things such as proper shot composition, steady pacing, or storytelling subtlety.

Next to "This is Law", "Dream of a Warrior" is a close contender to being the absolute worst film of the latest 'Korean New Wave'. There is absolutely no compelling reason for anyone to watch this ridiculous combination of lousy special effects, bad acting, incomprehensible storytelling, and production values befitting of a high school play. Even fans of Leon Lai's spotty filmography or the "Final Fantasy" videogame franchise are best advised to stay clear-- "Dream of a Warrior" is an absolute nightmare.

Yonggary (Reptilian) - 1999

Starring: Harrison Young, Donna Philipson, Dan Cashman
Director: Shim Hyung-rae
Availability: Korean-import VCD, North American DVD (Region 1)
Rating: •

Yonggary poster (*image courtesy of Sam Boo Entertainment*)

After the lows reached by "This is Law" and "Dream of a Warrior", you would think that the bottom of the barrel has already been scraped. Alas, Korea's answer to Godzilla, "Yonggary" (also known internationally as "Reptilian"), is so inept that it makes these two lackluster films look like strokes of brilliance in comparison. If you thought the writing, editing, and direction of "This is Law", and the special effects, acting, and production values of "Dream of a Warrior" were horrible, then "Yonggary" will redefine just how bad a movie can be.

"Yonggary" is actually a remake of 1967's rubber-suited "Grand Evil Master Yonggary", which was itself a remake of 1965's "Gamera, the Invincible". The film's titular creature, Yonggary, is a fire-breathing dinosaur that is being unearthed by mad paleontologist Dr. Campbell (Richard B. Livingston), despite the dire warnings of global apocalypse uttered by rival Dr. Wendel Hughes (Harrison Young, best known as the 'old' James Ryan in "Saving Private Ryan). Of course, Dr. Campbell doesn't listen, and Yonggary is brought back to life by aliens in an orbiting spaceship, who plan to use the 500-foot tall dinosaur to take over the world. With the help of Campbell's disenfranchised assistant Holly Davis (Donna Philipson), Dr. Hughes makes his way to a nearby military command post where Lt. Gen. George Murdock (Dan Cashman) is leading an effort to stop Yonggary. Unfortunately, regardless of what they throw at it (armed helicopters, F-16s, tanks, and even soldiers with rayguns and rocketpacks), Yonggary seems unstoppable.

With the cast being predominantly Western actors (bad ones at that) and hardly any signs that this is a Korean production (other than the presence of veteran

Korean 'monster movie' director Shim Hyung-rae in the credits and how almost everyone drives a Hyundai in the movie), it is fairly obvious that "Yonggary" was thrown together for purely export purposes. Alas, when one actually watches "Yonggary", the first question that comes to mind is, "Who would buy this?" (unfortunately… me).

Like all monster movies, such as Japan's long-running "Godzilla" or "Gamera" franchises, the script is an obvious area of weakness, with characters you don't care about, heavy exposition that passes for dialogue, and one big scene of destruction after another. The performances are a particular sore point in "Yonggary", as the implausibly cliché-ridden characters (for example, a reporter with "Time Magazine" named 'Bud' looks like he just got out of bed and speaks with a 'New Yock' accent befitting a movie from the 1950s) are compounded by unintentionally hilarious overacting.

Of course, nobody watches a monster movie for the nuances in writing or the thespian arts-- they want to see 'stuff get blowed up real good'. Unfortunately, "Yonggary" ends up cheating the audience out of this simple pleasure. Instead of a man in a rubber suit destroying intricately detailed miniatures, Yonggary makes heavy use of CGI to animate Yonggary and the military vehicles he trashes. But unlike the high-end CGI that Roland Emmerich used in his Hollywood version of "Godzilla", it looks as though director Shim used a Sony Playstation One to animate "Yonggary", with all its shiny textures and pixelated objects. And when these low-quality computer animations are blue-screened with live action, you'll be wishing that you had rented "Godzilla" movies from the 1960s instead.

Business-wise, "Yonggary" ended up being a financial success for all involved. In fact, "Yonggary" has been held up as a case study for how to export Korean films worldwide, as it was successfully sold to 90 countries and generated all sorts of press in CNN, Asia Week, and at the 1999 Cannes Film Festival. "Yonggary" even has its own theme park in its native Korea, and an 'extended version', entitled "Yonggary vs. Cyker", was released in 2001. But as a film that would appeal to fans of "Godzilla" and other monster movies, "Yonggary" is an unwatchable disappointment. As the film's tagline declares, "It's not what you expect"-- in fact, it's far, far worse.

Chapter 6: Hard Gore Thrillers – Horror Films

Up until the late nineties, Korean-made entries into the horror genre were rather sparse. However, the release of 1998's "The Quiet Family", which was actually more of a black comedy with horror elements, galvanized audience interest in horror films. Thus, in recent years, the output of horror and thillers has increased dramatically, as Korean filmmakers have cashed in on the pent-up audience demand for 'scary movies'. Unfortunately, not all entries in the nascent horror genre have lived up to their promise, as many have ended up being rehashes of mindless 'teen horror' films from Hollywood, or slow-burning and introspective pieces with little consideration for pacing or storytelling.

However, there are a few gems that have managed to take the genre into new and interesting directions. "Tell Me Something" reunited "Christmas in August" stars Han Suk-kyu and Shim Eun-ha in a "Se7en"-like serial-killer thriller, and though the story doesn't hold up well to detailed examination, the presentation is first-rate. "Say Yes" elevates the story of a vacationing couple's nasty run-in with an unbalanced individual above the usual 'mad slasher' trappings of the 'psycho killer road movie' genre to create a truly horrific film. Finally, "The Ring Virus" is an effective remake of the film that launched a best-selling Japanese horror franchise, while schoolgirl horror flick "Memento Mori" makes up for a muted ending with its creepy atmosphere and impressive technical credits.

The Quiet Family (Choyonghan kajok) - 1998

Starring: Go Ho-kyung, Song Kang-ho, Choi Min-shik, Lee Yeon-sung, Park In-hwan, Na Mun-hee
Director: Kim Ji-woon
Availability: Hong Kong-import VCD and DVD (multi-region)
Rating: ••••½

Na Mun-hee, Choi Min-shik, Go Ho-kyung, Song Kang-ho, Lee Yeon-sung, and Park In-hwan (*image courtesy of Myung Films*)

In his 1998 filmmaking debut "The Quiet Family", director Kim Ji-woon (who would go on to direct the comedy hit "Foul King") presents an inspiring story about how a crisis strengthens the bonds between the members of a dysfunctional family, bringing them closer together in a rare display of domestic solidarity. Unfortunately, the list of family-building activities represented in this South Korean black comedy includes murder, dumping the corpses into shallow graves, and, of course, staying quiet about it.

The family in question is the Kangs, who have moved from Seoul to operate the Misty Lodge, an isolated mountain inn. The family is dominated by no-nonsense father Tae-gu (Park In-hwan), with his loyal wife (Na Mun-hee) always by his side. The younger members of the family include sex-obsessed son Yeong-min (Song Kang-ho), clueless daughter Mi-su (Lee Yeon-sung), and sullen daughter Mi-na (Go Ho-kyung). Finally, rounding out the Kang clan is Tae-gu's younger brother (Choi Min-shik).

After a slow start, the Kangs finally receive their very first guest. The joy is short-lived though, as the man is found dead the very next morning, apparently having committed suicide during the night. Concerned that a dead body will 'kill' business and attract unwanted police attention, Tae-gu orders his sons to bury the man in the woods. Unfortunately, this is only the first entry in the Kangs' list of questionable deeds. Their next customers, a young couple, commit suicide after a passionate night of lovemaking (I dunno, maybe they saw Yoshimitsu Morita's "Lost Paradise"), and once again, the Kang's cover it up.

As the anarchy at the Misty Lodge increases, so does the body count. A hiker who tries to take advantage of Mi-su becomes acquainted with the business end of a shovel. A case of mistaken identity results in an assassination attempt at the lodge to go horribly wrong. To further add to their troubles, the Kangs receive word that the government plans to pave the road in front of the lodge, requiring them to find somewhere else to hide the bodies. And if juggling all these bodies and hiding the evidence wasn't difficult enough already, the police begin sniffing around as part of a missing persons investigation.

"The Quiet Family" finds an easy middle between the two extremes of its story. On the one hand, with its unconventional camerawork and bouncy Western pop soundtrack, the energetic production underscores the individual quirks of each family member (such as Mi-su's complete ignorance of what the rest of the family is up to), as well as the increasingly absurd situations they find themselves in (such as an attempt to incinerate the growing pile of cadavers that goes horribly wrong). However, at the same time, director Kim pushes the horror aspects of the script, and isn't squeamish at shocking the audience with some of the film's more grisly moments, such as the effect of a heavy rainstorm on the shallow graves that the Kangs have dug, or the shock when they one of the bodies unexpectedly comes back to life.

Kim also adds an additional layer of subtlety to "The Quiet Family" by hinting that the events depicted may be apocryphal, being the product of an overactive imagination. Clues are provided in that the story is told from the perspective of Mi-na, a 17-year old full of cynicism and gloom (think Christina Ricci in "The Addams Family"), and she appears in the film's opening scene, where she complains that "it's been thirteen days since we moved from the city... and still nothing has happened", as well as the curious closing scene, which upon an initial viewing, may make little sense.

The ensemble that Kim has gathered is strong. Park is perfect as the brutish family patriarch, and is ably supported by Na as his diligent wife. Popular actor Choi, who has made a career out of playing 'tough guys' (such as in "Failan" or "Shiri"), is cast against type as Tae-gu's dim-witted yet warm-hearted younger brother. The always likable Song, who would later star in Kim's follow-up feature "Foul King", shows off his gift for comic timing that helped establish his acting career. Finally, as the dour Mi-na, Go delivers an appropriately acerbic performance with the requisite amount of dry wit.

If you take your comedies black, then you need to look no further than "The Quiet Family". Straddling the fine line between humor and horror, "The Quiet Family" has developed quite a following at home and on the international festival circuit, including being remade in 2000 by cult Japanese director Takashi Miike as "The Happiness of the Katakuri's". Definitely not your run-of-the-mill 'family film'.

Tell Me Something - 1999

Starring: Han Suk-kyu, Shim Eun-ha, Jang Hang-seon, Yeom Jeong-ah, An Seok-hwan, Park Cheol-ho, Yu Jun-sang, Lee Hwan-jun
Director: Chang Yoon-hyun
Availability: North American DVD, Hong Kong-import VCD and DVD (multi-region), Korean-import DVD (multi-region)
Rating: • • • •

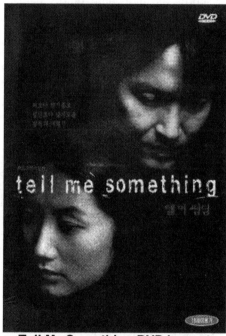

Tell Me Something DVD box art
(*image courtesy of Cinema Service*)

Dubbed a 'hard-gore thriller', 1999's "Tell Me Something" is South Korea's entry into the 'serial killer thriller' genre. Thanks to a big-budget marketing campaign, a slick trailer, and the drawing power of its two ultra-popular leads Han Suk-kyu and Shim Eun-ha (reunited from "Christmas in August"), "Tell Me Something" was a big hit in its native land, ranking third in the 1999 box office, just behind "Shiri" and "Attack the Gas Station!" With the film's rich cinematography, polished production values, and basis in an established Hollywood genre, it isn't surprising that "Tell Me Something" was subsequently picked up for a limited stateside theatrical release, as well as a North American DVD pressing. And though "Tell Me Something" is dead-on in matching the quality of bigger-budget Hollywood productions (such as "Seven"), it also encounters the same stumbling block as its North American 'serial killer thriller' brethren-- a less-than-cohesive script.

During the summer of 1999, a number of black garbage bags begin appearing around Seoul, filled with the assorted body parts of three murder victims. The high-priority case ends up falling into the lap of Detective Jo (Han Suk-kyu), a disgraced cop who he has just been put through the ringer by an internal affairs investigation. With the help of his partner Oh (Jang Han-seong) and a dedicated task force, Jo quickly learns that all three victims were former boyfriends of a comely but quiet museum curator named Chae Su-yeon (Shim Eun-ha).

With his attention focused on Su-yeon, Jo spends most of his time with her, uncovering clues from her troubled past as a means to track down the killer. Meanwhile, the body count continues to mount, and Jo soon finds himself in the killer's crosshairs. But who is behind these heinous crimes? Is it Kim Ki-yeon (Yu Jun-sang), an artist who is obsessed with Su-yeon? Or is it Su-yeon's best friend, a medical resident at a local hospital? Or could it be Su-yeon's estranged father, whom she has not seen in five years? Or could it be Su-yeon herself?

Using the neon- and rain-drenched settings to great effect, "Tell Me Something" is a slick and gritty piece of neo-noir, rivaling the stark urban tableau seen in Wong Kar-wai's "Fallen Angels" or Ridley Scott's "Black Rain". Director Chang Yoon-hyun has a good understanding of

Han Suk-kyu (*image courtesy of Cinema Service*)

creating the requisite atmosphere, as he infuses "Tell Me Something" with the creepiness and tension that you would associate with "Seven" or "The X-Files". This is also helped by the underplayed performances of Han and Shim, and the low-key script with a smoldering mystery that is gradually unveiled. Chang also earns the film's 'hard-gore' reputation by pulling no punches in the sporadic visualizations of the killer's crimes, which include dissections, severed limbs, decapitated heads, and copious amounts of blood. For the faint of heart, "Tell Me Something" is definitely best viewed on an empty stomach.

For most of its two-hour running time, "Tell Me Something" is engaging as it gradually ratchets up the suspense, drawing the audience deeper into the mystery while raising the stakes. Unfortunately, it is in the last act where the film starts to fall apart. Like the lesser entries in the 'serial killer thriller' genre (such as "Along Came a Spider" and "The Watcher"), the overly elaborate scheme of the killer ends up overwhelming the logical concerns of the narrative. While the film's climax is well-shot and executed with a great soundtrack (including the best use of "Red Right Hand" by Nick Cave and the Bad Seeds in a film, which was also used in "The X-Files" and "Scream"), it ends up not making sense when viewed in the context of what led up to it. Even more distressing is the film's coda, which introduces another logic-defying plot twist courtesy of what is dubbed the 'Kodak moment' cliché of murder-mysteries.

Though some of the plot points hold up on subsequent viewings of the film, a number of them do not, requiring character motivations and circumstances to jump through hoops in order for the story to remain cohesive. In fact, audiences in Korea have been so mystified that a number of Internet discussion groups have sprung up just to unravel the film's convoluted narrative. I suspect that part of the reason for the confusion could be due to the omission of a few key scenes, which may have been left on the cutting-room floor. Two obvious logical gaps would be how Detective Oh is able to link a seemingly unrelated crime scene to the murders, and a significant 'change of heart' experienced by one of the characters that triggers the film's climax.

If it were not for the confusing ending, "Tell Me Something" would gain a wholehearted recommendation. But if you are able to forgive the story's narrative missteps (as this reviewer was), then there is still a lot to like in "Tell Me Something", which is an entertaining, suspenseful, and visually arresting **Han Suk-kyu and Shim Eun-ha** (*image courtesy of Cinema Service*)

thriller that is on par with the better 'serial killer thrillers' that Hollywood has cranked out over the years. Just make sure you don't watch it alone.

Say Yes - 2001

Starring: Park Joong-hoon, Chu Sang-mi, Kim Ju-hyuk
Director: Kim Sung-hong
Availability: Korean-import DVD (multi-region)
Rating: ●●●½

Say Yes poster (*image courtesy of Cinema Service*)

Anyone planning a long-distance road trip is best advised to stay away from "Say Yes", in which a young couple's vacation takes a nasty turn after crossing paths with a psycho killer. And though the film covers familiar territory in other entries in 'psycho killer road movie' genre, such as "Joyride", "The Vanishing", or "Breakdown", while suffering from the occasional lapse in credibility, "Say Yes" ends up being a decent thrill machine that is capped off by a terrific ending.

The young couple in question are struggling writer Jeong-hyun (Kim Ju-hyuk) and Yun-hie (Chu Sang-mi), who have decided to take a weekend road trip to celebrate both their one-year wedding anniversary and Jeong-hyun's recent manuscript sale. During a stop at a roadside diner, Yun-hie is creeped out when she spies Em (Park Joong-hoon) staring at her. Later on, as Jeong-hyun drives out of the parking lot, he accidentally backs into Em and knocks him over. Feeling bad about what they have done, the young couple reluctantly accept Em's request for a ride. Unfortunately, their instincts prove to be right-- further down the road, Em declares that he hasn't decided... which one of them he plans to kill!

Not surprisingly, that little outburst gets him ejected from the car. Shaken up but undeterred, Yun-hie and Jeong-hyun continue on their trip and do their best to put the unfortunate incident behind them. However, they soon find themselves being stalked by Em and despite their best efforts to avoid him, the young couple end up playing right into Em's twisted little game. For example, Jeong-hyun ends up in jail charged with assault, after coming to blows with Em, and the only way that the charges are dropped is if Em is allowed to become their travelling companion. However, this is merely a drop in the bucket in terms of the horrors that await them....

Director Kim Sung-hong has crafted a competent thriller with "Say Yes", and it is primarily driven by the dynamics between the three main characters. On the outside, Yun-hie and Jeong-hyun seem to be an ideal couple, though Yeo Hye-young's script hints at their fatal flaws early on-- unbridled compassion in the case of Yun-hie, while Jeong-hyun prefers to 'go with the flow' and is subject to impulsive actions. Em, who is both smart and manipulative, mercilessly exploits the weaknesses of his prey and anticipates their every move. True, there are times where Yun-hie and Jeong-hyun seem a little too gullible to be going along with Em's demands, though in the context of their wishy-washy characters, it sort of does make sense.

Later on, the film goes into full-blown 'mad slasher' mode as Yun-hie and Jeong-hyun find themselves being chased by an almost unstoppable Em, who commandeers a dump truck and doesn't let anything stand in the way of running them down, including other vehicles and buildings. However, this pales in comparison to the film's shocking climax and ending. Whereas other 'mad slasher' films are content to end right after the protagonists have vanquished the villain (with the obligatory suggestion that the killer is not really dead yet), "Say Yes" closes on a chilling note by hinting at the viral nature of madness and how Em's reign of terror was but one signpost in an unending cycle of violence.

Performance-wise, the trio of lead actors acquit themselves nicely. Chu, no stranger to the horror genre with her prior work in "The Soul Guardians", and Kim are credible in the portrayal of their characters, which start off as a happy-go-lucky couple and end up enduring a truly harrowing experience. As the tormentor of Yun-hie and Jeong-hyun, Park's performance is a stark contrast to the keystone cop he played in "Nowhere to Hide" and the comedic roles that made him famous. It is doubtful that viewers will ever be able to see him in a positive light after such a menacing and sinister turn.

The satisfying "Say Yes" breathes new life into the well-tread 'psycho killer road movie' genre. Though it may push the credibility envelope at times, overall, the film shines with its energetic script, well-drawn characters, and an ending that blows other like-minded films away. 'Say yes' to "Say Yes".

The Ring Virus - 1999

Starring: Shin Eun-kyung, Jeong Jin-young, Bae Doo-na
Director: Kim Dong-bin
Availability: Korean-import DVD (multi-region)
Rating: ●●●½

Ring Virus DVD box art (*image courtesy of Hanmac Films*)

When Japanese author Suzuki Koji first penned "Ring", the opening chapter of a literary trilogy, little did he realize that this horror novel would become a cultural phenomenon, both at home and around the world. With a premise that sounds like the stuff of urban legends, where watching a videotape results in death after seven days, "Ring" has spawned three successful feature films (the first being the 1998 film "Ringu"), a radio drama, and two television series in its native Japan. "Ring" has also inspired at least one Hollywood production, Dreamworks SKG's 2002 remake of "Ringu", entitled "Ring", directed by Gore Verbinski ("The Mexican") and star Naomi Watts ("Mulholland Drive"), and perhaps influenced William Malone's 2002 horror film "FearDotCom", which revolves around a killer web site (you download, you die!).

"The Ring Virus" is the 1999 South Korean version of "Ringu", and it had the additional distinction of being the first-ever Japanese-Korean co-production. And though it is mostly a shot-for-shot remake, replicating a number of key scenes from the 1998 Japanese film, it also integrates some new elements from the original Suzuki novel, while infusing the story with a greater sense of mystery and atmosphere.

"The Ring Virus" kicks off with journalist Sun-joo (Shin Eun-kyung) investigating the sudden and mysterious deaths of her niece Sang-mee and three of her friends. Not only did they all die at the exact same time, but they also all appear to have died from heart attacks. In going through her niece's things, she finds an old message on her pager that cryptically says that 'they should not have watched it'. Sun-joo also learns that Sang-mee and her friends had stayed at a seaside hotel the week before. There, she discovers that they had seen a videotape containing enigmatic and disturbing imagery, that ends with the warning, "You will die in a week. If you want to survive..." Unfortunately, someone has taped over the rest of the message.

With potentially only one week remaining before she succumbs to the videotape's curse, Sun-joo enlists the help of Choe-yol (Jeong Jin-yeoung), a cynical neurosurgeon with some wild theories of his own about the mysterious deaths and the tape. Together, they investigate further, and find that the tape is connected to a young woman named Eun-suh (Bae Doo-na) who disappeared a long time ago. Unfortunately, this knowledge does not bring them any closer to finding out how to break the seven-day curse.

Though "The Ring Virus" essentially retreads material from the 1998 Japanese film, director Kim Dong-bin skilfully ratchets up the tension gradually as Sun-joo and Choe-yol's investigation unfolds, while his visual style imparts an atmosphere of imminent doom to the proceedings. Particularly chilling are the disturbing montage on the cursed videotape, the horrifying scene that the tape's victims see before they die, and the film's grim ending, which reveals that because of Sun-joo's investigation, a Pandora's Box has been unleashed upon the world. Performances by Shin and Jeong are also good, with the former becoming increasingly frustrated and panic-stricken as the days count down, and the former gradually turning from skeptic to a true believer.

Unfortunately, this remake does have its share of problems, mainly with respect to keeping the audience abreast of all the twists, turns, and revelations of the investigation. The script suffers from several logical gaps, making it difficult to understand how Sun-joo and Choe-yol move forward in their investigation or leap to the conclusions they make. There is also little explanation given as to the whys behind the tape and its curse, which would have provided for some fascinating detail. Finally, the Korean-import multi-region DVD is plagued with spotty English subtitles, which may have contributed to the aforementioned problems.

Overall, "The Ring Virus" does not offer anything substantially new for those familiar with the Japanese original, "Ringu". Nevertheless, "The Ring Virus" is a polished effort that drips in atmosphere and successfully places the focus more on the mystery than on pure visceral scares, creating a truly infectious horror film.

Memento Mori (Yeogo goedam II) - 1999

Starring: Kim Min-sun, Park Ye-jin, Lee Young-jin, Kong Hyo-jin, Kim Min-heui
Director: Kim Tae-yong, Min Kyu-dong
Availability: Hong Kong-import VCD and DVD (multi-region), Korean-import DVD (multi-region)
Rating: ● ● ●½

Memento Mori poster (*image courtesy of Cinema Service*)

Though it is labelled as a 'sequel' to 1998's surprise hit "Whispering Corridors", "Memento Mori" shares only the title, all-girls' school setting, and supernatural elements of its predecessor, while involving an entirely new cast of characters and story. With rookie filmmakers Kim Tae-yong and Min Kyu-dong at the helm, "Memento Mori" gets off to a good start with the intrigue surrounding a lesbian relationship between two students and a mysterious death as a hook for the audience. Unfortunately, the film starts to fall apart as the emphasis on exaggerated supernatural happenings and special effects quickly overwhelm the story, leading to an unsatisfying conclusion.

The story begins with high school student Min-ah (Kim Min-sun) finding the shared diary of fellow students Shi-eun (Lee Yeong-jin) and Hyo-shin (Park Ye-jin). As Min-ah flips through the diary, a series of flashbacks details the rise and decline of Shi-eun and Hyo-shin's 'special relationship'. However, Min-ah also begins experiencing a number of strange hallucinations of a paranormal nature, which only become intensified when Hyo-shin falls off the roof of the school in an apparent suicide. With the help of two classmates (Kim Min-heui and Kong Hyo-jin), Min-ah begins her own investigation of Hyo-shin's suicide, particularly in fleshing out the potential involvement of Shi-eun and a male teacher named Goh (Baek Jong-hak).

Given that homosexuality is a subject generally avoided in South Korea (for example, Wong Kar-wai's gay drama "Happy Together" is banned there), kudos go to Kim and Min for the audacity to present this theme, particularly in a supernatural tale set in an all-girls' high school. However, it seems that the directors were a little too daring, as some rare production photos hint at a few deleted scenes with more overt lesbian sexuality. But aside from this iconoclastic challenge to the South Korean establishment, "Memento Mori" ends up being only a passable horror film.

The first half of "Memento Mori", though a bit on the slow side, is perhaps the most interesting, as the two directors engage the audience with a narrative structure that seamlessly glides between flashbacks and the present, offering tidbits of exposition on the relationship between Shi-eun and Hyo-shin. In addition, Min-ah begins experiencing the first of many hallucinations, which are

Lee Young-jin and Park Ye-jin (*image courtesy of Cinema Service*)

punctuated by the use of startling sound effects and stunning cinematography. However, by the halfway mark, the suspenseful story of love gone sour slowly begins to lose its way, as the ghost of Hyo-shin lays siege to the school, trapping the students inside. "Memento Mori" then becomes a simple supernatural scarefest that all but jettisons the careful and suspenseful plotting that came before it.

Since its release in 1999, "Memento Mori" has developed a cult following, as well as become a favorite at film festival midnight screenings. Unfortunately, I found it difficult to get caught up in all the hoopla. While the slow-burn build-up about love, betrayal, and vengeance is worthy of attention, the film's unsatisfying finale left me wondering what the fuss was all about, if not wanting more.

Sorum - 2001

Starring: Kim Myeong-min, Chang Jin-young, Ki Ju-bong
Director: Yoon Jong-chan
Availability: Korean-import DVD (Region 3)
Rating: ● ● ●

Sorum DVD box art (*image courtesy of Buena Vista International Korea*)

Yoon Jong-chan's directorial debut "Sorum" straddles the line between horror and psychological drama. Unfortunately, despite a setting thickly coated in atmosphere, this 2001 entry almost ends up failing in both respects, done in by its confusing script, laggard pacing, and scares that seem to go nowhere.

The story is kicked off when cab driver Yong-hyun (Kim Myeong-min) moves into room 504 of the crumbling Migum Apartments. On the outside, he appears to live a quiet life, looking after his pet hamster and being an avid fan of Bruce Lee movies. However, a few hints about his unsettled past are revealed, such as being fired from his previous job after his ex-girlfriend stole some money and disappeared. Hopefully, with a new home and new surroundings, he can get back to a normal life.

Unfortunately, Yong-hyun quickly learns that there is little that is normal about the building or his new neighbors. He becomes closest with Sun-yeong (Chang Jin-young), a young woman who works in the local 7-11 and bears bruises from constant beatings by her no-good husband. Sun-yeong's best friend, Eun-soo, is a piano teacher and she also lives in the building. Yong-hyun also comes to know a hack writer named Lee (Ki Ju-bong) who is writing a ghost-story novel based on events that actually happened in 504-- thirty years ago, apparently, a baby was almost burned to death after his father killed his mother and ran off with a woman living next door. And to further add to 504's cursed reputation, it seems that the apartment's previous tenant, aspiring writer Kwang-tae, whom Eun-soo was in love with, had also died in a mysterious fire.

Yong-hyun's life takes a sharp left turn when Sun-yeong shows up at his door one night, covered in blood-- she has just killed her abusive husband and needs help in burying the body. Yong-hyun agrees, and after the dirty deed is done, they start a physical relationship. Unfortunately, this murder sets in motion a series of events that lead to a return of the curse which plagues 504 and its unfortunate tenants, destroying both Yong-hyun and Sun-yeong in the process.

The biggest detriment of "Sorum" is director Yoon's scatterbrained approach to storytelling. This is the type of film where the audience will always be ten minutes behind, and there will be plenty of head scratching. There are a number of intriguing scenes that suggest that there are ghosts or supernatural forces at work in the Migum Apartments. Unfortunately, not only are these scenes abruptly inserted, but they also seem to have little bearing to what is actually happening when the larger picture becomes clear. Are these scenes attempts at misdirection, suggesting that the tenants of the building are suffering from some sort of collective madness, or are they merely 'cheap scares' for the sake of living up to the film's title (which translated, means 'goosebumps')?

The other problem is how the story takes a long time to get where it is going. This is most apparent in the second act, where the story essentially grinds to a halt. With so many questions having been raised by the unexplained supernatural happenings and the characters aimlessly wandering from one scene to the next, sitting through "Sorum" becomes an exercise in frustration. Thankfully, as the third act gets into gear, not only does a sense of urgency return to the film, but some major revelations divulge an unexpected connection between Yong-hyun and Sun-yeong, as well as the common fate that damns them both.

Despite being saddled with meandering and confusing material, the performances by the two leads are decent. Kim, who has more than a passing resemblance to Hong Kong's Leon Lai, is an enigmatic young man who mostly keeps to himself, yet he seems to have a dark side to his character-- one revealing scene finds him laughing hysterically at the victim of a fatal car accident. Chang, who is completely unrecognizable from her memorable turn in "The Foul King", is also good as the somber and slightly disturbed Sun-yeong.

In the end, the horror found in "Sorum" comes not from restless spirits or supernatural phenomena, but from the madness that arises from human frailty. Unfortunately, it is disappointing to see these concepts being undermined by Yoon's erratic execution. Despite its atmospheric build-up and an ending that defies audience expectations, the slow-boil approach that Yoon takes, along with his penchant for scares that go nowhere, severely tests the patience of viewers, and mars an otherwise fascinating film.

Secret Tears (Bimil) - 2000

Starring: Kim Seung-woo, Yun Mi-jo
Director: Park Ki-hyeong
Availability: Korean-import DVD (Region 3)
Rating: ● ●½

Secret Tears DVD box art (*image courtesy of Cinema Service*)

"Secret Tears" is the sophomore feature of "Whispering Corridors" director Park Ki-hyeong. And though "Secret Tears" does possess supernatural elements like Park's 1998 debut feature, it is more of a supernatural romance with some heavy psychological drama thrown in. And though the film's production values are strong, including some stunning cinematography and impressive special effects, the script is not, as the film fails to do anything meaningful or even of interest with its intriguing premise.

The story begins during a heavy downpour. While 33-year old insurance man Ku-ho (Kim Seung-woo) is driving co-workers Hyeon-nam (Jeong Hyeon-woo) and Do-kyung (Park Eun-suk) home, they accidentally run over 15-year old schoolgirl Mi-jo (Yun Mi-jo). They scoop up the unconscious girl and bring her back to Ku-ho's place, where they are shocked to learn that she has survived without even have a scratch on her. However, Mi-jo is unable to speak and seems to have lost her memory.

Though she is a teenager, Ku-ho finds himself intrigued by the mysterious Mi-jo. He also accidentally discovers, after Mi-jo gets lost in an amusement park, that he shares a telepathic link with the girl. Ku-ho also begins digging into Mi-jo's past, and makes some startling discoveries. And as his fascination with Mi-jo grows into feelings of love, the girl's psychic powers begin escalating to deadly levels.

The slowly paced and contemplative "Secret Tears" is at its best during the first half, as the audience uncovers the mystery surrounding Mi-jo alongside Ku-ho. The script, which was also penned by Park, does dabble in some social commentary through its examination of the isolating behaviors of modern life via the silent interaction between Ku-ho and Mi-jo, or the sterile exchanges among Ku-ho's friends. In addition, the developing relationship between Ku-ho and a teenage girl eighteen years his junior will also surely raise more than a few eyebrows. On top of this, cinematographer Mun Yong-shik's pristine and stylish lensing helps create the right mood for the story's supernatural happenings.

Unfortunately, the further along you get in "Secret Tears", the less interesting it becomes, with the film's interesting build up being sabotaged by an unfocused second half. Instead of providing a satisfying payoff to all the questions raised by the intriguing set up, the film's rising action is muted, lacking in any sense of urgency, tension, or answers. Performances by the cast are similarly lethargic.

"Secret Tears" starts off interestingly enough, as it toys with a few interesting ideas and sets up what could be an intriguing tale of the supernatural. Unfortunately, Park Ki-hyeong's follow-up to his immensely popular "Whispering Corridors" ends up being an increasingly frustrating disappointment, a film where the mood and introspection end up overwhelming everything else.

The Soul Guardians (Toemarok) - 1998

Starring: Ahn Sung-ki, Chu Sang-mi, Shin Hyun-june, Oh Hyeon-chul
Director: Park Kwang-choon
Availability: Hong Kong-import VCD (no subtitles) and DVD (multi-region)
Rating: ••½

The Soul Guardians DVD box art
(*image courtesy of Winson Entertainment*)

Fantasy-horror pic "The Soul Guardians" is the film adaptation of an on-line novel inspired by the real-life mass suicide of a Seoul cult, and served as the debut for first-time director Park Kwang-choon, who had previously served as an assistant director on "The Gingko Bed". But despite a strong start, "The Soul Guardians" ends up mixing "The Exorcist", "The Terminator", and "End of Days" into an unsatisfying jumble of erratic storytelling and ho-hum special effects.

The film's opening sequence has heavily armed police crashing the mass suicide by a group of Satan-worshippers. They find a pregnant woman lying on an altar, and she is rushed to a nearby hospital. Though the woman eventually dies, her baby girl is saved. Twenty years later, the baby girl has grown up into auto mechanic Seung-heui (Chu Sang-mi), who is troubled by strange nightmares and inexplicable events.

Meanwhile, five other survivors of the mass suicide are being killed off by an unknown supernatural force, which soon turns its attention to Seung-heui. Sensing that Satan wishes to use Seung-heui as his vehicle to enslave the human world, a disparate group of three would-be exorcists step up to save her: surgeon-turned-Catholic-priest Father Park (Ahn Sung-ki), Taoist videogame fan Jun-hu (Oh Hyeon-chul), and the mysterious Hyun-am (Shin Hyeong-jun), who is armed with a 'haunted' knife.

Despite what could have been an interesting premise, "The Soul Guardians" ends up being completely unremarkable. The script is short on exposition, which will certainly leave more than a few viewers scratching their heads as they try to figure out where the gifted kid came from and why is he working with Father Park, what Hyun-am's motives are, and why Seung-heui is so damn important. As a result, the story just seems to ramble aimlessly from one scene to the next, punctuated by the occasional (not to mention obvious) use of CGI. It also doesn't help that the cookie-cutter characters (Park is the tormented one, Jun-hu is the lippy-kid sidekick, Hyun-am is the silent lone wolf, while Seung-hi is perpetually in need of rescuing) end up being played mechanically by the cast.

It is also quite obvious that director Park borrows heavily from Hong Kong horror films and Western actioners. Taoists and their paper charms figure heavily into the story, while some of the action sequences seem to have been lifted out of the "Terminator" films. For example, Seung-heui being chased by a possessed soldier echoes "The Terminator" on more than a couple of instances, while an escape in an elevator eerily mimics a similar scene in "Terminator 2: Judgement Day".

Though the film shows promise during the first half hour, it is quickly snatched away by the confusing plot, herky-jerky direction, and flat performances. And though "The Soul Guardians" was a groundbreaking film in South Korea at its time for its extensive use of CGI, with the advances in moviemaking technology that have occurred since 1998 (witness "Volcano High"), the visual effects end up being lackluster by today's standards. Alas, short in both coherence and originality, "The Soul Guardians" is a disappointing early entry in Korean genre filmmaking, following in the dubious footsteps of "The Gingko Bed".

Nightmare (Gawi) - 2000

Starring: Kim Kyu-ri, Ha Ji-weon, Yoo Ji-tae
Director: Ahn Byeong-ki
Availability: Hong Kong-import DVD (multi-region), Korean-import DVD (Region 3)
Rating: • •

Mixing "I Know What You Did Last Summer" plotting with traditional Japanese horror aesthetics, "Nightmare" (also known as "Horror Game Movie" and "Scissors") features well-scrubbed college students being gradually picked off by a vengeful spirit. The film starts off promisingly enough with a prologue that details the accidental death of Eun-ju (Ha Ji-weon), one of the female members of a group of eight students who call themselves 'A Few Good Men'. However, it is made abundantly clear that Eun-ju won't take this lying down-- as her body is being prepared in the morgue, Eun-ju's eyes pop open despite having been sewn tightly shut.

Two years later, the remaining members have pretty well put the unfortunate incident behind them. However, it becomes dragged out into the open again when Hye-jin (Kim Kyu-ri) becomes convinced that her former friend Eun-ju is still alive. Of course, no one else believes her, though that quickly changes when aspiring filmmaker Se-hun (Jun Jeong) is found dead with his eyes gouged out and actress Mi-ryeong (Jo Hye-yeong) is stabbed to death in the shower. One by one, the remaining members of 'A Few Good Men' bite the dust in painful and gruesome ways, and it is up to Hye-jin to uncover the truth about Eun-ju's death and the role that 'A Few Good Men' played.

Technically speaking, "Nightmare" is a polished production that has excellent camerawork, effective lighting, and a host of special effects at its disposal. Unfortunately, the pristine production values are wasted on a lackluster story that rehashes the tired conventions of Japanese and Hollywood horror films, such as the 'spontaneous appearance out of thin air' scare, the 'making sharp objects fly dangerously through the air' scare, among others. The film also suffers from Kim's lethargic performance as the protagonist, which leaves the audience no other choice but to root for the murderous Eun-ju. And in a bid to make the film more 'arty', director Ahn Byeong-ki gives the film a convoluted non-linear narrative structure, hoping that the audience won't notice how similar it is to every other 'dead teenager' movie out there.

Alas, it seems that "Nightmare" is just a bad dream.

Ghost Taxi (Gongpo taxi) - 2000

Starring: Lee Seo-jin, Choi Yu-jeong, Lim Ho, Jeong Hae-gyu, Jeong Jae-yeung
Director: Heo Seung-jin
Availability: Hong Kong-import VCD
Rating: •

Flying taxis with beating 'hearts' instead of engines under the hood. Phantom taxi drivers preying on the living to fuel their cars, which run better on blood. Ghosts roaming the streets of the city after the sun goes down. If it weren't Korean, "Ghost Taxi" would easily fit right into the supernatural *oeuvre* of Hong Kong über-producer Tsui Hark, whose repertoire includes fantasy classics such as "A Chinese Ghost Story", "The Wicked City", and more recently, "Legend of Zu".

While on his way to propose to his long-time girlfriend Yu-jeong (Choi Yu-jeong), taxi driver Gil-nam (Lee Seo-jin) is involved in a fatal car crash. Exactly forty-nine days later (which, according to Asian folklore, is how long it takes for the dead to return), Gil-nam finds himself back behind the wheel of his taxi. Unfortunately, he is now in the world of the dead, and his only companions are other ghosts, such as fellow phantom taxi drivers OK (Jeong Hae-gyu) and Non-stop (Jeong Jae-yeong), who enjoy freaking out unsuspecting passengers with their deadly road etiquette. Unfortunately, a malevolent spirit named Mantis, who has been responsible for a series of automobile fatalities in the real world, is now threatening Yu-jeong. Limited by what he can do in the spirit world, Gil-nam enlists the help of his long-time friend Byoung-su (Lim Ho).

While the concept is interesting and the scenes of 'road rage' are certainly worth a gander, "Ghost Taxi" eventually gets bogged down by a nonsensical script and annoying characters, particularly Jeong Hae-gyu's OK, whose penchant for throwing out poorly pronounced English slang gets old very quickly. Director Heo Seung-jun never really gives the audience a decent understanding of how the 'ghost world' works or what motivates the characters. Why does Gil-nam still drive a taxi after he is dead? Why do ghosts need to take cabs when they can appear and disappear at will? And perhaps the biggest question of all: why bother watching at all?

The Record (Zzikhimyeon jukneunda) - 2000

Starring: Kang Seong-min, Choi Ji-woo, Park Eun-hye, Han Chae-young
Director: Kim Gi-hun, Kim Jong-seok
Availability: Hong Kong-import VCD and DVD (multi-region)
Rating: •

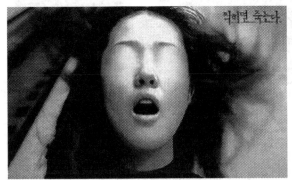

The Record artwork (*image courtesy of Sam Wu Communications*)

It seems that South Korean cinema has not been immune to the revival of the teen-horror genre. "The Record" might as well have been called "I Know What You Taped Last Summer", because it follows the same beats as "I Know What You Did Last Summer", only with the innovations of the video camera and the World Wide Web thrown into the mix. Unfortunately, this piece of 'Hitchschlock' has the same annoying characters who don't try very hard to stay alive, idiotic banter, and plot holes that plagued the type of films that inspired it, only with lower production values.

The senseless teen murders are kicked off by one of the most idiotic schemes ever conceived by movie teenagers. Sung-wook (Lee Young-ho) is the resident punching bag of his high school class, as his constant coughing, the result of his chronic asthma, irritates the hell out of his schoolmates. However, he ends up getting invited to a cottage in the country by the prettiest girl in the class, Eun-mi (Han Chae-young). However, just as he seems on the verge of scoring with Eun-mi, several masked men burst through the door and stab Sung-wook to death, while capturing the gory details on a video camera…

… and then 'cut'. It turns out the masked men are some of the school toughs who regularly beat Sung-wook up, the knife is fake, and they were merely taping a realistic murder scene for a horror movie they are filming. The only problem is that this prank has gone a little too far and as implausible as it may sound, Sung-wook has indeed been stabbed to death. Scared that their crime will be discovered, which would severely limit which universities they could attend after graduation, they decide to bury Sung-wook and the incriminating videotape in the woods and make a pact to never speak of this again.

Fast-forward one year later, and Sung-wook's murderers receive a web address.

After visiting the site, they find that someone has uploaded the video of Sung-wook's murder. In addition, they find themselves being killed off by a mysterious figure wearing a raincoat and wielding a very big knife...

If you have managed to sit through the likes of "I Know What You Did Last Summer", "Urban Legends", or any of those other "Scream"-wannabes, you should pretty well know what to expect. Co-directors Kim Gi-hun and Kim Jong-seok don't bring anything new to the genre, other than

Park Eun-hye and Han Chae-young (*image courtesy of Sam Wu Communications*)

directing it like a music video and rehashing scenes from equally inferior horror films. Thus, the audience must sit through one tired scene after another of stupid, stupid people being knocked off by a masked killer without the benefit of any true suspense, consistent logic, or wit. Even fans of this sort of mindless drivel will find themselves checking their watches and wondering when it's all going to end.

Chapter 7: True Love and Time Travel – Romance Films

Romantic melodramas have always been a staple in Korean cinema. This is partly due to the country's long history of censorship by governments, both foreign (such as during the Japanese annexation) and domestic (particularly during the Park and Chun regimes), making romantic melodrama one of the few 'safe' genres that filmmakers could dabble in. Thus, even to this day, romantic melodramas still comprise a sizable portion of the output of local movie studios. Furthermore, romantic melodrama has even managed to infiltrate other genres, such as in the case of the espionage actioner "Shiri", which mined the plight of a conflicted North Korean spy for full melodramatic effect.

One of the most noticeable characteristics of Korean romantic melodramas is that the protagonists often find themselves separated by insurmountable barriers, a reflection of the country's psyche that has been divided by ideology and war into the democratic South and the communist North. For example, class distinctions create a wedge between the son of a governor and the daughter of a courtesan in "Chunhyang", while reincarnation poses a problem for a schoolteacher when his long-dead first love returns as one of his male students in "Bungee Jumping of Their Own".

Staying true to the theme of overcoming seemingly insurmountable barriers is a new sub-genre that has been steadily currying favor among South Korean moviegoers in the past few years, blending the traditional staple of melodrama with some science-fiction or fantasy time-travel elements that unite two lovers otherwise separated by time. 1996 saw the first entry into what I dub the 'love across time' genre with "Shiri" director Kang Je-gyu's "The Gingko Bed", where an antique bed reunites a man in present-day Korea with his long-lost love from a previous life. Since then, true genre has grown to include a number of films, including "Il Mare", where a 'magic mailbox' unites two people living two years apart, and "Ditto", in which a ham radio connects two students living in different decades, as well as a couple that have already been mentioned in other chapters: "Peppermint Candy" ("Forrest Gump" meets "Memento" as a man travels back in time through the events that have unraveled his life) and "Failan" (a low-level thug finds dignity in the letters written by his deceased wife whom he never knew).

In all its shapes, sizes, and colors, Korean melodramas are at the top of their game, blending imaginative storytelling and heartwrenching drama in a fashion that will drive even the most cynical of moviegoers to tears. With films such as "An Affair", "Art Museum by the Zoo", "Last Present", and "The Harmonium in My Memory", be prepared to have plenty of tissues on hand.

Il Mare - 2000

Starring: Jeon Ji-hyun, Lee Jung-jae
Director: Lee Hyun-seung
Availability: Hong Kong-import VCD, Korean-import DVD (Region 3)
Rating: ●●●●½

Il Mare poster (*image courtesy of Sidus*)

"Il Mare" (Italian for 'the sea') is the unlikely title for a captivating South Korean romance. An audience favorite at the 2000 Pusan International Film Festival, "Il Mare" combines the correspondence of "You've Got Mail" with the time-travel complexities of "Frequency" to create a refreshing and heartfelt story about two lonely people who become connected via a 'magic mailbox'. "Il Mare" also has the distinction of being the fourth film to have its U.S. remake rights purchased by a major Hollywood studio, following in the footsteps of "My Wife is a Gangster", "Hi, Dharma", and "My Sassy Girl".

The story begins at the tail end of 1999, as voiceover actress Eun-joo (Jeon Ji-hyun) moves out of a seaside home named 'Il Mare'. Before leaving, Eun-joo leaves a Christmas card in the mailbox, with a message asking the next owner to forward any mail of hers to her new address in the city. Meanwhile, exactly two years prior in 1997, Il Mare's first owner, architect Sung-hyun (Lee Jung-jae), receives Eun-joo's card. Thinking it to be a joke, he writes back to Eun-joo and asks her not to tamper with his mailbox anymore, while pointing out that the 'current year' is 1997.

However, after a bit of back-and-forth banter, all doubt about the magical properties of the mailbox are soon erased, and Eun-joo and Sung-hyun begin sending regular correspondence to each other. In addition to finding out that they are both kindred spirits, they come up with new uses for their unique connection: Sung-hyun is able to return a tape recorder that Eun-joo lost two years ago, while Eun-joo is able to send back a still-unpublished book written by Sung-hyun's estranged father. Eventually, they agree to meet in person-- an uneasy task given their separate time periods. Though the agreed-upon day is only a week away from Eun-joo's perspective, it is still a full two years from where Sung-hyun stands. Will these two lovelorn pen pals meet?

The most obvious standout aspect of "Il Mare" are the time-constrained interactions between Eun-joo and Sung-hyun's, which result in a number of gee-whiz moments and thought-provoking scenes, such as the film's ending, which is heart-wrenching, uplifting, and mind-blowing at the same time. However, what makes "Il Mare" so memorable is the well-told love story at its core. Without resorting to overt melodrama, director Lee Hyun-seung chronicles the blossoming romance between his two protagonists and how their regrets of the past threaten to tear them apart, brought to life by the natural performances of the two leads. In addition, Lee conveys a mood of both warmth and melancholy through some stunning cinematography that makes good use of the seaside setting. There is also some good tension generated as Eun-joo and Sung-hyun edge closer towards meeting each other in person, though at times, it seems a little needlessly drawn out. Thankfully, this oversight ends up being redressed with a third-act revelation that only heightens the emotional resonance of their connection.

Despite what could have been a 'gimmicky' premise, "Il Mare" is far from insincere in how it details the emotional bond that develops between two people separated by time. Like two other recent Korean romances of note, "Christmas in August" and "Art Museum by the Zoo", "Il Mare" goes about its business with a quiet eloquence. True, the script may strain some credibility in

Jeon Ji-hyun (*image courtesy of Sidus*)

terms of delaying the eventual union of its two lovers, but overall, "Il Mare" remains a smart and stirring entry in the romance genre, a bittersweet confection that is not easily forgotten.

Last Present (Seonmul)- 2001

Starring: Lee Young-ae, Lee Jung-jae, Kyeon Hae-hyo
Director: Oh Ki-hwan
Availability: Hong Kong-import VCD and DVD, Korean-import DVD (Region 3)
Rating: ● ● ● ●½

Last Present poster (*image courtesy of Cinema Service*)

After tripping through her English dialogue in "Joint Security Area" and testing the patience of audiences in "One Fine Spring Day", actress Lee Young-ae finally gets a chance to shine in "Last Present", director Oh Ki-hwan's touching follow-up to "Ghost in Love". Lee plays Jeong-yeon, who is married to struggling comic Yong-gi (Lee Jung-jae), who happens to be a complete loser. Yong-gi has been virtually disowned by his parents, who disapprove of his marriage to Jeong-yeon and resent having a 'clown' for a son. Unable to get steady work on television, where he aspires to be, Yong-gi is content to work at third-rate comedy clubs and play the role of 'curtain riser' for better and more successful comedians.

Though Jeong-yeon constantly nags Yong-gi for not getting his act together, deep down, she truly cares about her husband. When she is not busy running her baby goods store, she works hard behind the scenes to help Yong-gi's career, such as speaking to television producers on his behalf, or failing that, buying gifts to curry favor with the producers' wives. Meanwhile, Jeong-yeon is also dying of a terminal illness, which she has kept secret from Yong-gi, as she does not want his sadness to diminish his ability to make people laugh.

But unknown to Jeong-yeon, Yong-gi learns about his wife's condition by accident. Knowing how prideful she is, Yong-gi keeps his discovery secret from Jeong-yeon and begins redoubling his efforts to become a success. In addition, he coerces two conmen (Kyeon Hae-hyo and Lee Mu-hyun) to help him locate three people whom his wife has not seen in years. Unfortunately, Jeong-yeon's health continues to slowly deteriorate, leaving little time for either of them to put the finishing touches on their 'last presents' to each other.

Though the film's ending is a foregone conclusion given the set-up, "Last Present" still manages to be an involving and suspenseful film. In addition to the intrigue of the husband and wife toiling away in secret for the benefit of each other, a mystery is also developed as the conmen speak to Jeong-yeon's old school chums and learn that the love of her life might actually be someone other than Yong-gi. The film's climax, as Yong-gi is about to finally taste success as a television comedian, is also too beautiful for words.

At the center of attention in "Last Present" are the performances by the two leads. Lee Young-ae apparently earned the unofficial title of 'most desirable wife' in Korea for her work here. Indeed, the actress makes a career-defining performance with her touching portrayal of Jeong-yeon, whose abrasive outer shell hides a caring and gentle soul who only wants the best for her

Lee Jung-jae and Lee Young-ae (*image courtesy of Cinema Service*)

daydreaming husband. Lee Jung-jae, no stranger to romantic melodrama with his roles in films such as "Il Mare" and "An Affair", acquits himself nicely also as a man who must grow up very quickly and becomes increasingly torn between his growing fame and the need to look after his ailing wife. In supporting performances, Kyeon Hae-hyo is a scene-stealer as an incompetent con man with a heart of gold, while Kong Hyeong-jin is passable as Yong-gi's comedy partner.

Though "Last Present" is firmly rooted in romantic melodrama territory, particularly with its use of the 'terminal disease' device to lend emotional weight to the proceedings, the film still manages to be an effective and well-told story with never a dull moment during its two-hour running time. As this film most aptly demonstrates, there is nothing more heartbreaking than the tears of a clown.

Ditto (Donggam) - 2000

Starring: Yoo Ji-tae, Kim Ha-neul, Ha Ji-weon, Kim Min-ju, Park Yong-woo
Director: Kim Jung-Kueon
Availability: Hong Kong-import VCD and DVD (multi-region), Korean-import DVD (multi-region)
Rating: ● ● ● ●

Ditto poster (*image courtesy of Hanmac Films*)

One of the more popular entries in the 'love across time' genre is Kim Jeong-kweon's "Ditto (Donggam)", which appeared in Korean movie houses four months prior to the release of "Il Mare" and racked up an impressive one million admissions in 2000. The story details the relationship between two college students, So-eun (the lovely Kim Ha-neul) and In (Yoo Ji-tae) which connect via ham radio one night. However, when they decide to meet on campus and miss each other, it is revealed that they are separated by 21 years, with So-eun in 1979 and In living in the present day, 2000.

Eventually, they become comfortable with the supernatural phenomenon that has brought them together, as well as their correspondence. She relates her camaraderie with her best friend Seon-mi (Kim Min-ju) and her pining for fellow student Dong-heui (Park Yong-woo), while he talks about the unwanted attention he receives from fellow co-ed (Ha Ji-weon). However, as the on-air relationship deepens, it is revealed that their ties go far deeper than ever imagined.

True, the plot of "Ditto" is eerily similar to a Hollywood production released that same year, "Frequency", in which a young man is able to communicate with his late firefighter father through a ham radio. However, there is a difference between the two films with respect to intent. Whereas "Frequency" was more-or-less a sci-fi suspense-thriller, "Ditto" ends up being a bittersweet drama that offers up some interesting perspectives on the national psyche of country that has moved from one political extreme to the other within the span of a single generation.

Screenwriter Jang Jin (who also wrote the Korean political satire "The Spy") anchors the young and naïve So-eun in the month of October of 1979, a period of major political upheaval that was triggered by the assassination of Park on the 25th of that month. On the other hand, In is a child of the Internet era, who perhaps takes the relative stability of modern South Korea for granted. As the story develops, Chang makes it very clear in one of the film's genuine 'gee-whiz' moments that the destinies of these two protagonists are irrevocably intertwined, with the decisions made and actions taken by So-eun having significant implications for In, not unlike how South Korea's political strife during the Sixties and Seventies helped set the stage for reform during the Eighties and Nineties. Unfortunately, like much of the 'lost generation' of Koreans during the Park and Chun regimes, So-eun ends up becoming a casualty of history, which is eloquently conveyed in the film's sad coda in the present day.

Technically speaking, director Kim Jung-kueon has crafted "Ditto" with some top-notch production values. Kim makes good use of some stunning cinematography to contrast the two eras, such as the missed meeting at the clock tower, which has So-eun under sunny skies and In soaked by a downpour. The film's judiciously chosen soundtrack also highlights the differences between the two time periods, and heightens the sense of bittersweet remorse that dominates the film's ending. Coupled with a strong performance by Kim Ha-neul, who capably demonstrates So-euns emotional maturation against the film's historical backdrop, "Ditto" is in the league of "Il Mare" and "Peppermint Candy" as a shining example of the genre.

With the growing prominence of Korean films on the world stage, it is not surprising to see that the 'love across time' genre has crossed over into other markets, such as with the 2001 release of "Second Time Around", essentially a Hong Kong take on the genre starring Ekin Cheng and Cecilia Cheung (who also starred in "Failan"). However, whereas "Second Time Around" is purely aimed at cashing in on a growing cinematic phenomenon, "Ditto", along with the other films of the Korean 'love across time' genre, is a thoughtful reflection of the national psyche of South Korea, a country that has matured into a functioning democracy in a relatively short time, yet still bears the scars of that long and difficult struggle.

An Affair (Jeongsa) - 1998

Starring: Lee Mi-sook, Lee Jung-jae, Kim Min-jeong, Song Yeong-chang
Director: E J-Yong
Availability: Hong Kong-import VCD and DVD (Region 3), Korean-import DVD (Region 3)
Rating: ●●●●

An Affair DVD box art (*image courtesy of Nine Films*)

"An Affair", the 1998 directorial debut of E J-Yong, is a sad tale of a middle-aged housewife who falls in love with a younger man, the fiancé of her younger sister. The housewife is Seo-hyun (a comeback role for veteran Korean actress Lee Mi-sook), a woman trapped in a loveless marriage to an architect (Song Yeong-chang) who would rather spend most of his time at work. Her younger sister Ji-hyun (Kim Min-jeong) is working in the United States, but she is soon expected to rejoin her fiancé Wu-in (Lee Jung-jae, who would also appear in E J-Yong's follow-up "Asako in Ruby Shoes"), who has already arrived in Seoul. In the interim, Ji-hyun asks Seo-hyun to lend Wu-in a hand in settling down.

At first, things go well, as Seo-hyun provides some sisterly support, meeting Wu-in for coffee, helping with house shopping, and making wedding preparations. Unfortunately, as she spends more time with him, Seo-hyun finds herself attracted to Wu-in, despite the fact that he is ten years her junior, and of course, is her sister's fiancé. For Wu-in, the feelings are mutual, and he begins to use aggressive measures to consummate the relationship-- measures that eventually succeed. Of course, keeping such an affair under wraps proves to be difficult, as Seo-hyun's husband and son begin to notice her conspicuous absences, or she runs into friends on the street while arm-in-arm with Wu-in. But the biggest challenge comes when Ji-hyun finally returns to Seoul, leaving Seo-hyun caught between two equally undesirable alternatives.

What is most remarkable about "An Affair" is its neutral presentation of the relationship between Seo-hyun and Wu-in, and the uncompromising look at the consequences of Seo-hyun's choices. Just as there are no easy answers in such a situation, the script offers no simplistic solutions to the moral dilemma that she faces.

To establish the desperation of Seo-hyun, Director E J-Yong brilliantly conveys the loneliness of her life through a series of vignettes. Though she is married, has a son, and enjoys an upper-class lifestyle, she is virtually ignored by her husband, subject to her son's unkind remarks, and spends most of her time alone-- one telling scene has Seo-hyun keeping to herself at a dinner party with her husband's co-workers, while another catches her through the frame of a fishbowl as a metaphor for her lonely existence. However, as the affair begins, we see a remarkable transformation in Seo-hyun from bored housewife to a vibrant and passionate woman. Though Seo-hyun knows that what she has done is wrong, she cannot help but continue with the affair, as it has awoken the long-dormant feelings of true love and happiness that her tired marriage has long denied-- feelings that she does not want to leave behind. This conflict is readily apparent in the deeply expressive performance of Lee Mi-sook, who easily becomes the emotional hook for the audience.

The other piece of the puzzle is Wu-in, whose motivations remain much of a mystery throughout the film, adding an element of suspense to the proceedings. Are his actions stemming from a combination of attraction and loneliness, or are more sinister motives at work? At times, he seems to be a quiet man reduced to acts of desperation when he finds himself irresistibly attracted to Seo-hyun, while at others, his pathological behavior suggests that he may in fact be manipulating her to his will. For most of the film, the director leaves either interpretation open, leaving it up to the audience to make the call on his sincerity, which is even more difficult given Lee Jung-jae's chilling performance that lends credence to both possibilities.

Overall, "An Affair" is a powerful, thought-provoking, and sobering film. With E J-Yong's solid direction, Lee Mi-sook's sympathetic and credible performance, and the tension brought to the table by Lee Jung-jae's portrayal of her love interest, "An Affair" is a stark portrayal of choices made and consequences endured in the name of love.

Art Museum by the Zoo (Misuhlgwa yup dongmulgwon)- 1998

Starring: Shim Eun-ha, Lee Sung-jae, Ahn Sung-ki, Song Seon-mi
Director: Lee Jeong-hya
Availability: Hong Kong-import VCD, Korean-import DVD (multi-region)
Rating: ● ● ● ●

Art Museum by the Zoo DVD box art
(*image courtesy of Cinema Service*)

The 1998 film "Art Museum by the Zoo" actually mocks the very genre it represents, the romantic comedy. But despite its irreverent attitude, "Art Museum by the Zoo" still manages to be a heartwarming experience that benefits greatly from the luminous presence of the ever-popular Shim Eun-ha and her chemistry with costar Lee Sung-jae.

Apparently a semi-autobiographical reflection of director Lee Jeong-hya's own life, the story kicks off with a soldier, Chul-su (Lee), returning to his girlfriend's apartment while on leave. Unfortunately, what Chul-su doesn't know is that his girlfriend Da-hye (Song Seon-mi) moved out a few months ago and is about to marry someone else. To further complicate matters, the apartment is now being rented by videographer/aspiring screenwriter Chun-hi (Shim). But because he has nowhere else to go, Chun-hi reluctantly allows Chul-su to sleep on the couch until he can patch things up with Da-hye, while she tries to finish a screenplay for an upcoming contest and snag the man of her dreams, a senator's aide (veteran Korean actor Ahn Sung-ki).

Stealing a page from the book on romantic comedies, Chun-hi and Chul-su initially don't get along, as the former is an Oscar-like slob while the latter is an arrogant and chauvinistic male. However, what they both share is a difficulty in finding true love. Chun-hi is unable to start a relationship because of both her shy character and the unrealistic expectations she has about romance. On the other hand, though Chul-su is cynical about love, he clings to the relationship with his estranged girlfriend out of desperation, allowing her to trample all over him in the process.

However, where these two diametrically opposed personalities finally find some common ground is with Chun-hi's romantic-comedy script. After reading it, Chul-su poo-poos all over her efforts-to-date, labeling it as hackneyed and implausible, and decides to help her write a new draft. They begin writing the new script together, projecting their own insecurities and desires into the story's characters. The audience is then privy to a 'movie within a movie' as the two collaborators imagine their script, "Art Museum by the Zoo", coming to life. Ironically enough, what they imagine their film to be plays out like your typically Tom Hanks/Meg Ryan romantic comedy, as it is about the unlikely pairing between an art museum curator (whom Chul-su envisions as his estranged girlfriend) and a veterinarian who works in a nearby zoo (whom Chun-hi imagines as her unattainable senator's aide). Of course, in the process of crafting their romantic screenplay, Chul-su and Chun-hi begin to fall for one another...

"Art Museum by the Zoo" was very popular in Korea in 1998, especially among women, and after watching this charming film, it's not hard to see why. Though the film looks and feels like your typical Hollywood-style romantic-comedy, it doesn't take the easy road of films such as "She's All That" or "America's Sweethearts", where the heroine's only hope of finding true love is to do a make-over. Instead, Chun-hi remains a disheveled and awkward slob throughout the film, and she is able to find true love by merely 'being herself' and through her shared experience with Chul-su. Another nice touch is how director Lee plays with the viewer's expectations by having some fun with the film's self-aware 'movie within a movie' segments, parodying every well-worn cliché of lesser romantic comedies.

However, a key aspect that makes "Art Museum by the Zoo" work is the performance of its lead actress. Shim carries the film with her effortless and natural portrayal of the unlucky-in-love heroine that makes it easy for her likable character to connect with the audience. In many respects, Shim exudes the same naiveté and vulnerability that marked her unforgettable performance in another film that year, "Christmas in August", and it is easy to see why she is the most popular actress in Korean cinema. In addition, Shim is also nicely balanced with Lee's portrayal of the boorish Chul-su, a turn that subtly reveals the 'nice guy' underneath all the abrasive male bravado.

"Art Museum by the Zoo" may not necessarily break any new ground in the romantic-comedy genre, and you can pretty well guess how things will turn out, but it is still very easy to fall under its spell. Backed by a self-reflective script, quaint production values, and two heartwarming performances with chemistry to spare, "Art Museum by the Zoo" is an absolute delight.

Chunhyang (Misuhlgwa yup dongmulgwon)- 1998

Starring: Lee Hyo-jeong, Cho Seong-woo, Lee Jung-hun, Cho Sang-hyun, Kim Myung-hwan
Director: Im Kwon-taek
Availability: North American DVD (multi-region)
Rating: •••

Chunhyang DVD box art (*image courtesy of Lot 47 Films*)

Pansori, which roughly translates into 'songs in a place of entertainment', has a long tradition in Korean performance art. The typical *pansori* is usually performed by two people, with one person playing the *puk*, or *drum*, while the other 'sings' a lengthy narrative to the beat. In addition to providing a rhythmic foundation for the performance, the drummer (*gosu*) also provides emotional emphasis for key parts of the 'song' by varying the tempo or providing shouts of encouragement, or *chuimsae*, to the singer. The singer (*myeongchang*), who usually sports a handkerchief and fan, recites the story, which can go on for hours, with a combination of *sori* (singing), *aniri* (recitation), and *pallim* (gestures). Though there used to be twelve *pansori*, only five of them are still performed today, including *Jeokbyeokga, Heungboga, Sugungga, Simcheongga*, and *Chunhyangga*. It is the latter that the South Korean film "Chunhyang", which saw a limited release in North America in 2000 and a DVD release the following year, is based. And though the film's initial slow pacing and narrative style take some getting used to, overall, "Chunhyang" is a pleasant take on an age-old folk tale.

The plot of "Chunhyang" is your typical story about two lovers separated by class, such as the doomed romance between a penniless writer and a showgirl seen in "Moulin Rouge", or even the pairing of a corporate shark and a hooker-with-a-heart-of-gold seen in "Pretty Woman". In this case, the forbidden love is between Mongyoung Lee (Cho Seung-woo), a governor's son, and Chunghyang Sung (Lee Hyo-jeong), the beautiful daughter of a courtesan, who marry in secret after a brief courtship. Unfortunately, Mongyoung cannot tell his father about his class-defying union, as it will not only bring shame to the family name, but also potentially jeopardize a future appointment to the Royal Court.

Their married bliss is short-lived though, as the governor is transferred to Soeul, and Mongyoung is obligated to follow, leaving Chunhyang behind only with a promise to return some day. Unfortunately, years go by, and a new governor (Lee Jung-hun) takes office in the region, who wishes to have Chunghyang as his mistress. Determined to remain faithful to her absent husband, Chunghyang refuses the governor's demands. Enraged by such insolence, the new governor has Chunghyang beaten, thrown in prison, and sentenced to death.

"Chunhyang" is framed by a modern-day *pansori* performance by Cho Sang-hyun and Kim Myung-hwan, which provides the voiceover narration for the film. However, for those unfamiliar with the art form, this does take some acclimatization, as it is not singing in the traditional Western sense. The 'singing' of a *pansori* is more like chanting, and unlike other forms of song, there is an emphasis on creating a slightly rough and husky sound in the throat, or *tongseong*. Thus, Cho's 'narration' is often at times musically dissonant from what one would expect, and can even be jarring against director Im Kwon-taek's vibrantly captured scenery or handsome leads.

However, once the initial shock has worn off, the use of *pansori* as narration does work, such as when guards are dispatched by the new governor to detain Chunhyang. At other times, the reactions of the audience and performers are effectively used to heighten the emotional pull of a scene, such as when Mongyoung sets out on the road to be reunited with Chunhyang, or the pained expression on Cho's face as he recounts Chunghyang's repeated beatings by the new governor.

"Chunhyang" has the distinction of being the first Korean film to ever compete in the Cannes Film Festival, and is a much-deserved global debut for Im Kwon-taek, who is considered to be Korea's leading director, with a filmography that stretches four decades and numerous awards to his name. True, it may be rather unconventional in execution, but the film's sheer beauty and familiar yet heartfelt story make "Chunhyang" a rare and uplifting moviegoing experience, whether you are familiar with *pansori* or not.

Love Wind, Love Song (Yeonpung yeonga)- 1999

Starring: Jang Dong-gun, Ko So-young
Director: Park Dae-yeong
Availability: Hong Kong-import VCD and DVD (multi-region), Korean-import DVD (multi-region)
Rating: ● ● ● ●

Love Wind, Love Song poster (*image courtesy of Cinema Service*)

If it wasn't for the sincere performances of leads Jang Dong-gun and Ko So-young, Park Dae-yeong's "Love Wind, Love Song" would have been another namby-pamby 'boy meets girl' melodrama, as suggested by the film's bland-sounding title. The boy in this case is Tae-hie (Jang), a young professional from Seoul whom we see turning down a big promotion for reasons unknown in the film's opening scene. We are then introduced to the girl, Young-seo (Ko), a perky tour guide who lives and works on the picturesque Cheju island.

They first meet when Tae-hie has a run-in with a pickpocket and retrieves a wallet stolen from one of Young-seo's customers. Appreciative of the assistance, Young-seo agrees to Tae-hie's request to serve as his personal tour guide while he visits the island. As they spend time together amidst the beautiful scenery, it is hardly surprising that they fall in love with each other. Unfortunately, pursuing a relationship with Tae-hie goes against Young-seo's own philosophy of becoming involved with 'mainlanders', particularly those on vacation, as they are bound to leave at some time. In addition, it seems that Tae-hie is wrestling with a few issues of his own, one of which includes looking after his crippled father.

There are very few surprises in "Love Wind, Love Song". When Tae-hie talks to Young-seo about his ex-girlfriend (Kim Min-jeong), you know that she's going to show up sooner or later and put a damper on things. When Tae-hie promises to meet Young-seo under a specific tree before heading back to Seoul, it comes as no surprise when he doesn't show up. And when Young-seo takes a trip to Seoul to track down her delinquent new boyfriend, you know she will likely be disappointed by what she finds. Finally, during the film's ending, where the two would-be lovers are brought back together (three guesses as to exactly where they meet up), what transpires is a no-brainer. Given the abundance of such predictable material that has been borrowed from countless other romantic melodramas, why is "Love Wind, Love Song" still watchable? The performances.

The down-to-earth portrayals of Tae-hie and Young-seo bring an unparalleled degree of warmth and humanity to an otherwise oft-told story. Jang is solid as the quiet and shy Tae-hie, making a nice change of pace from his more high-profile roles, such as in "Nowhere to Hide", "Friend", and the more recent "2009 Lost Memories". However, the best performance in the film belongs to Ko for her affecting turn as the love-struck tour guide. Ko is credible and sympathetic as a young woman whose bubbly personality is but a thin mask for her deep-rooted insecurities, and it is difficult not to be moved by the work she does here.

Ko So-young (*image courtesy of Cinema Service*)

Though "Love Wind, Love Song" hardly breaks any new ground, it ends up being a decent entry into the romance genre. Benefiting greatly from the charisma of its two leads and the natural beauty of the Cheju Island setting, "Love Wind, Love Song" makes up for its lack of originality with its tenacious, not to mention satisfying, emotional hooks.

Wanee & Junah (Waneewa Junah)- 2001

Starring: Joo Jin-mo, Kim Hee-sun, Cho Seung-woo, Choi Kang-hie
Director: Kim Yong-gyun
Availability: Korean-import DVD (multi-region)
Rating: ●●●½

Wanee & Junah poster (*image courtesy of Warner Bros.*)

On the surface, "Wanee & Junah" might appear to be yet another unremarkable and dull Korean romantic melodrama propped up by two eye-pleasing leads, the ruggedly handsome Joo Jin-mo and beauty Kim Hee-sun. Fortunately, you cannot always judge a book by its cover, and "Wanee & Junah" is a case in point. Smartly directed by Kim Yong-gyun, this film takes the well-tread throughline of 'a character being unable to move forward in the present due to romantic trauma in the past' and spins a compelling story with the help of a fluid flashback-laden narrative style and good performances.

The titular characters are animator Wanee (Kim) and aspiring screenwriter Junah (Ju), who have been living together for quite some time and have settled into quiet domestication. However, their stable relationship becomes rocked by the imminent return of her half-brother Yeong-mi (Cho Seung-woo), who has been studying abroad for the past few years. Through a series of flashbacks, it is gradually revealed that Yeong-mi was Wanee's first and unattainable first love, and it seems that he still weighs heavily on her heart in the present. To further complicate matters, Wanee receives a visit from old school chum So-yeong (Choi Kang-hie of "Whispering Corridors"), who secretly held a flame for Yeong-mi back in high school. Will Wanee try once again to recapture the forbidden love of her youth? Will Junah stick by Wanee in this most trying time?

Though the story is hardly innovative, it is the presentation that makes "Wanee & Junah" so remarkable. In addition to the judicious use of flashbacks to gradually reveal Wanee's path, director Kim brings the audience into Wanee's state of mind by making such flashbacks almost seamless with the present. For example, one scene has Wanee in the present sitting at the dinner table. As she remembers something from the past, the camera slowly pans to the living room where the scene in the past begins. Another interesting bit of visual storytelling has Wanee imagining that the people she speaks to over the telephone, such as her mother or Yeong-mi, are actually sitting across from her in the same room.

In addition to these bits of whimsy, the film features some stunning animation that emerges from or dissolves into live action. Highlights include the pages of Wanee's old sketchbook 'coming to life' as Junah flips through it, and a seemingly unrelated 'boy meets girl' animation that opens and closes the film that actually reveals some backstory about Wanee and Junah.

Rounding out the film's distinct visual style are the credible performances of leads Ju and Kim. Ju is quite good as the compassionate and understanding Junah, while Kim redeems herself for the lifeless and stilted performances she gave in "Calla" and "Bichunmoo" with her down-to-earth portrayal of the conflicted and confused Wanee, making this possibly the best performance of her career.

Joo Jin-mo and Kim Hee-sun (*image courtesy of Warner Bros.*)

"Wanee & Junah" is a delightful surprise from start to finish. Though the distinct visual dynamic is enough to maintain audience interest, underneath what appears to be yet another staid romantic melodrama is an involving and reaffirming film, one that poetically examines the ties that bind in the matters of the heart.

The Harmonium in My Memory (Nae Maeumeui punggeum) - 1999

Starring: Lee Byung-heon, Jeon Do-yeon, Lee Mi-yeon
Director: Lee Young-jae
Availability: Hong Kong-import VCD and DVD (multi-region)
Rating: ●●●½

The Harmonium in My Memory DVD box art (*image courtesy of Modern*)

Those familiar with Zhang Yimou's "The Road Home" will have a sense of cinematic déja vu upon viewing "The Harmonium in My Memory", even though this South Korean melodrama came out a year before Zhang Ziyi's breakthrough feature. Based on the Ha Keum-chan novel "Female Student" and serving as the feature film debut of director Lee Young-jae, "The Harmonium in My Memory" draws an interesting love triangle between a recently arrived teacher in a small town, his beautiful colleague, and one of his students.

Reminiscent of the setting of "The Road Home", the film opens in the early Sixties with the arrival of 21-year old Kang Su-ha (Lee Byung-heon) in the country village of Sanri, where he has landed his first teaching job at the local school. The greenhorn teacher quickly gets more than he bargained for when he is faced with the undisciplined students in his class, the teaching challenges posed by many of the students' impoverished parents being illiterate themselves, and the few diversions available in such a backwater town.

However, Kang soon finds one good reason to stick it out in Sanri-- the unrivalled beauty of fellow teacher Yang Eun-hee (Lee Mi-yeon), which encourages the young bachelor to try and pursue a romantic relationship. However, Kang remains unaware of the growing feelings that 17-year old Yun Hong-yeon (Jeon Do-yeon), one of his students, has towards him, triggering a love triangle that results in some unexpected turn-of-events.

Production-wise, "The Harmonium in My Memory" is simplistic, and the rural country setting may be jarring to those more familiar with the typical urban and modern-day settings of Korean films. However, once the initial shock wears off, the viewer is quickly pulled into the emotionally resonant drama that unfolds. Like "The Road Home", "The Harmonium in My Memory" is a story that details the trials and tribulations of first love. However, unlike the one-sided approach that Zhang Yimou used, the well-balanced love story is told through the eyes of two romantically naive characters, Kang and Yun. Their romantic aspirations, changing perceptions, and bitter disappointments are exquisitely detailed, providing much of the film's emotional pull. One nice touch is how Kang's love of records, most notably those of Connie Francis, while initially seen as a means of adding color to Kang's character, becomes the lynch pin for the film's heartwarming conclusion.

Similar to how Zhang Ziyi held "The Road Home" together, actress Jeon is the emotional center of this film. The chameleon-like actress is almost unrecognizable as the rebellious and amorous Yun, especially in light of her memorable leading role in the Internet romance "The Contact" only one-year prior. Lee Byung-heon is no slouch either in his earnest portrayal of Kang, while

Jeon Do-yeon (*image courtesy of Korea Image Investment & Development*)

Lee Mi-yeon acquits herself decently as a female colleague who maintains her distance for a good reason.

Right up until the final credits, "The Harmonium in My Memory" is a touching film of simple beauty and raw emotion. Romanticizing how teachers can become a powerful influence in shaping young lives, while depicting the bittersweet emotional discovery of first love, "The Harmonium in My Memory" is a pure masterpiece of storytelling.

Indian Summer - 2001

Starring: Park Shin-yang, Lee Mi-yeon
Director: Noh Hyon-jung
Availability: Hong Kong-import VCD and DVD (multi-region)
Rating: ●●●½

Indian Summer poster (*image courtesy of Cinema Service*)

According to the dictionary, the term 'Indian summer' refers the period of unseasonably warm weather that occurs in late autumn, or the tranquil time just before the end of something. Appropriately enough, the 2001 directorial debut of Noh Hyo-jung "Indian Summer" is about the brief respite a woman has from death row for the murder of her husband, executed with equal parts of compelling courtroom drama and stirring romantic melodrama.

The first half follows the typical episode of the television show "The Practice", with lawyer Suh Jun-ha (Park Shin-yang) being appointed by the court to defend Lee Shin-young (Lee Mi-yeon). Lee is accused of butchering her husband with a scalpel, and a guilty conviction will result in the death penalty. However, she seems resigned to her fate and refuses to say anything in her own defence. Despite the uncooperative nature of his client and pressure from his boss to not waste too much time on a court-appointed case, Suh builds a defence on Lee's history of abuse at the hands of her husband, as well as the prosecution's lack of physical evidence directly linking her to the murder.

The film's second half falls into the domain of traditional Korean melodrama, after reasonable doubt results in an acquittal. Spurred by sympathy for his client, Suh befriends Lee outside of the courtroom and a romance blooms. Unfortunately, such bliss ends up being short-lived when the prosecution turns up new evidence and plans to overturn the acquittal.

"Indian Summer" is essentially a two-character piece, contrasting the youthful optimism of Suh with the world-weary melancholy of Lee. Like many other recent Korean melodramas where two star-crossed lovers find themselves kept apart by insurmountable barriers, such as time in "Il Mare" or distance in "Asako in Ruby Shoes", it is their differing worldviews that separates them and ultimately results in the story's tragedy. The determination of Lee's guilt or innocence gives the film much of its momentum, and serves as an excellent frame for the budding relationship of these two characters.

Complementing the good script are the strong performances turned in by the two leads. Park, who actually spent almost half a year hanging out at a law firm to prepare for the role, is affable and charismatic as the young and idealistic lawyer, a sharp contrast to his role as the tough big boss in "Hi, Dharma" or the corrupt cop in "Kilimanjaro". As the story's woman of mystery, Lee is credible and sympathetic as a

Lee Mi-yeon and Park Shin-yang (*image courtesy of Cinema Service*)

woman who has all but lost the will to live in the face of what she has endured and done.

Prior to directing "Indian Summer", Noh was already an accomplished screenwriter, with a number of film credits to her name. With "Indian Summer", she makes the leap into the big chair and her passion for the material is evident throughout this well-written, assuredly directed, and superbly acted bittersweet courtroom melodrama.

Ghost in Love (Jaguimo) - 1999

Starring: Kim Hee-sun, Lee Sung-jae, Cha Seung-won, Chang Jin-young
Director: Lee Kwang-hoon
Availability: Korean-import DVD (multi-region)
Rating: • • •

Ghost in Love DVD box art (*image courtesy of Cinema Service*)

Despite its sometimes-confusing plot, 1999's "Ghost in Love" blends elements of "Ghost" and "City of Angels" to create a satisfying and technically proficient supernatural romance. In addition, "Ghost in Love" also features a number of actors who have become familiar faces over the years, including Kim Hee-sun, Lee Sung-jae, Cha Seung-won, Chang Jin-young, and Park Kwang-jung.

The film kicks off with Jin Chae-byul (Kim) finding out that her fiancé Nah Han-soo (Cha) has been cheating on her with another woman-- his boss' daughter. Distraught, Chae-byul contemplates suicide while waiting for a subway. Though Chae-byul changes her mind the very last second, a phantom-like 'recruiter' (Park) for the Society for Suicide Ghosts (SSG for short) gives her a little push and she ends up being hit by the train.

When Chae-byul comes to, she learns that she is dead and is led to the headquarters of SSG, whose members all committed suicide and allegedly are not allowed to enter the afterlife. In order to sustain their numbers, the group actively recruits new members by any means possible, including putting suicidal ideas into people's heads or giving them a nudge as they lean over the edge of a tall building. However, Chae-byul gradually adapts to her new 'life' and becomes good friends with another spirit, Diety (Lee Yeong-ja).

Meanwhile in the human world, despite Chae-byul's sudden death, Han-soo has quickly moved on with his life and proposed to the boss' daughter, as he considered his previous fiancée to only be a 'sex partner'. Driven by feelings of anger and a thirst for revenge, Chae-byul decides to make Han-soo's life a living hell, following the lead of a fellow spirit named Pale Face, who is tracking down and killing the men who had raped her before she died.

Unfortunately, interfering with the human world is a big no-no in the afterlife, and as a result of Chae-byul's and Pale Face's extracurricular activities, two 'messengers' (Jeong Won-jung and Jang Se-jin) are sent to arrest and execute them (apparently, you can die twice). Meanwhile, another spirit, Kantorates (Lee), tries to convince Chae-byul to leave the human world alone and move on, as he struggles with leaving behind the woman he had loved deeply in his previous life, Lee Young-eun (Chang).

"Ghost in Love" uses its interesting premise to spin an age-old tale about characters who must let go of the past in order to move on in the present, and this theme is common throughout many of the story threads in the film. It is also particularly touching how all these story threads and this central theme end up coming together in the film's last act, where Chae-byul, Kantorates, Lee, and Pale Face must confront the consequences of clinging the tragedies and misdeeds of the past. In addition the film's technical credits are impressive, as the film is well shot and the special effects are surprisingly decent. Compared to "The Soul Guardians", which came out in 1998, the use of CGI has improved tremendously in this outing.

Unfortunately, despite such thematic cohesiveness and visual splendor, "Ghost in Love" also suffers from some confusing plotting and lack of internal consistency. The 'rules' of the afterlife world are presented in a haphazard fashion, and there will likely be times that viewers will be a few minutes behind in trying to figure exactly out what is going on. There is also some inconsistencies in terms of what these disembodied spirits can and cannot do, though these typically plague other films of this ilk, such as how the spirits can pass through walls yet not fall through the floor of an elevator or a subway car (which also occurred in "Ghost", by the way).

Despite the script's shortcomings, performances are good. Kim acquits herself decently as a woman who is torn between her former life in the human world and the new possibilities offered to her by the afterlife. Lee also acquits himself decently as a spirit, who despite his sermonizing about not interfering with the human world, is just as vulnerable to revelations about how life has moved on with him. "Ghost in Love" also serves as the feature-film debut for Chang, who would go on to make a name for herself as the cutie in 2000's "The Foul King".

Like many romances of the latest 'Korean New Wave', "Ghost in Love" offers a story of love that must overcome a seemingly insurmountable barrier-- in this case, death and the tenacious hold of history. And though the story may lack polish, overall, "Ghost in Love" ends up being a decent romance that benefits from an intriguing concept, adequate special effects, and credible performances.

Bungee Jumping of Their Own (Beonjijeompeureul hada) - 2001

Starring: Lee Byung-heon, Lee Eun-ju, Yae Hyun-soo
Director: Kim Dae-seung
Availability: Korean-import DVD (multi-region)
Rating: ● ● ●

Lee Eun-ju and Lee Byung-heon (*image courtesy of Walt Disney*)

It may not be everyone's cup of tea, but the oddly titled "Bungee Jumping of Their Own" is another imaginative entry in the romance genre in the spirit of "Il Mare" and "Ditto". However, instead of time being the barrier that separates the two would-be lovers, the directorial debut of former Im Kwon-taek assistant director Kim Dae-sung uses the notions of reincarnation and gender in a thoughtful, though flawed, take on romantic melodrama.

The film begins in 1983, when college student In-woo (Lee Byung-heon) falls hopelessly in love with Tae-hee (Lee Eun-ju), who briefly shares his umbrella while waiting for the bus. After a vigorous pursuit, as well as some initial awkwardness, In-woo and Tae-hee finally realize that their destinies are entwined and begin a serious relationship with a vow to never leave one another. Unfortunately, not long after, In-woo finds himself waiting at the train station for Tae-hee, who never shows up.

Seventeen years later, In-woo has become a languages teacher at a high school. Married and with a child, thoughts of Tae-hee has long faded from In-woo's mind. However, the memories of his first love are rekindled by one of his male students, the smug yet bright Hyun-bin (Yae Hyun-soo). Hyun-bin's phrases and mannerisms echo those of Tae-hee, as do his sketches that eerily mimic her style of drawing. Convinced that Tae-hee has somehow been reincarnated as this student, In-woo becomes obsessed with Hyun-bin and tries to get closer to him. Not surprisingly, vicious rumors begin circulating around the school that both In-woo and Hyun-bin are gay lovers, which have serious implications for both teacher and student.

Unfortunately, the biggest weakness of "Bungee Jumping of Their Own" is how the script resolves the dilemma facing In-woo and Hyun-bin. Some viewers might feel a sense of unease watching societal norms being trashed in the name of love, particularly since Hyun-bin offers a triple-whammy of lines being crossed, as he is (a) a teenage (b) male (c) student of In-woo's. It also doesn't help that Lee's portrayal of In-woo lacks sympathy, as he appears to be more like a lecher than a conflicted individual. However, given that homosexuality is still a taboo subject in South Korea, the on-screen depiction of In-woo and Hyun-bin's interactions never gets physical. Unfortunately, there is a sense that the script by Ko Eun-nim tries too hard to play it safe in the third act, as they are brought together by Hyun-bin's sudden and unconditional acceptance of his fate. As a result, the story's bittersweet resolution ends up coming across as contrived, robbing the film of some emotional resonance.

Regardless of how the material is handled, Kim's flawless direction is a joy to watch throughout the entire film. The film's first half, detailing the courtship of In-woo and Tae-hee, is beautifully handled with a judicious blend of awkwardness and passion, such as In-woo's clumsily obvious attempts to get close to Tae-hee, or their difficulties in overcoming shyness when they decide to consummate their love for the first time in a motel. There is also some spectacular camerawork on display throughout the film, such as a magnificent crane shot that is used when In-woo and Tae-hee take in a magnificent view while hiking in the mountains, or a sweet scene where Tae-hee teaches In-woo how to waltz on the beach as the sun sets behind them.

"Bungee Jumping of Their Own" takes a daring leap with its story of true love in the face of societal norms and morality. Unfortunately, it ends up stumbling on its last step with a disappointingly contrived third act that tries too hard to please everyone. But despite this weakness, it is still an unconventional take on romantic melodrama with an intriguing premise. And coupled with Kim's imaginative direction, "Bungee Jumping of Their Own" ends up doing more things right than wrong.

I Wish I Had a Wife (Nado anaega isseosseumyeon johgessda) - 2000

Starring: Sol Kyung-gu, Jeon Do-yeon, Jin Hee-kyung
Director: Park Heung-shik
Availability: Hong Kong-import VCD and DVD (multi-region), Korean-import DVD (Region 3)
Rating: ● ● ●

I Wish I Had a Wife poster (*image courtesy of Cinema Service*)

This South Korean romantic comedy from 2000 is a rather unglamorous and slowly paced story about how two plain-looking people get together. Kim Bong-soo (Sol Kyung-gu) is a shy bank clerk who lives alone and longs for a wife, or at least a steady girlfriend. Jung Won-ju (Jeon Do-yeon) is a homely schoolteacher who works across the street from Bong-soo's bank branch. As expected, these two lonely souls keep bumping into each other both inside and outside the bank. At first, their run-ins are completely by accident, but later, they are by design, as Won-ju finds herself attracted to Bong-soo and begins conspiring reasons to interact with him. Unfortunately, not only does Bong-soo rebuff her advances, which he considers to be some kind of joke, but he also begins to have a relationship with another woman (Jin Hee-kyung).

"I Wish I Had a Wife" takes a long time to get to where one would expect. In fact, the film is about three-quarters of the way through before finally Bong-soo gets around to seriously pursuing Won-ju, and even then, they both have serious emotional hang-ups that need to be worked through before they can truly be considered a couple. And after what seems to be an eternity (actually, only two hours), the film comes to an abrupt stop without a sense of proper closure.

That said, the film does have its share of brilliant moments, courtesy of director Park Heung-shik (who was assistant director in "Christmas in August"), which make the pedestrian pacing and predictable plotting far more tolerable. Included among the film's small but great moments is a scene where Bong-soo is stuck on a darkened subway lit only by the glow from the cells phones of passengers calling their spouses. Another scene has Bong-soo watching the tape from the bank machine surveillance camera that has captured patrons confessing their deepest secrets to the camera, including Won-ju declaring her love for him and carrying on a dialogue that eludes her in real life.

Another high point of "I Wish I Had a Wife" is the pairing of Sol and Jeon, who both deliver amiable performances. In sharp contrast to his breakthrough role in "Peppermint Candy", where he played the volatile, combative, and tortured protagonist, Sol is sympathetic as the quiet and reserved Bong-soo. Jeon ably demonstrates why she is one of Korea's most versatile actresses with her suitably de-glamorized portrayal of the daydreaming Won-ju, who is so plain that even her female students are insulted when compared to her-- a sharp contrast to her sexually liberated performance in "Happy End" or her Meg Ryan aspirations in "The Contact".

"I Wish I Had a Wife" exemplifies many of the shortcomings of traditional Korean melodrama and is burdened with a slow and unassuming plot. However, these deficiencies are offset by the earnest performances of leads Sol and Jeon which, in combination with a few sparkling moments of brilliance by director Park, make this charming little romantic comedy a worthwhile effort.

The Contact (Cheob-sok) - 1997

Starring: Han Suk-kyu, Jeon Do-yeon, Chu Sang-mi
Director: Chang Yoon-hyun
Availability: Hong Kong-import VCD
Rating: ● ● ●

Guns & Talks poster (*image courtesy of Myung Films*)

Despite the relatively recent innovation of the Internet, the central conceit of the Internet romance genre has been around for decades. Having two characters who can't stand each other or are strangers in real life, only to be intimate in another medium (such as via telephone or letter writing) has served as the basis of several romances and romantic comedies in the past. 1940's "The Shop Around the Corner" had two antagonistic coworkers who didn't realize that they were each other's secret pen pal. This was then remade into a Judy Garland musical in 1949 called "In the Good Old Summertime", which changed the setting to a music shop but essentially kept the story the same. The 1959 sex comedy "Pillow Talk" had Rock Hudson and Doris Day sharing a 'party line' (shared telephone line) without knowing each other's identity. And in 1998, "The Shop Around the Corner was updated as Nora Ephron's "You've Got Mail", an America Online commercial disguised as a romantic comedy.

With one of the highest rates of Internet penetration in the world, it is not surprising that South Korea's homegrown film industry was one of the first to come out with an Internet romance, beating Hollywood to the punch by one year. "The Contact" features the ever-popular Han Suk-kyu as radio producer Dong-hyun, who is suffering from a broken heart even though six years have passed since being dumped by girlfriend Young-hae. One day, he receives an old Velvet Underground record in the mail from Young-hae, and decides to play it on the radio. The song makes a strong impression on Su-hyun (Jeon Do-yeon), who hears the broadcast over her car radio while witnessing a fatal car crash. Unable to get the song out of her head, Su-hyun sends an e-mail to the radio station to request the song.

Thinking that the requestor might be his long-lost love, Dong-hyun begins an online chat with Su-hyun. At first, Su-hyun raises some false hopes in Dong-hyun by pretending to be Young-hae. However, her increasing discomfort forces her to reveal her true identity. Despite the charade, Dong-hyun continues his online correspondence with her, and they soon discover that they have very much in common, including the pangs of unrequited love. And unbeknownst to the would-be lovers, they have actually crossed paths numerous times in the past without realizing it.

Despite their chat-room intimacy, they are both reluctant to meet face to face. And to further complicate matters, they both must deal with some real-life romantic entanglements-- Dong-hyun finds himself in a love triangle with best friend Tae-ho (Park Yong-su) and an overly aggressive writer named Eun-hee (Chu Sang-mi), while Su-hyun is secretly in love with her roommate's boyfriend (Kim Tae-woo). Will these two cyberspace soul mates ever meet in the real world?

"The Contact" is not a bad film, but on the other hand, there isn't anything here that makes it an exceptional one either. Though the production values are quite good, director and co-scribe Chang Yoon-hyun (who would go on to direct "Tell Me Something" in 1999) doesn't really offer anything new in this rather conventional melodrama. As the two romantic leads stumble towards each other over the course of two hours, there is little on the screen to engage audience interest. The characters of Dong-hyun and Su-hyun have few distinguishing features that separate them from other run-of-the-mill lovelorn protagonists of the genre, making them rather dull to spend time with. It also doesn't help that Han's delivers a very low-key and understated performance as Dong-hyun, leaving it up to Jeon to carry the entire film with her sympathetic portrayal of Su-hyun. In addition, the script misses some opportunities to explore some potentially relevant themes, such as the juxtaposition of increased connectedness with increased alienation in modern society.

With a story about two lonely hearts who find true love via an Internet connection, "The Contact" enjoyed both critical and financial success when it was released in 1997. In addition to being credited with rejuvenating flagging audience interest in homegrown moviemaking, thereby paving the way for the latest 'Korean New Wave', "The Contact" garnered a number of awards, both at the Grand Bell and the Blue Dragon Awards (both of which honor Korean filmmaking). In addition, "The Contact" became the first Korean film to be remade outside the country-- the German version "Frau2 sucht HappyEnd" was released in 2001. However, despite such success at home and abroad, "The Contact" ends up being an underwhelming entry into the Internet romance genre. With its slow approach to storytelling, uninteresting characters, and the inexplicably bland performance of lead actor Han Suk-kyu, "The Contact" fails to connect.

Asako in Ruby Shoes (Sun ae bo) - 2000

Starring: Lee Jung-jae, Misato Tachibana, Kim Min-heui, Urara Awata
Director: E. J-yong
Availability: Hong Kong-import VCD and DVD (multi-region), Korean-import DVD (Region 3)
Rating: ●●●

Asako in Ruby Shoes DVD box art (*image courtesy of Cinema Service*)

Though it might be easy to dismiss the 2000 Korean-Japanese co-production "Asako in Ruby Shoes" as yet another Internet romance, à la 1997's "The Contact", it is actually a sobering examination of the depths of desperation reached by two lonely souls in search of happiness and true love. And though some of the film's elements, such as a fixation on basal bodily functions, make E. J-yong's follow-up to his "An Affair" from 1998 at times repulsive, it ends up being surprisingly clever in how it links the destinies of its two romantic leads.

The two forsaken protagonists of "Asako in Ruby Shoes" live in different countries, with shiftless civil servant U-in (Lee Jung-jae) eking out a living in South Korea, and young woman Aya (Misato Tachibana) fairing poorly in her college preparatory classes in Japan. The former is an introverted and socially awkward man who is obsessed with a red-headed girl named Mia (Kim Min-heui) who helps out at a nearby cooking class, yet lacks the courage to approach her. Meanwhile, a few thousand miles away, the chronically depressed Aya drops out of school, skips her anti-depressant medication, and dreams of committing suicide by holding her breath until she dies.

Though the film drops numerous hints about the invisible connections linking U-in and Aya together (reminiscent of Krzysztof Kieslowski's "Three Colors: Red"), the most overt connection begins when U-in stumbles across an adult webcam site featuring an Asian woman named 'Asako in Ruby Shoes'. With her short red hair, she is a spitting image of Mia, spurring U-in to apply for a credit card such that he can become a regular subscriber to the service. Turns out that 'Asako in Ruby Shoes' is none other than Aya, who has answered an ad in search of extra income. Through the convoluted machinations of fate and circumstance, these two kindred spirits eventually find comfort in each another's company.

On one hand, "Asako in Ruby Shoes" is almost fairy tale-like in how it unites the two would-be lovers, which includes some fanciful scenes, such as Aya's best friend (Urara Awata) straddling between U-in and Aya's worlds, or a strange scene that has the two of them bumping into each other on the subway, even though they are in two completely different cities at the time. On the other

Misato Tachibana (*image courtesy of Cinema Service*)

hand, the director tries a little too hard at cinematic realism, particularly in the disturbing fashion in which he pulls no punches in illustrating U-in's numerous bodily functions, including a stomach-churning scene where actor Lee actually vomits into a toilet (which I'm sure deserves some type of recognition for pure moxie).

But despite such a 'Jekyll and Hyde' execution, "Asako in Ruby Shoes" ends up being an absorbing and fascinating off-kilter romance, due in part to the convincing and melancholy performances of its two leads, and the clever way in how the story eventually brings them together. Though "Asako in Ruby Shoes" has a basis in the 'Internet romance' genre, director E J-yong takes this oft-told type of story in new and unexpected directions.

Calla (Chara) - 1999

Starring: Song Seung-heon, Kim Hee-sun, Kim Hyeon-ju
Director: Song Hae-seong
Availability: Hong Kong-import VCD, Hong Kong-import DVD (multi-region)
Rating: ••

Calla poster (*image courtesy of Modern*)

"Calla" is one of the earlier entries in the 'love across time' genre-- it also happens to be one of the weakest. In it, a man is given the chance to relive a day to set things right, and hopefully save the life of the woman he loves. And though this film speaks to similar themes found in other entries of the genre, particularly the importance of reinterpreting past events in the context of the present, the credibility of the "Groundhog Day"-type script is undermined by a protagonist who never seems to think more than two minutes ahead.

Seon-woo (Song Seung-heon), who rides the same bus every day, catches sight of the lovely Ji-hee (Kim Hee-sun) during his morning ride and is instantly smitten. He then begins finding a bouquet of flowers, calla, on his desk at work every morning, without any clue as to who sent them. Seon-woo eventually tracks down the flowers to a local florist where Ji-hee happens to work. Convinced that Ji-hee feels the same about him as he does about her, Seon-woo doggedly works up the nerve to ask her out. Ji-hee agrees over the telephone, and they arrange to meet in a hotel restaurant on Christmas Eve, after Seon-woo returns from a business trip.

Unfortunately, when Seon-woo arrives at the restaurant at the appointed time, he finds the place swarming with police. Seon-woo races up to the restaurant just in time to see Ji-hee and an unknown man holding her hostage leap through a glass window and fall to their deaths. However, some time later, a supernatural occurrence returns Seon-woo to the morning of that fateful Christmas Eve, giving him a second chance to save the woman he loves.

"Calla" is hardly a new concept, though at times, the plot machinations are rather interesting, particularly after Seon-woo goes back in time. Through the added perspective of Ji-hee's coworker (Kim Hyeon-ju), it is revealed that Seon-woo's perceptions of the Ji-hee and the events that led up to her death are far from the truth, and that his true love may lie elsewhere. Unfortunately, as a man motivated to prevent his supposed beloved from dying again, the actions of Seon-woo strain credibility, as he seems to wander about without purpose or forethought. This is most apparent when he foolishly decides to take on some drug dealers in a bar for no good or convincing reason, who end up beating him to a pulp. Good work brainiac!

Despite what could have been a promising premise, "Calla" ends up squandering it with a poorly conceived plot that requires a giant leap of faith on behalf of the audience. Coupled with the lukewarm performances of the leads, "Calla" just doesn't smell as sweet as its namesake.

The Gingko Bed (Eunhaengnamoo chimdae) - 1996

Starring: Han Suk-kyu, Shim Hye-jin, Jin Hee-kyung, Shin Hyun-june
Director: Kang Je-gyu
Availability: Cantonese-dubbed Hong Kong-import VCD and DVD (multi-region),
Korean-import DVD (multi-region)
Rating: • •

Gingko Bed DVD Box Art (*image courtesy of Tai Seng*)

Before making "Shiri", Kang Je-gyu's claim to fame was his 1996 supernatural romance/horror film "The Gingko Bed", which also featured "Shiri" star Han Suk-kyu. With its paranormal story elements and decent production values, "The Gingko Bed" was one of the first homegrown productions in recent years to develop a following outside its native Korea, particularly in Hong Kong, where it called to mind the fantasy films of Tsui Hark, such as "A Chinese Ghost Story". However, when one actually watches the film, it seems that the merits of "The Gingko Bed" have been grossly misrepresented.

You can actually get a pretty good idea of what to expect from the rest of the film from the first fifteen minutes. First, the film opens with an atrociously low-budget 'special effect' sequence where a hawk uses a lightning bolt to destroy one of a pair of gingko trees (all in model railroad HO scale). Second, when the film fast-forwards to the present day, one of the first scenes depicts a woman being raped in a dark alley, which smacks of the sexual exploitation that was rampant in 'old school' Korean filmmaking.

After these two unimpressive expectation-lowering scenes, "The Gingko Bed" settles down into its story, which revolves around art teacher Su-hyeon (Han) and his live-in surgeon girlfriend Seon-young (Shim Hye-jin, who would star opposite Han once again in 1997's "Green Fish"). Su-hyeon begins to have vivid dreams about a mysterious woman, which become intensified after he makes an impulse purchase of an antique gingko bed. It turns out that the bed contains the spirit of Princess Midan (Jin Hee-kyung), who was Su-hyeon's lover in a past life, and now wants to be reunited with him. Unfortunately, their reunion is cut short by another spirit, General Hwang (Shin Hyun-june), who has emerged from the afterlife to claim Midan for himself.

While the central concept of "The Gingko Bed" is certainly interesting, the execution is deplorable. The story is downright confusing, and the film's scatterbrained script strains credibility at every turn. This is partly due to a lack of consistent internal logic in what happens in the story, such as how the spirits interact with the human world, or the laziness of the film's *deus ex machina* conclusion.

To further confuse audiences, extraneous plot elements are freely thrown into the mix, such as Seon-young's political troubles at her hospital. This awkwardly inserted exposition grinds the film's pacing to a halt, and serves only as a desperate attempt to inject some additional conflict during the film's overcooked climax. There is also a lack of credibility in the motivations of Su-hyeon, who immediately falls in love with the ghost of Midan despite already being in a steady relationship, and Seon-young, who not only tolerates her boyfriend's wandering eye, but is even willing to risk her life for it. And though Shin is rather imposing figure, the one-dimensionality of his character and a corresponding lifeless performance make General Hwang a villain who has much better luck in putting the audience to sleep than placing the protagonists in any true danger.

In comparison to Kang's superior follow-up "Shiri", a film that irrevocably changed the face of Korean cinema, "The Gingko Bed" is pure amateur hour. However, despite its numerous flaws, "The Gingko Bed" is at least interesting from a film history perspective. In addition to serving as a primer for "Shiri", "The Gingko Bed" would end up laying the foundation for other time-twisted romances, what I dub the 'love across time' genre-- films that explore the invisible connections between the past and present, and ultimately reveal the national psyche of a divided country.

White Valentine (Hwaiteu ballenta-in) - 1999

Starring: Jun Ji-hyun, Park Shin-yang
Director: Yang Yun-ho
Availability: Hong Kong-import VCD and DVD (no English subtitles, multi-region),
Korean-import DVD (multi-region)
Rating: •

White Valentine DVD box art (*image courtesy of Tae Chang Entertainment*)

Like "The Contact", "White Valentine" is another one of those romances conceived around the notion of two people who are strangers in the real world yet familiar via a communication medium. However, instead of the Internet, the would-be couple in this 1999 offering are pen pals.

In the film's prologue, we learn that teenager Jung-min (Jun Ji-hyun) is corresponding by mail with a soldier named Hyun-jin (Park Shin-yang). Unfortunately, Jung-min has misrepresented herself in her letters as a much-older schoolteacher, and when Hyun-jin arrives in town to meet her for the first time, she is too embarrassed to show up.

Fast-forward a few years later, and Jung-min has grown into beautiful, yet aimless young woman who spends her days helping out at her belligerent grandfather's bookstore. Unbeknownst to her, Hyun-jin lives nearby and now runs a pet store specializing in birds. They even run into each other on a number of occasions, though without realizing who the other person actually is. Can they rekindle the intimacy they once had?

Unfortunately, after sitting through the film's first fifteen minutes, it is doubtful you will want to stick around long enough to find out. About the only thing going for "White Valentine" (and the only reason why people would spend money on it) is that it was Jun's first feature film role, though her performance is nowhere near as engaging or credible as the far superior work she did in "Il Mare" or "My Sassy Girl". Park, who played the big boss in "Hi, Dharma" and the tortured cop in "Kilimanjaro", is similarly bland as a love interest who spends his days talking to the birds. And if the plain characters and performances weren't bad enough, Yang Yun-ho's direction is equally uninspired, with an over-reliance on static camerawork, sluggish pacing, and an aversion to the use of close-ups.

Overall, "White Valentine" is as namby-pamby as the title suggests. Even rabid fans of Jun Ji-hyun, the type whose lives would be incomplete unless they get their hands on every piece of memorabilia, should stay clear of this lackluster love story. This is one 'valentine' that should be returned to its sender.

Chapter 8: Tears & Turmoil – Dramas

Drama is probably one of the most diverse categories among Korean films. Included in its wide berth are some of the most compelling, tragic, and unforgettable films of the latest 'Korean New Wave', such as a cuckolded husband's brutal retribution against his cheating wife in "Happy End", the heartbreaking quest of a sterile couple to have a child of their own in "A Day", the sci-fi exploration on matters of memory in "Nabi", or the unflattering examination of the undue influence of the American military during the Korean War in "Spring in My Hometown" and "Address Unknown".

But despite such diversity, one common theme does seem to dominant in this genre: the downside of South Korea's liberalizing reforms and emergence as an economic powerhouse over the past few decades, which some see as having brought about corruption and created greater disparity between the haves and have-nots. Lee Chang-dong's "Green Fish" is a case in point as it details the tragic descent of a soldier who returns to his hometown with dreams of starting his own business, only to see them destroyed after falling in with the local mob. This sort of 'broken dreams' drama plays out repeatedly throughout the genre, such as the vicious circle of violence that erupts around the economically motivated kidnapping of a little girl in "Sympathy for Mr. Vengeance", the bleak perspective on violence-ridden gangland life in "Die Bad" and "Beat"; the struggles and evolving relationships of five female high school graduates with few economic prospects in "Take Care of My Cat"; or the films of Korea's 'bad boy' director Kim Ki-duk, such as "The Isle" and "Bad Guy", who leaves no stone uncovered in detailing the seedy underbelly of Korean society.

It has been said the best art comes from the deepest pain, and in the case of the latest 'Korean New Wave', tears and turmoil are the key ingredients for some of the most compelling and provocative dramas in the world.

Happy End (Haepi endeu) - 1999

Starring: Choi Min-shik, Jeon Do-yeon, Joo Jin-mo
Director: Jung Ji-woo
Availability: Hong Kong-import VCD and DVD (multi-region)
Rating: • • • • •

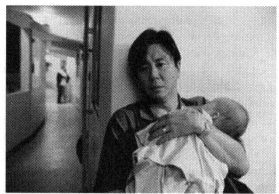

Choi Min-shik (*image courtesy of CJ Entertainment*)

In the highly controversial "Happy End", a man learns that his wife is cheating on him and comes up with an extreme solution to the problem. And despite what is implied by the title, the film's resolution leaves the protagonist debating whether or not he has achieved his 'happy end', or merely substituted one torment with another.

In a scene that borders on soft-core pornography, the film's startling opening graphically depicts a vigorous lovemaking session between career woman Bo-ra (Jeon Do-yeon) and her lover Il-beom (Joo Jin-mo), a former college sweetheart. This is then sharply contrasted with Bo-ra's staid domestic life and her passionless marriage to the older Min-ki (Choi Min-shik). An out-of-work former banker, Min-ki has had little luck and ambition in finding gainful employment, and prefers to spend his days reading romance novels in a used bookstore, or watching soap operas on television. Together, Bo-ra and Min-ki have a baby daughter, and raising her seems to be the only thing they have in common.

However, as the film unspools, Min-ki gradually pieces together the evidence of Bo-ra's infidelity, and is devastated by what he finds. And though the shiftless side of his character seems quietly resigned to live with what his wife has done, he is soon galvanized into taking far more aggressive measures when his wife's indiscretions threaten the well being of their infant daughter. Taking cues from the mystery books that have become the new staple of his reading habits, Min-ki meticulously plots and executes his uncompromising solution.

What is most striking about "Happy End" is how first-time writer/director Jung Ji-woo portrays each of the characters in the love triangle, who each have their reasons, both right and wrong, for what they do. Min-ki is shown initially in an unsympathetic light, as he seems content to enjoy a couch-potato lifestyle on his wife's salary. However, by the second half, he is perhaps the most sympathetic character on the screen, as he is reeling from the discovery of his wife's infidelity and abhorred by how her irresponsibility lands their daughter in the hospital. Similar mixed emotions arise out of Min-ki's radical response to the affair, which is gruesomely depicted. And even though Min-ki is successful in exacting his revenge, it is clear that Min-ki is haunted by what he has done and his expected sense of satisfaction remains elusive.

In contrast, Bo-ra's motivation for the affair seems credible in the film's first half as she seems trapped in a marriage with a shiftless husband who barely says a word to her. However, towards the second half, her character becomes far more complex, as she tries desperately to break off her relationship with Il-beom, leading to a tragic lapse in judgement. Finally, even the interloper, Il-beom, is given some credible motivation for wanting to stay with Bo-ra, depending on how audiences interpret a key conversation where he asserts that Bo-ra's daughter is in fact his.

As the cuckolded and quiet husband, Choi's performance is in contrast to his recent high-profile roles in "Shiri" and "Failan", yet no less effective. Popular actress Jeon, who starred opposite popular actors Han Suk-kyu in the 1997 hit romance "The Contact" and Sol Kyung-gu in 2001's "I Wish I Had a Wife", casts off her usual warm and perky screen persona in her portrayal of the complex and sexually liberated Bo-ra. Finally, Jun is passable as Il-beom, with his portrayal of the strong and silent type a little too reminiscent of his similar work in the historical epic "Musa".

"Happy End" has developed quite an international following since its controversial run in South Korea in 1999. It has become a favorite programming piece at numerous film festivals around the world, and was nominated for Best Asian Film at the 2002 Hong Kong Film Awards. Though the subject matter and execution is rather disturbing, director Jung has created a compelling and suspenseful drama that uncompromisingly details an explosive situation for which there can never be a happy ending.

Sympathy for Mr. Vengeance (Boksuneun naeui geos) - 2002

Starring: Song Kang-ho, Shin Ha-kyun, Bae Doo-na
Director: Park Chan-wook
Availability: Korean-import DVD (Region 3)
Rating: ● ● ● ● ●

Song Kang-ho, Bae Doo-na, and Shin Ha-kyun
(*image courtesy of CJ Entertainement*)

"Sympathy for Mr. Vengeance" may share two of the same male leads (Song Kang-ho and Shin Ha-kyun) as director Park Chan-wook's last feature, the critically acclaimed "Joint Security Area", but it is entirely different type of film, if not superior. Whereas Park's runaway hit from 2000 was a military drama that focused on the human toll of a divided Korea, "Sympathy for Mr. Venegeance" is an uncompromisingly grim psychological thriller about the vicious circle of violence that erupts around the botched kidnapping of a child.

The key players in this tragedy are deaf factory worker Ryu (Shin), his gravely ill sister (Im Ji-eun) who is in dire need of a kidney transplant, his left-wing activist girlfriend Cha Yeong-mi (Bae Doo-na), Ryu's boss Park Dong-jin (Song), and Dong-jin's young daughter Yu-sun (Han Bo-dae). Events are set in motion when Ryu is fired after having taken too much time off work to look after his sick sister. But because he is deaf, he is unable to communicate the extenuating circumstances to his foreman.

To make matters worse, he hands over his life savings to a black market organ trafficking ring in the hopes of exchanging one of his kidneys for one that is suitable for his sister. Unfortunately, he wakes up after the operation only to discover his kidney removed and the organ traffickers (as well as his money) gone. And to further compound the situation, a suitable donor for his sister ends up being found through normal channels. But with his money gone, Ryu now cannot pay for the legitimate transplant.

It is here that the woman at the center of the vicious circle, Yeong-mi, suggests that they kidnap and ransom the daughter of Ryu's former boss, Dong-jin, as a means of securing the necessary funds. At first, it seems as though the plan will work. Yu-sun thinks that she is being babysat by Ryu and Yeong-mi, and is completely unaware that she is being ransomed; Dong-jin obeys all the ransom instructions without involving the police; and Ryu's sister is also in the dark about what is actually transpiring.

Unfortunately, like all best-laid plans, things start to go terribly wrong. Ryu's sister uncovers what is really going on and decides to takes her own life, while Yu-sun is accidentally killed. These calamities then set in motion the terrible acts of violence that follow in the film's bloody second half, as Ryu and Yeong-mi plot their revenge against the organ traffickers, while Dong-jin is hot on their trail, plotting his.

Those viewers familiar with the uncompromising violence, black humor, and degradation of Japanese cinema, particularly the films of Takeshi Kitano and Takashi Miike, will find the style that Park employs in "Sympathy for Mr. Vengeance" to be very familiar. This slowly but assuredly paced film places viewers in the uncomfortably claustrophobic and bleak lives of its characters, particularly Ryu, whose lack of hearing seems to detach him from reality-- a condition that ends up having tragic implications.

And as the characters plot their revenge on those who have wronged them, it is sometimes difficult to determine whether or not to be appalled or to feel "Sympathy for Mr. Vengeance". True, there is a sense of satisfaction from seeing these characters righting painful wrongs, but at the same time, their desperation and fury transform them into inhuman monsters that are capable of unspeakable evil. And to further drive home how very similar the 'hero' and the 'villain' are in the story, Park uses a divergent narrative structure to parallel the trails of revenge taken by these two men, whose motivations and actions are not that dissimilar. And indeed, they both end up in a very similar place, destroyed by the same spiral of violence that neither of them had the courage to stop.

Song Kang-ho and Shin Ha-kyun (*image courtesy of CJ Entertainement*)

Supporting such an ambitious production are a number of great performances. Song, who rose to fame with a number of high-profile comic roles (such as "The

Foul King" or "No. 3") and action roles (most notably "Shiri"), delivers a tour de force as an ordinary man who gradually becomes consumed by his rage. Shin, who starred alongside Song in both "The Foul King" and "Joint Security Area", does an impressive job playing a character whose inability to speak results in his being taken advantage of at every turn. Finally, Bae delivers some of her best work since "Take Care of My Cat" as the rhetoric-spouting miscreant who unwittingly orchestrates the tragedy to its bitter end.

Bae Doo-na (*image courtesy of CJ Entertainement*)

Unfortunately, at the start of 2002, many Korean moviegoers went into "Sympathy for Mr. Vengeance" expecting something akin to "Joint Security Area II". Not surprisingly, many went away disappointed. Regardless of such audience misconceptions, "Sympathy for Mr. Vengeance" ends up being a powerful and stimulating follow-up effort that undoubtedly illustrates Park's gift as a director-- perhaps one of the best to come out of the latest 'Korean New Wave'.

A Day (Haru) - 2001

Starring: Ko So-young, Lee Sung-jae
Director: Han Ji-seung
Availability: Korean-import DVD (multi-region)
Rating: ● ● ● ● ●

A Day DVD box art (*image courtesy of Cinema Service*)

Han Ji-seung's "A Day" is a great example of a film that demonstrates the mastery of Korean filmmakers in the art of melodrama. This unassuming film, released at the start of 2001, tells the story of a young couple faced with an agonizing decision in regards to their unborn child.

The couple in question is Jin-won (Ko So-young) and Sok-yun (Lee Sung-jae), who have been married for six years. Like all young married couples in Korea, they are expected to have children not long after tying the knot. Unfortunately, despite countless efforts, Jin-won has yet to bear a child. Meanwhile, adoption is out of the question because, as Jin-won puts it, "Why should I embrace the misfortune of others?" However, after their last attempt at artificial insemination, they receive wondrous news-- Jin-won has finally become pregnant. Overjoyed, Jin-won and Sok-yun immediately start preparations for the new baby, which includes moving into a new house and preparing the nursery...

...but then they receive what could be the worst possible news -- the foetus is anencephalic, meaning that it lacks a brain and not live more than twenty-four hours after birth. They are then given a choice: bring the child to term only to watch it die, or abort the fetus now. Despite the grim reality of the situation, Jin-won still prefers to keep the baby-- nothing is more important than to hold her own child in her arms, even if it is only for a day.

From start to finish, "A Day" never fails to delight, entertain, and involve with a down-to-earth script that is rife with laughter and tears. The film's beginning focuses on how much importance Jin-won ascribes to becoming a mother, such as her embarrassment when a nosy co-worker assumes that she already has a child, or some exposition that reveals how she never experienced what it felt like to have a father and a mother as she was raised by her spinster aunt. There is even some great humor at play, such as when the pert Jin-won discovers that she is ovulating and militantly orders Sok-yun to 'get to it'. And when they receive the news that Jin-won is pregnant, I'm sure the audience will find their elation to be contagious.

However, as the film heads into the second-half, their short-lived elation turns into denial and grief, emotions that soon become a wedge between Jin-won and Sok-yun. And like any well-written film, director Han 'shows, not tells' the severe toll that such a difficult situation takes on them, both as a couple and as individuals. And though the story's resolution does end up as a 'happy ending', it is earned and qualified through Jin-won's acceptance of the situation and the realization of her responsibilities.

In all her film roles, such as in Kim Sun-su's "Beat" or Park Dae-yeong's "Love Wind, Love Song", Ko has proven herself to be an exceptional young actress with impressive dramatic range. True to this reputation, "A Day" revolves around her well-rounded portrayal of Jin-won, exuding equal parts of chutzpah and vulnerability, well suited to the film's lighter moments, as well as its weightier ones. Complementing her memorable performance is Lee's turn as Sok-yun, who would rather omit the truth or even lie than rock the boat. Supporting these two leads are Kim Chang-wan as their doctor and veteran actress Yun So-jeong in a touching performance as Jin-won's aunt.

With its well-written script and excellent performances, there is not a single false moment or misstep to be found in "A Day". In the hands of a lesser director, the subject matter could have easily become fodder for an unremarkable movie-of-the-week. But with its earnest, charming, and ultimately heartfelt script, along with emotionally intense performances by its leads, "A Day" is a film of rare emotion and depth.

Die Bad (Jukgeona hokeun nabbeugeona) - 2000

Starring: Park Seong-bin, Ryu Seung-wan, Ryu Seung-beom, Bae Jung-shik
Director: Ryu Seung-wan
Availability: Korean-import DVD (Region 3)
Rating: • • • •

Die Bad DVD box art (*image courtesy of Mirovision*)

"Die Bad" is the indie-filmmaking Cinderella story of South Korea cinema. This impressive debut by Ryu Seung-wan was cobbled together from two of the director's previous short films and two newly shot segments. And though the film's low-budget roots are betrayed by the fuzzy 16mm production and the mono sound, Ryu exhibits tremendous skill from both a narrative and visual sense in this violent drama that traces the tragically intertwined lives of two high-school friends.

The film's first segment was originally shot in 1998 and is entitled "Rumble". Tech school students Sung-bin (Park Seong-bin) and Suk-hwan (played by the director himself) are shooting pool when they get into a fight with some students from a rival art school. During the scuffle, Sung-bin accidentally kills one of the art students, an act that sends him to jail and ends up haunting him for the rest of his life.

This segues into the next segment, "Nightmare", in which recently paroled Sung-bin gets a job as an auto mechanic. One night, he witnesses a local big boss, 'President Kim', being beaten by four thugs. Though he is still haunted by the murder he committed seven years prior and is being watched like a hawk by his parole officer (Im Won-hee), Sung-bin jumps into the fray and rescues the gangster, sealing his fate to a life of crime.

The story then jumps into the next segment, which is centered around Ryu's 1999 short "Modern Man", in which Suk-hwan, who has now become a cop, gets into a drawn-out fisticuffs with President Kim. As the cop and criminal beat each other senseless, the pugilistic action is intercut with interviews of both combatants, revealing that despite their being on the opposite sides of the law, they aren't that different.

This is followed by the film's longest and most devastating vignette, "Die Bad". Shot in black-and-white, it draws the narrative's disparate threads into a devastating conclusion. Suk-hwan's younger brother (played by the director's younger brother, Ryu Seung-beom) and his friends, frustrated by school and enamored with the gangster lifestyle, ask Sung-bin if they can join his gang. Unfortunately, Sung-bin accepts, culminating in a bloody confrontation befitting the film's title.

"Die Bad" apparently only cost around $3,000 US to make, and Ryu stretches the miniscule budget with a clever script, some inventive camerawork, and a punchy soundtrack. The most notable aspect would be the many fight sequences that pepper "Die Bad", such as the artfully done "Rumble", the almost endless battle royal between Suk-hwan and President Kim in "Modern Man", and the brutality of the film's final scenes. However, instead of presenting violence for violence's sake, the pervasive pugilism serves a purpose here. Like other Korean gangland sagas of note, such as "Friend" and "Beat", the violence underscores the world that the characters find themselves in-- a bleak place where violence is the only common language and pain is the only basis of understanding.

After the success of "Die Bad", Ryu became the director to work with and was given wide latitude for his sophomore feature "No Blood No Tears". Though his 2002 follow-up feature benefited from more recognizable stars, a bigger budget, and more technical wizardry, it lacked the skin-of-your-teeth edginess, creativity, and emotional intensity of "Die Bad". It may not be pretty, but "Die Bad" sure packs a punch.

Take Care of My Cat (Goyangireul buiakhae) - 2001

Starring: Lee Yu-won, Bae Doo-na, Ok Ji-yeong, Lee Eun-sil, Lee Eun-ju
Director: Jeong Jae-eun
Availability: Korean-import DVD (multi-region)
Rating: ●●●●

Take Care of My Cat DVD box art (*image courtesy of Warner Bros.*)

Virtually ignored when it was released in South Korea at the tail end of 2001 but revived by a legion of dedicated fans, "Take Care of My Cat" is a well-written and smartly directed feature film debut for Jeong Jae-eun. Though at first glance the film appears to be a 'chick flick' version of Kwak Kyung-taek's gangland saga "Friend", as it details how the relationships of five female friends evolve after graduating from high school, "Take Care of My Cat" ends up being a carefully orchestrated character study that illuminates the insecurities and challenges of South Korea's marginalized youth.

The film's opening scene has five young women taking a picture to commemorate their graduation from high school: Hae-ju (Lee Yu-won), Tae-hee (Bae Doo-na), Ji-yeong (Ok Ji-yeong), and Chinese twin sisters Bi-Ryu (Lee Eun-sil) and On-jo (Lee Eun-joo). Unfortunately, their elation and vows to always remain friends eventually give way as they awaken to the harsh reality of their post-high school lives.

When we catch up with these young women some time later, their lives are beginning to diverge onto different paths, and their differing personalities come to the surface. The vain and ambitious Hae-ju has landed herself an entry-level position at an upscale brokerage, and her growing arrogance quickly becomes a source of conflict with the other girls, particularly when she decides to leave their working class hometown of Inchon for the bright lights of Seoul. In contrast, the shy but artistically gifted Ji-yeong is at the other end of the economic strata, drifting from one low-paying job to the next while sharing a crumbling hovel with her impoverished grandparents. In-between is the rebellious yet considerate Tae-hee, whose strong ties with both Hae-ju and Ji-yeong often relegate her to the role of peacekeeper. She also has dreams of her own, as she longs to become a sailor, though her rigid patriarchal family life limits her choices. Finally, twins Bi-ryu and On-jo, who lighten the heavy atmosphere with some comic relief, operate a stall in Inchon's Chinatown selling their homemade fashion accessories.

The film's title stems from a stray cat that Ji-yeong picks up and names 'Titi'. As the story unfolds and the dynamics of the relationships between the characters change, it is revealed that the cat becomes a symbol for these five women who, because they never had the opportunity to go to college, are looked down upon (one character muses that most people love dogs, but some hate cats). However, as the cat is passed between these girls for various reasons, the act of giving Titi to one another becomes a symbol of their friendship, and each character's reaction to the responsibility is rather revealing.

The bulk of the film, except for the last act, has very little plot to speak of, as it essentially details the interactions between these five friends. Though this may sound uninteresting and pointless, writer-director Jeong actually does a superb job of fleshing each of the five main characters, particularly their insecurities, and distilling compelling drama from the everyday. Most of the tension comes from the escalating animosity between Hae-ju and Ji-yeong, with the former's insensitivity and the latter's pride being the catalysts. For example, when Ji-yeong confides that she wishes to study art abroad, Hae-ju shoots the idea down by telling her that studying requires money-- something she clearly doesn't have. Another memorable scene has Hae-ju inviting the rest of the gang to go shopping, a situation that creates some visible discomfort for Ji-yeong.

Ok Ji-yeong, Lee Eun-sil, Lee Yu-won, Bae Doo-na, and Lee Eun-ju (*image courtesy of Warner Bros.*)

Jeong also injects plenty of great character moments into the film. One telltale scene reveals that Ji-yeong is not immune from the influence of Hae-ju's lifestyle aspirations, as she ends up living beyond her means when she plunks down her meager earnings for a sleek new cell phone, buying a brief respite from the dreariness of her everyday life. And despite her arrogance, Hae-ju is wrestling with a few demons of her own, constantly concerned about her looks (even to the point of spending thousands on laser eye surgery and contemplating plastic surgery in the future) and the limitations to her career path, given that she does not have a university degree. Another scene has Tae-hee lashing out at her father in a Western restaurant after he decides that everyone will eat the restaurant's most popular dish, rather than conceding that he cannot read the menu. These character studies are ably backed up by strong performances from the cast, particularly by Bae, Ok, and Lee as the core triumvirate.

Another refreshing aspect of "Take Care of May Cat" is how Jeong grounds his film in reality. The film's setting is the port city of Inchon, which is a sharp contrast to the typically cosmopolitan settings of other youth-oriented Korean films ("My Sassy Girl" or "A.F.R.I.K.A." for example). Like the lives of its characters, the settings used in "Take Care of My Cat" are cold, bleak, and firmly rooted in the lives of the working class. And instead of spending their days wondering if a certain boy likes them or what to wear to an upcoming party, the issues that the characters must deal with are far more mundane but far more gripping and universal, such as trying to find a job, coping with being glossed over for advancement at work, trying to get a belligerent landlord to fix a hole in the roof, and dealing with death in the family.

Finally, production-wise, "Take Care of My Cat" is very slick, with a particularly noteworthy aspect being the use of on-screen text to highlight the text messages that the girls send to one another over their cell phones. Jeong also makes good use of contemporary beats in the film's soundtrack.

"Take Care of My Cat" is an unforgettable character study cum coming-of-age story that resonates from start to finish, thanks to a strong script, excellent performances, and purposeful direction. And as a result of overwhelming critical and fan support, "Take Care of My Cat" has recently enjoyed a special edition multi-region DVD release-- though the case does specify 'Region 3', it will work on all players. Hopefully, this new lease on life will allow an even wider audience the opportunity to appreciate such an uncommon film.

Green Fish (Chorok mulkogi) - 1997

Starring: Han Suk-kyu, Shim Hye-jin, Moon Sung-keun, Song Kang-ho
Director: Lee Chang-dong
Availability: Hong Kong-import VCD, Korean-import DVD (multi-region)
Rating: •••

Green Fish poster (*image courtesy of Cinema Service*)

Despite its fairly straightforward narrative, director Lee Chang-dong's 1997 directorial debut "Green Fish" has much in common with his 2000 follow-up "Peppermint Candy", which used a reverse chronology to detail the downfall of a man over twenty years of recent South Korean history. Like "Peppermint Candy", "Green Fish" is a pessimistic look at the dark side of South Korea's transformation into an economic powerhouse, detailing the loss of innocence and corruption that have followed in its wake. The theatrical release of "Green Fish" could not have been better timed, as South Korea was hit by an economic crisis at the tail end of 1997, a meltdown in which government scandals over fraudulent loans played a factor.

The story begins with Mak-dong (Han Suk-kyu) on a train ride home after completing his military service. While on the train, he sees a woman, Mi-ae (Shim Hye-jin) being accosted by a group of ruffians. Unfortunately, Mak-dong ends up receiving a beating, losing his luggage, and missing his train for all his trouble. When he finally returns to his hometown after a long walk, he finds things have changed dramatically and for the worse in his absence. The old home is gone, having been demolished to make way for new high-rises, and his mother and retarded brother have moved into smaller quarters on the edge of town. Meanwhile, the remaining members of Mak-dong's family have moved out, with each one trying to make ends meet on their own-- for example, his sister (Oh Ji-hye) has resorted to becoming a coffee shop hooker.

Mak-dong then receives a call from Mi-ae, who has been holding his misplaced luggage since the incident on the train. Mi-ae works in a local nightclub as a singer and is the girlfriend of powerful gangster Bae Tae-gon (Moon Sung-keun). Grateful for how he helped Mi-ae on the train, Tae-gon gives Mak-dong a job in one of his enterprises and makes him an official member of his gang. Faced with a tight job market and few opportunities for meaningful employment, Mak-dong easily accepts Tae-gon's offer, seeing it as a means to save up enough money to open a restaurant where his whole family could live and work together. Unfortunately, as Mak-dong is drawn into the underworld, the more dangerous it becomes. In addition to becoming romantically entangled with Mi-ae, Mak-dong becomes caught in-between a power struggle between Tae-gon and a gangland rival.

Like "Peppermint Candy", "Green Fish" is a tragedy borne of unbridled ambition, avarice, and corruption. From director's Lee perspective, in today's world, human life is cheap, and relationships can be bought and sold. Like the time-traveling protagonist of "Peppermint Candy", Mak-dong is just another naïve innocent who becomes chewed up by the compromised morality and materialism of modern Korea. This contrast between the 'old' and 'new' ways is illustrated at every turn in the film, such as the juxtaposition of shiny new apartment buildings against the small home of Mak-dong's mother, or the film's iconic scene where Mak-dong tearfully reminisces over the phone about a happier time from his childhood. And like Lee's 2000 follow-up, "Green Fish" has its share of disturbing scenes, particularly an outdoor birthday celebration that goes terribly wrong.

Han received a Best Actor award at both Korean national film award ceremonies that year, and they are well deserved. As Mak-dong, Han capably handles the descent from a starry-eyed young man full of big hopes and dreams to a broken, desperate, and tragic victim. Shim also received Best Actress nods for her turn as the film's resident *femme fatale*, while Moon's portrayal of the ruthless and domineering Tae-gon is chilling and unforgettable. Other recognizable faces in the cast include Song Kang-ho (who would eventually star with Han in "Shiri"), Jeong Jin-young, and Yu Yeon-su (who would also go on to appear in "Peppermint Candy").

At times, the slowly paced "Green Fish" does lapse into cliché-ridden melodrama, however, such missteps are easily forgivable in light of director Lee's expert handling of the material. Though "Green Fish" is not as memorable as Lee's more recent "Peppermint Candy", it still remains a powerful film with its disturbing and uncompromising depiction of a man's destruction, a tragic end set against the amoral wasteland of Korea's unchecked economic prosperity.

Beat - 1997

Starring: Jung Woo-sung, Yoo Oh-sung, Im Chang-jeong, Ko So-young
Director: Kim Sun-su
Availability: Korean-import DVD (multi-region)
Rating: ● ● ● ●

Beat DVD box art (*image courtesy of Sidus*)

Based on a popular comic book, "Musa" director Kim Sun-su's 1997 feature "Beat" could easily be mistaken as the Korean remake of the 1988 Hong Kong drama "As Tears Go By". With its neon-meets-acid-wash cinematography, stop-motion action sequences, and a main character caught between true love and his gangland obligations, "Beat" certainly seems to hit all the notes of Wong Kar-wai's breakthrough film. Fortunately, Kim has a few more tricks up his sleeve to make "Beat" stand on its own. Indeed, "Beat" is a gritty and unforgettable look at youth alienation borne of broken dreams and economic marginalization.

Similar to Kwak Kyung-taek's smash hit "Friend", "Beat" details how the friendship and loyalties of four youths are strained by time, differing ambitions, rampant corruption, and plain bad luck. At the core of the story is the relationship between natural-born pugilist Min (Jung Woo-sung) and best friend Tae-su (Yoo Oh-sung). Tae-su quits school to join a gang, while Min stays behind and ends up befriending Hwan (Im Chang-Jeong), a kid with a knack for getting into trouble. Rounding out the quartet is Romi (Ko So-young), a girl with college aspirations whom Min meets in a nightclub.

As the years pass, life puts these four individuals through the ringer. Tae-su does some jail time for murdering a gangland rival; Min and Hwan open up a restaurant, only to fall victim to local toughs and corruption, while Romy is mentally traumatized by the death of a close friend. Unfortunately, as time passes, Min increasingly becomes the nexus for his three friends, and his choices, both right and wrong, have devastating consequences for all.

For those familiar with "As Tears Go By", much of what happens in "Beat" will seem very familiar. Min is obviously the Andy Lau character, with Romi, despite her personal problems, being the Maggie Cheung character who offers him salvation from the vicious circle of gangland violence. In addition, the Jacky Cheung character, representing the path to destruction, is split between the loyalty-bound Tae-su and the volatile Hwan. Even the film's numerous fight scenes are reminiscent of Wong Kar-wai's stop-motion visual style, as are a number of visual set pieces that seem to have been plucked from Wong's *oeuvre*, particularly "Fallen Angels". However, unlike Kim Yui-Seok's pretentious "Holiday in Seoul", this attempt at emulating Wong Kar-wai has a point and actually manages to score a few emotional beats along the way, most notably in the film's tragic ending. Performances are also strong, with Jung and Yoo leading a strong ensemble.

Like "Green Fish", which came out just a few months prior, the release of "Beat" could not have been more timely, given the turmoil that would befall the South Korean economy in 1997. Like Lee Chang-dong's critically acclaimed drama, "Beat" is a sobering tale about the downside of Korea's economic and political rejuvenation during the Nineties, only told from the perspective of the country's disaffected youth.

Jung Woo-sung (*image courtesy of Sidus*)

Nabi - 2001

Starring: Kim Ho-jung, Kang Hea-jung, Jang Hyun-sung
Director: Moon Seung-wook
Availability: Korean-import DVD (multi-region)
Rating: ●●●½

Jang Hyun-sung, Kang Hea-jung, and Kim Ho-jung (*image courtesy of Buena Vista International Korea*)

In the not-too-distant future, South Korea has become an environmental wasteland. The frequent bouts of acid rain can irritate exposed skin, even to the point of causing cancer in the worst-case scenario, while storms of toxic 'yellow dust' occasionally blow in from nearby mainland China. In addition, lead poisoning has reached crisis levels, with brain-damaged victims being rounded up by the police and pregnant women being subjected to abortions to reduce the incidence of birth defects. However, despite such chaos, Korea's tourist industry continues to thrive. The reason? The outbreak of the so-called 'oblivion virus', a disease that wipes out the memories of those who become infected, has turned the country into a mecca for thousands of pilgrims who wish to purge themselves of painful memories. This is the intriguing set-up for "Nabi", a low budget, independently produced digital-video feature from 2001 that blends science fiction with arthouse sensibilities, albeit with mixed results.

The Korean title translates to "The Butterfly", which refers to how butterflies signal the presence of the virus, as well as the name of a company that conduct excursions for those wishing to erase their memories, Butterfly Tours. The film begins with the arrival of Butterfly Tours' latest customer Anna Kim (Kim Ho-jung), a woman who is visiting Korea for the very first time after having spent most of her life growing up in Germany. Because the virus is always on the move, Anna is provided a 'virus guide' named Yuki (Kang Hea-jung) and a driver named K (Jang Hyun-sung). Unfortunately, finding the virus and erasing her painful memories ends up not being such a straightforward process, as Anna becomes drawn into the complex lives of her two new acquaintances.

The focus of "Nabi" is on the three main characters and it draws several parallels between them. It is gradually revealed that Anna has come to Korea to forget the loss of her unborn child, who died in her womb at seven months-- though it is not explicitly stated, it is implied that the child was aborted. Similarly, Yuki is seven-months pregnant, though her chances of being allowed to keep the baby or even surviving childbirth are slim, as she suffers from lead poisoning. Finally, the driver K, who was orphaned at a young age, is desperately seeking anyone who might know anything about his family-- in addition to placing video ads on the Internet, he picks up every passenger he can in the hopes that someone will recognize him.

Despite the potential to be an interesting film, "Nabi" ends up losing its way by the halfway mark. The connections drawn between these three players are hardly compelling, and any emotional resonance appears to be forced, as the motivations of the characters remain muddled. It is also difficult to discern exactly the point that director Moon Seung-wook is trying to make, which triangulates somewhere between the persistence of memory and how the past provides context for the present. Indeed, for the most part, it seems "Nabi" is little more than an existential road movie, as the characters wander around Seoul aimlessly, each of them dazed by their own introspective haze. Also, given that the budget was very low, the film also offers little in the way of spectacle, other than making the best use of existing locations in Seoul, such as the most cosmopolitan parts of the city or a dingy construction site.

The film's true stroke of brilliance does not come until close to the end, when Anna finds evidence that she may have actually been to Korea before and been on a 'virus tour' before. Unfortunately, little is done with this clever twist, which could have provided the basis for a far more interesting and compelling film. Nevertheless, the film's ending hints that those exposed to the oblivion virus, such as Anna, are doomed to live their lives repeating the same mistakes over and over again, not unlike the amnesia-suffering protagonist of Christopher Nolan's "Memento".

To director Moon's credit, "Nabi" has a fascinating premise and the potential to be a Wong Kar-wai style discourse on the double-edged blade of memory. Unfortunately, with its lack of focus and all the unremarkable detours that it takes along the way, "Nabi" ends up being a passable drama rife with missed opportunities-- not as unforgettable as one would hope.

The Isle (Seom) - 2000

Starring: Seoh Jung, Kim Yu-seok
Director: Kim Ki-duk
Availability: Hong Kong-import VCD and DVD (Region 3), Korean-import DVD (Region 3)
Rating: ●●●½

The Isle poster (*image courtesy of CJ Entertainment*)

There is one scene in Kim Ki-duk's "The Isle" that perfectly encapsulates what this beautiful yet twisted film is all about. The two main characters catch a fish, only to discover that someone has hacked off two large strips off its sides, leaving the skeleton partially exposed. But despite having experienced such terrible physical trauma, the fish is remarkably still alive. The characters then decide to throw the strange fish back into the lake, where it swims off and disappears into the murky depths. Like the fish, the two lead characters of "The Isle" bear the ugly scars of violence and trauma, yet they both manage to go on living. Unfortunately, the same cannot be said for their bruised and battered psyches, the manifestations of which unfold in the idyllic and mist-covered vistas of "The Isle".

The two main characters in question are Hee-jin (Seoh Jung) and Hyun-shik (Kim Yu-seok). Hee-jin is the beautiful yet mute woman who runs a fishing spot in the Korean countryside. During the day, she ferries food, bait, and other supplies to the 'house boats' that the fishermen rent, and at night, she returns again to sell sexual favors. Hyun-shik arrives one day to rent one of the house boats, though he is not there to fish-- instead, he seems to be on the run from the police and has come to this tranquil place to kill himself. Hee-jin finds herself immediately intrigued and then attracted to this most recent arrival. And after she stops one of his suicide attempts and nurses him back to health, a strange and perverted relationship develops between these two wounded souls, who find fleeting comfort in one another-- that is, until their respective pasts catch up and destroy them.

When "The Isle" was released in Korea in 2000, it became the type of film that audiences hate and critics love. Audiences could not look beyond the graphic sexuality, the seemingly misogynistic tone, the bloody violence, or Kim's vulgar attempts at cinematic realism (case in point-- the underwater perspective of a man defecating). Critics, on the other hand, were able to look beyond the visceral indecencies, and see the film for what it was. Like the rest of his filmography, Kim lays bare the dark and rotten underbelly of Korean society in "The Isle", an allegorical construct that touches on subjects such as the second-class status of women, the country's underground economy that is fuelled by pornography and prostitution, and how love becomes perverted into violent possession.

Many of the story elements create a microcosm of Korean sexual politics. On the one hand, Hee-jin, who has no voice of her own, is dependent on her lodgers, as she earns a living from their continued patronage, as well as from satisfying their sexual appetites. But on the other hand, Hee-jin also wields some power of her own, such as having the only operating boat on the entire lake, leaving the

Seoh Jung and Kim Yu-seok (*image courtesy of CJ Entertainment*)

lodgers completely under her control for transportation between the shore and the house boats. Hee-jin also exercises her power in more violent ways, such as stabbing a rude john that insulted her, or kidnapping and disposing of Hyun-shik's sometimes girlfriend (Seo Weon) after she drops by for a visit. And in the spirit of the proceedings, every female character in "The Isle" ends up being a prostitute.

Unfortunately, like Kim's other films, the deep metaphorical examination quickly overwhelms the rest of the film, as "The Isle" becomes subject to Kim's directorial indulgences and dull pacing. The first half is the best, as Kim gently eases the viewer into the story, creating suspense as he reveals the odd habits, warped personality, and violent nature of Hee-jin, as well as the death wish Hyun-shik, all to the tune of cinematographer Hwang Suh-shik's immaculate lensing. Unfortunately, as the film evolves into a perverse romance, replete with repulsive imagery, "The Isle" starts to run out of steam and becomes more and more like an arthouse exercise run amuck.

However, one aspect that does remain strong throughout is the quiet yet intense performance delivered by Seoh, whom some astute viewers will recognize from "Peppermint Candy". Without any dialogue for her character, Seoh is able to communicate the intense emotions of her character with only gestures and facial expressions. And despite her character's despicable acts, Seo is able to make Hee-jin sympathetic in the context of the miserable existence she leads. As her opposite, Kim acquits himself decently, though his performance is limited by a sketchily defined character. Viewers will also recognize Jang Hang-sun of "Tell Me Something" as the fisherman who carves up the fish and throws it back, as well as Jo Jae-hyun of "Interview" who plays a pimp that shows up to claim his 'property'.

Beautiful, vicious, thought provoking, and ultimately depressing, it is doubtful you have seen anything like "The Isle" before. Director Kim Ki-duk has a number of films to his name, but "The Isle" would have to be one of his most original and gripping with its allegorical take on the misery and pain that lies beneath the surface of modern Korean society. If it wasn't for the fact that Kim was unable to maintain such momentum and conviction all the way through, I'm sure audiences would have been completely hooked.

Spring in My Hometown (Areumdawoon sheejul) - 1998

Starring: In Lee, Kim Jung-woo, Ahn Sung-ki, Bae Yoo-jung
Director: Lee Kwang-mo
Availability: Korean-import VCD and DVD (multi-region)
Rating: ●●●½

Spring in My Hometown poster
(*image courtesy of SKC*)

An example of 'function over form', "Spring in My Hometown", was the most critically acclaimed film of 1998. Offering a critical view of the American military presence during the war, and using the lost innocence of its child protagonists as a metaphor for the undue influence it has had on the nascent South Korean nation, "Spring in My Hometown" is a powerful and thought-provoking drama-- that is, if you can manage to sit through director Lee Kwang-mo's uninspired and patience-testing direction.

The story is told through the eyes of two 13-year old boys growing up near a US military base as the Korean War rumbles in the distance. The family of Sung-min (In Lee) benefits greatly from the American presence, as his older sister is dating an American soldier, while his father (Ahn Sung-ki) gets a lucrative job as a translator on the base. In sharp contrast is the impoverished family life of Sung-min's friend Chang-hee (Kim Jung-woo). With her husband gone as a result of the war, Chang-hee's mother (Bae Yoo-jung) must accept handouts from Sung-min's mother (Song Wok-suk) to put food on the table.

However, despite their differing backgrounds, Sung-min and Chang-hee are best of friends and they have fun at the expense of the US soldiers, from chasing after their jeeps, stealing whatever American trinkets they can get their hands on, or getting their kicks from watching local girls prostituting themselves at the local mill. Unfortunately, this happy-go-lucky attitude changes when the two boys spy Chang-hee's mother bedding down with an American soldier.

Judging from the vignettes he presents in "Spring in My Hometown", there is little doubt that Lee is critical of the influence that the United States has had on his country. For example, the film's opening scene features a suspected communist sympathiser being dragged away from his family by an angry pro-American mob. At school, the boys chant slogans to the effect of "Kill all communists!" with the sort of fervor that would make even Chairman Mao Tse-tung blush. And as mentioned before, the prostitution of the town's local women becomes a metaphor for how Lee views his country's dealings with the United States. Whether you agree with Lee's politics or not, these provocative statements do add a level of poignancy to this coming-of-age tale, with the boys gradually coming to see the world with a critical eye-- as men.

Unfortunately, many viewers will likely tune out of this stirring drama too quickly, turned off by Lee's un-cinematic and lifeless handling of the material. With its turgid pacing, over-reliance on static camera shots, and lack of close-ups (which not only makes it difficult to figure out who is talking to whom, but also ends up distancing of the viewer from the on-screen action), "Spring in My Hometown" is frustrating to sit through. Even the stunning compositions by cinematographer Kim Hyung-ku (who also lensed "Musa") cannot compensate for such minimalist direction.

"Spring in My Hometown" is a very personal film for director Lee Kwang-mo, as it is based on the experiences of his late father during the Korean War. Despite its lack of accessibility on the part of Lee's direction, it is evident that a lot of care and reflection went into writing "Spring in My Hometown", making this coming-of-age drama a film of remarkable thoughtfulness and emotional depth.

My Beautiful Days (Seumulnet) - 2002

Starring: Kim Hyun-sung, Kim Min-sun, Byun Eun-jong, Pang Eun-jin, Myung Kye-nam
Director: Im Jong-jae
Availability: Korean-import DVD (Region 3)
Rating: ● ● ●

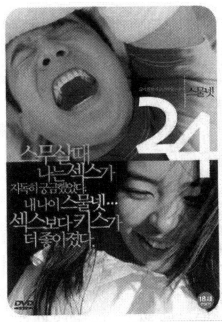

My Beautiful Days DVD box art
(*image courtesy of Cinema Service*)

"My Beautiful Days" is about an aimless young man named Jun (Kim Hyun-sung) whose life is passing by, one missed opportunity after another. Unfortunately, the same could be said about the film itself, which intentionally plods along without any sense of direction and ends without any sense of accomplishment.

The Korean title of "My Beautiful Days", "Seumulnet" or "24", refers to the protagonist's age. With only a month left before his military reserve duty is up, Jun spends his days supervising a parking lot at a government office as part of his official duties, and helping out at a small dry cleaning store run by the similarly named but older Mr. Jun (Myung Kye-nam). As the story unfurls, Jun becomes romantically involved in varying degrees with three different women. At first, we see him involved in sexual callisthenics with Mi-young (Pang Eun-jin), an older, married mother of one who works in the same office as Jun. And even though Jun feels that his relationship with Mi-young is wrong, his own apathy prevents him from walking away.

Enter Eun-ji (model Byun Eun-jeong, in her feature film debut), the former girlfriend and first love of Jun, who is now working as a newscaster at a local television station. However, similar to how they lost contact with each other so many years ago, a lack of chemistry and interest on both sides prevents them from picking up where they left off. Instead, Jun finds himself attracted to Eun-ji's effervescent younger sister Hyeon-ji (Kim Min-sun), who enjoys long runs and watching Bruce Lee movies-- the only problem is that Hyeon-ji doesn't feel the same way about him, especially since he's supposed to be dating her older sister.

"My Beautiful Days" is more of a character study than a drama, as the script focuses on the disappointing consequences that arise from Jun's inaction and inertia. And though Jun is given a taste of where all of this can lead through the experiences of the older Mr. Jun, who gave up painting and lost contact with his true love, it doesn't seem to make much of an impression on the young man. By the end of the film, which comes suddenly and without warning, Jun ends up exactly where he started from, wasting time with Mi-young, as Eun-ji has gone abroad to study and Hyeon-ji has never been heard from again. Even Jun's proactive attempts to revitalize Mr. Jun's dry cleaning business seem to fizzle. Not particularly inspiring or interesting, but at least it remains true to the story's central theme.

Kim Hyun-sung, Kim Min-sun, and Byun Eun-jong (*image courtesy of Cinema Service*)

Unfortunately, other than this melancholic examination of Jun's pathological inability to commit, there is little else that is worthy of note in the slowly paced "My Beautiful Days". Performance-wise, each of the lead actors fill their roles out nicely, with the most interesting being Kim's free-spirited turn as Hyeon-ji, Byun's portrayal of the shy and guarded Eun-ji, and Pang as a woman whose ravenous carnal desires are a mere distraction from her sad and lonely existence. Director Im Jong-jae's direction is also decent, despite the low-key material.

Bad Guy (Nabbeun namja) - 2001

Starring: Jo Jae-hyeon, Seo Weon
Director: Kim Ki-duk
Availability: Korean-import DVD (Region 3)
Rating: ● ● ●

Jo Jae-hyeon and Seo won (*image courtesy of CJ Entertainment*)

Buoyed by more straightforward plotting and the popularity of its lead actor, "Bad Guy" became director Kim Ki-duk's most financially successful film to date. Like his internationally acclaimed "The Isle", this 2001 film forges a twisted romance in the darkest recesses of Korean society, which in the case of "Bad Guy", is a red-light district. Unfortunately, whereas "The Isle" created an intriguing microcosm of Korean sexual mores in its fishing-hole setting, "Bad Guy" plays out more as a misogynistic fantasy, detailing the melancholy relationship that emerges after a low-level thug forces a pretty college student into prostitution.

"Bad Guy" begins with gang leader Han-ki (Jo Jae-hyeon) catching a glimpse of middle-class college student Seon-hwa (Seo won), who is sitting on a park bench awaiting the arrival of her boyfriend. Enamored by her beauty while lacking the word 'subtlety' in his vocabulary, Han-ki forces himself on her. Not surprisingly, Seon-hwa spits in his face and he is beaten up by some passers-by.

However, Han-ki does not give up so easily. He later finds out that Seon-hwa is deeply in debt and hatches a scheme to gain control over her, which succeeds. Desperate for cash, Seon-hwa begins turning tricks at a brothel under Han-ki's control. And as Seon-hwa's life descends into degradation and depravity, little does she know that Han-ki is secretly watching her every move through a two-way mirror. However, this is only the first step of the obsessive and destructive relationship that develops between the predator and his prey.

Like Kim's other 'in yer face' films, "Bad Guy" generated its fair share of controversy when it was released at the tail end of 2001, with the bulk of it centered on the character of Seon-hwa. Indeed, the biggest flaw with the film is the implausibility of her transformation. When we first see Seon-hwa, she seems to be a fierce young woman who takes crap from no one, yet she seems to have a sudden change of heart when she begins to prostitute herself. Not only does she submit a little too willingly to her new station in life, but she even seems to enjoy it and doesn't even bother trying to extricate herself from her predicament. Furthermore, she even develops romantic ties to Han-ki, the very man who destroyed her life. Though Kim prides himself on depicting the uglier elements of Korean society, his take on Seon-hwa's descent and Han-ki's domination simply reeks of misogynistic male fantasy.

On the positive side, "Bad Guy" is probably one of the most accessible (in terms of narrative structure) of Kim's films, as the film remains focused on the story's central concept without wandering off on obscure tangents. And like "The Isle", the cinematography in "Bad Guy" is stunning, thanks to the work of lenser Hwang Cheol-hyeon ("My Boss, My Hero"), who makes good use of the film's tawdry and decrepit settings. Performances are also strong, with Jo actually being able to make his distasteful character somewhat sympathetic using only facial expressions and gestures (he only speaks one line throughout the entire film), while Seo (who also appeared in "The Isle") is able to handle the wide dramatic demands of her character, even if the switch from sassy girl to powerless victim lacks credibility.

If you are familiar with Kim's filmography, then what transpires in "Bad Guy" should be of little surprise. Though "Bad Guy" is perhaps the most straightforward of Kim's films, indicating that the director is moving towards injecting more mainstream sensibilities into his work, the manner in which this sex- and violence-laden 'romance' unfolds might leave some viewers reeling in disgust. But then again, maybe that is exactly what the 'bad boy' director of Korea wants.

On the Occasion of Remembering the Turning Gate (Saenghwalui balgyeon) - 2002

Starring: Kim Sang-gyong, Ye Ji-won, Chu Sang-mi
Director: Hong Sang-soo
Availability: Korean-import DVD (multi-region)
Rating: ● ● ●

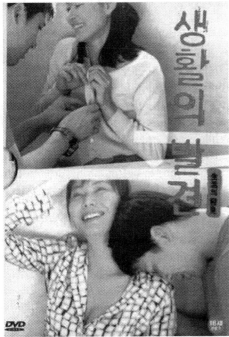

On the Occasion of Remembering the Turning Gate DVD box art (*image courtesy of Cinema Service*)

In addition to being a mouthful, "On the Occasion of Remembering the Turning Gate" is acclaimed director Hong Sang-soo's most successful film to date. It is labelled as a comedy, though the film plays out more as a rather frank look at the small quirks and ironies of male-female relationships, some of which approach the absurd-- hence, the 'comedy'. Though Hong should be lauded for trying to inject as much realism into the proceedings as possible, such zeal quickly bogs down the film with every mundane and depressing detail, making "On the Occasion of Remembering the Turning Gate" as long-winded as its title.

The film takes its title from a Chinese legend that tells of a man who was executed for falling in love with the king's daughter. However, his love is so strong that he ends up being reincarnated as a snake and wraps himself around the princess. After all attempts to remove the snake fail, the princess travels to Chongpyong-sa temple, located where the town of Chunchon in Kangwon Province is today. Before the princess enters the temple, she asks the snake to disengage himself momentarily and wait for her while she prays. The snake agrees and waits outside for her return. However, the princess never re-emerges, and before the snake is able to enter the temple to look for her, a rainstorm washes him away. Thus, the gate to Chongpyong-sa temple became to be known as the 'Turning Gate'. It is only toward the end of the film that the rationale behind the title becomes apparent.

The story revolves around two successive romantic entanglements of theatre/film actor Kyong-su (Kim Sang-gyong). After failing to land a role in an upcoming movie, Kyong-su travels to Chunchon to visit an old friend, which is where he meets Myong-suk (Ye Ji-won), a professional dancer with whom he has a one-night stand. Kyong-su ends up getting far more than he bargained for when Myong-suk falls for him and begins pursuing him obsessively. Eventually, the pressure from Myong-suk gets to be too much, and Kyong-su runs away to Pusan.

While on the train to Pusan, he becomes infatuated with Son-young (Chu Sang-mi), a married woman who is a fan of his theatrical work. He follows her off the train at Kyongju and once again, he has a one-night stand, only this time, he is the one who ends up being left outside the 'Turning Gate'.

Unlike the typical romantic comedy or even romantic melodrama, presenting everyday realism in Kyong-su's romantic foibles is director Hong's intent in this film. Hong diligently offers up little tidbits of humanity throughout the film, which sometimes even border on the painful. Even the film's sex scenes are not spared this philosophy, as they are shot with the uncompromising frankness of de-glamorized soft-core pornography. While some viewers will recognize the little moments and strange absurdities from Kyong-su's encounters as their own, the truth is that after a while, the minimalist plot and mind-numbing attention to detail make the film tedious to watch.

This is unfortunate, because there are certainly some interesting ideas at work in the film. In addition to the obvious parallel between the legend of the 'Turning Gate' and Kyong-su's entanglements, both of which are mirror images of each other, one of the recurring ideas in the film is how people fall into patterns. After a falling out with a producer at the beginning of the film, Kyong-su proceeds to use the producer's last words to him, "It's hard enough to be human, let's not be monsters," as a parting statement in his own dealings. Similar to how easy it is for his speech to become stuck in a pattern, Kyong-su's expectations of sex and love fall into the predictable, as his failing with Son-young results from his unreal expectation that she will be exactly the same as Myong-suk.

When I first saw the trailer for "On the Occasion of Remembering the Turning Gate", my hopes were raised by the use of a song from Wong Kar-wai's "Days of Being Wild" (the 'cha cha cha' number that Leslie Cheung dances to in his underwear). Like most Wong Kar-wai films, there are definitely some golden nuggets of wisdom to be found here. Unfortunately, with its slow pacing, excessive focus on the minutiae of human interaction, and static camerawork, "On the Occasion of Remembering the Turning Gate" ends up being a challenge to sit through, requiring audiences to dig, and dig hard, for those rare moments of brilliance.

Virgin Stripped Bare by Her Bachelors (Oh! Su-jeong) - 2000

Starring: Lee Eun-ju, Jeong Bo-seok, Moon Sung-keun
Director: Hong Sang-soo
Availability: Korean-import DVD (Region 3)
Rating: ● ● ●

Virgin Stripped Bare By Her Bachelors poster (*image courtesy of Buena Vista International Korea*)

Under the potentially racy title of "Virgin Stripped Bare by Her Bachelors", which is actually a play on the name of a Marcel Duchamp sculpture, director Hong Sang-soo offers a rather mundane 'he said, she said' look at romantic relationships. Alas, other than some impressive black-and-white lensing and offering audiences a chance to puzzle together the truth from two widely varying perspectives, "Virgin Stripped Bare by Her Bachelors" suffers from the same minimalist attention to minutia that plagued his follow-up feature, "On the Occasion of Remembering the Turning Gate".

The film, shot entirely in black and white, is divided into five main sections. The first chapter is "Day's Wait", where art gallery owner Jae-hoon (Jeong Bo-seok) arrives at a hotel room on Cheju Island and awaits the arrival of television scribe Yang Su-jeong (Lee Eun-ju), presumably for a romantic interlude. The second section, entitled "Perhaps Accident", then takes the audience back to how Jae-hoon met Su-jeong, which was through his television-producer friend Yeon-su (Moon Sung-keun), who also happens to be Su-jeong's boss. Jae-hoon falls hard for the beautiful Su-jeong, and awkwardly tries to get the young woman in bed with him. However, in the end, Jae-hoon prevails when Su-jeong agrees to meet in a hotel room.

"Suspended Cable Car" returns the action to the present and shifts the perspective to Su-jeong, who is on her way to the hotel room but is unsure of whether or not she is doing the right thing. Though she eventually decides to go through with the meeting, a power failure traps her on a cable car. The story then segues into "Perhaps Intention", which revisits the events in "Perhaps Accident" from Su-jeong's perspective, revealing her true backstory and motivation in meeting Jae-hoon. Finally, the last segment "Naught Shall Go Ill When You Find Your Mare" reveals the outcome of the planned rendezvous.

The most intriguing aspect of "Virgin Stripped Bare by Her Bachelors" is how the perspectives of Jae-hoon and Su-jeong diverge. While most of the action syncs between "Perhaps Accident" and "Perhaps Intention", there are a few significant differences. For example, in the first-time through, Jae-hoon forces himself onto Su-jeong in an empty alley, only to be pushed away. However, from Su-jeong's perspective, it was Yeong-su with her in the alley. Such alterations, some large and some small, are rampant between the two perspectives, leaving it up to the audience to decide what actually happened behind the characters' subjective interpretations of events.

Unfortunately, other than giving the audience some "Rashomon"-style detective work, the 'he said, she said'-style back-and-forth fails to make any interesting observations about male-female politics. The film is also a chore to sit through, a combination of laggard pacing, the extensive use of static camerawork, a sparse soundtrack, and attention to even the most mundane detail.

Thankfully, the film is made somewhat tolerable with the strong performances of the cast. Lee, who has been seen more recently in "Bungee Jumping of Their Own", delivers the standout performance, and her charismatic turn as the quiet but determined Su-jeong is one of the highlights of the otherwise drab film. Ably supporting Lee are Jeong as Su-jeong's clueless would-be suitor, and Moon, who previously displayed his acting chops in Lee Chang-dong's "Green Fish".

Fans of director Hong will probably find "Virgin Stripped Bare by Her Bachelors" of interest, as it combines the non-linear storytelling of his highly acclaimed 1998 feature "The Power of Kangwon Province" and the examination of male-female relationships in "On the Occasion of Remembering the Turning Gate". Unfortunately, viewers unaccustomed to Song's style will probably find this film frustrating to sit through, in which the monotony is only broken by the character's opposing and puzzling perspectives.

Interview (Intyebyu) - 2000

Starring: Lee Jung-jae, Shim Eun-ha
Director: Daniel H. Byun
Availability: Hong Kong-import VCD and DVD (multi-region), Korean-import DVD (multi-region)
Rating: ••½

Interview poster (*image courtesy of Cine 2000*)

Established in Copenhagen during a 1995 conference of Danish directors (including Lars von Trier and Thomas Vinterberg), the 'Dogme 95' movement was created to inject realism and character-driven drama back into cinema, a so-called 'rescue operation to counter certain tendencies in film today'. This cinematic 'vow of chastity' opposed the use of 'make-up, illusions, and dramaturgical predictability', such that the plot would be justified purely by the 'inner lives of the characters'. Among the strict rules that Dogme 95 filmmakers have to follow include shooting on location without additional props, recording only natural sounds, avoiding genre conventions, and not using any 'superficial action', such as murder or firearms. Since its inception, the principles of the Dogme 95 manifesto have been seen at work in Thomas Vinterberg's "Festen" and Lars von Trier's "Dancer in the Dark".

Though the Dogme 95 movement has maintained a low profile in the last few years with only the occasional Danish feature adhering to its rules, its influence has been felt around the world, including South Korea. Daniel H. Byun's 2000 directorial debut "Interview" was billed as the first Asian Dogme 95 film, presumably because of the large amount of digital video shot for the film. However, in addition to violating many of the technical constraints of the Dogme 95 'vow of chastity', "Interview" is pretentious as hell, wasting the talents of ever-popular lead actors Lee Jung-jae and Shim Eun-ha.

The story begins with filmmaker Eun-seok (Lee) in the midst of filming a documentary that involves interviews of people talking about love and relationships. Eun-seok eventually becomes enamored with one of his interview subjects, a quiet and reserved hairdressing assistant named Yeong-heui (Shim), who becomes involved in the film after tagging along with her actress friend (Kweon Min-jung, playing herself). Through his numerous interviews with Yeong-heui, Eun-seok learns of her traumatic heartbreak resulting from the untimely death of her soldier boyfriend. However, when Eun-seok and his crew go to conduct one last interview with Yeong-heui on the day of an important hairdressing exam, the young woman has disappeared and it seems as though she never actually existed.

The film then backtracks a few months to provide some back-story on mystery woman Yeong-heui, who is revealed to actually be a ballerina recovering from the death of her long-time dance partner and lover. The film then presents a number of extended scenes from the film's first half, along with some new ones, to reveal the actual truth behind Yeong-heui, as well as the budding relationship with Eun-seok.

Mind you, the idea explored in "Interview" is certainly interesting, as it peels back the lies in front of the camera that are accepted as 'the truth' in Eun-seok's documentary, and provides some context for the true reality of the story. Unfortunately, "Interview" ends up being an overwrought and pretentious piece of filmmaking that dulls the impact of the revelations in the second half. This is particularly noticeable in the scenes shot in France (apparently director Byun's old stomping grounds), the majority of which could have been easily excised without diminishing the clarity of the story. Also distracting are the numerous digital video interviews conducted with other interviewees that further derail what little narrative momentum that Byun is able to sustain. Even the luminous presence of the country's top actress can't salvage "Interview", as Shim delivers a flat and understated portrayal of the troubled Yeong-heui.

Other than being of interest to cinephiles who dig Dogme, there is very little in "Interview" to maintain or even elicit audience interest. And given the torturous two-hour plus running time of this student-film-gone-awry, this "Interview" fails to do the job.

Holiday in Seoul - 1997

Starring: Kim Min-jong, Jin Hee-kyung, Choi Jin-shil, Jang Dong-gun
Director: Kim Yui-seok
Availability: Hong Kong-import VCD and DVD (multi-region)
Rating: ●●½

Holiday in Seoul DVD box art (*image courtesy of Universal Laser & Video*)

With "Holiday in Seoul", it is abundantly clear that director Kim Yui-seok is a big fan of Hong Kong auteur Wong Kar-wai ("In the Mood for Love"). From start to finish, not only does Kim copy Wong's unmistakable style, but he also recreates a number of key scenes from the veteran Hong Kong director's most famous films. Unfortunately, this 1997 South Korean production lacks what is probably the most compelling part of Wong Kar-wai's films, a thematically rich narrative with multiple layers of subtlety. Thus, "Holiday in Seoul" ends up being little more than an exercise in style with nothing meaningful to say.

Similar to "Chungking Express", "Holiday in Seoul" is divided into two halves, each with a separate story that takes place in and around the same location, the Holiday Inn Seoul. The first story involves an unnamed hotel bellboy (Kim Min-jong) who falls in love with a regular guest of the hotel, a professional leg model (Jin Hee-kyung). The film's second half deals with the odd nocturnal activities of one of the hotel's telephone operators (Choi Jin-shil), which include having telephone conversations with her dead father or taking complete strangers to bed. One night, after taking a cab home and realizing she has no money, she offers the cab driver (Jang Dong-gun) sex in exchange for the fare. Thus begins a very strange relationship, where the cab driver does his best to act as her protector-- something she adamantly refuses to accept.

Those familiar with the films of Wong Kar-wai will immediately recognize the degree that Kim has emulated his style. The most noticeable aspects include the handheld camera work and washed-out lensing reminiscent of Wong's long-time cinematographer, Christopher Doyle. The characters, all disconnected from emotional contact by virtue of their 'middlemen'-type vocations (for example, the bellboy is virtually ignored by guests as he carries their bags, while the telephone operator is only responsible for connecting other people's calls), speak incessantly through voiceovers (another Wong trademark), waxing poetically about the interminable loneliness of their sad existences. Kim also wallpapers his film with a soundtrack that combines contemporary pop songs (such as Eric Clapton or Tracy Chapman) with more ethnic sounds, similar to the effect used by Wong in "Fallen Angels".

A number of scenes also mimic key scenes in a number of Wong's films, such as a scene where the leg model imagines being embraced by her dead boyfriend, paralleling similar scenes in "Ashes of Time". Other pilfered moments include a nighttime motorcycle ride reminiscent of the closing scene in "Fallen Angels", numerous scenes that take place in a convenience store ("Chungking Express"), and two scenes at the end of the film, one where the cab driver catches sight of the telephone operator decked out in a military uniform, and the other with the leg model not being recognized by the newly-promoted bellboy, which make reference to the endings of "Fallen Angels" and "Chungking Express", respectively.

Unfortunately, other than providing an opportunity to play 'spot the Wong Kar-wai reference' drinking games with your friends, there is little else going on under the hood in "Holiday in Seoul". Though Kim tries to pursue the themes of loneliness and emotional isolation in today's world, themes that are common throughout Wong's films, the minimalist plot sheds little light on exactly what the director is actually trying to say, other than merely flattering through imitation.

Wong Kar-wai fans will probably find some pleasure with "Holiday in Seoul", as it is probably the closest they will ever come to seeing what a Korean film by the celebrated Hong Kong director would look like. Unfortunately, as a Wong Kar-wai film, it is not very good, and its pointless, pretentious, and meandering plot only serves to reinforce why many people have heard of the name Wong Kar-wai, and not Kim Yui-seok.

Address Unknown (Soochwieen boolmyung) - 2001

Starring: Yang Dong-kun, Ban Min-yung, Kim Young-min, Pang Eun-jin, Mitch Malum
Director: Kim Ki-duk
Availability: Korean-import DVD (multi-region)
Rating: ••½

Kim Young-min, Ban Min-yung, and Yang Dong-kun (*image courtesy of Tube Entertainment*)

Kim Ki-duk's "Address Unknown" covers similar thematic territory as Lee Kwang-mo's "Spring in My Hometown" in depicting how the American presence in the country has had an undue influence on life in South Korea. However, with Kim best known for putting together some of the more disturbing films of the latest 'Korean New Wave' such as "The Isle" and "Bad Guy", it goes without saying that the subtlety of Lee's coming-of-age drama is nowhere to be found in "Address Unknown". Instead, Kim offers his usual brand of 'in yer face' storytelling where no indignity or violent act is off-limits, including sharp objects being thrust into eyes, rape, mutilation, and yes, even a hint of bestiality.

The film is set during the Seventies in the small town of Pyongtaek, where a group of broken lives revolves around the local US military base. Half-Korean-and-half-African-American Chang-guk (Yang Dong-kun) lives with his mentally disturbed mother (Pang Eun-jin), who writes letters non-stop to Chang-guk's father, an American soldier who returned to the States long ago. Unfortunately, all her letters end up being returned marked 'address unknown'. In his spare time, Chang-guk works for his mother's latest boyfriend, a butcher called Dog Eyes (Kim regular Cho Jae-hyun), so-named because he specializes in making mincemeat out of stray dogs.

Meanwhile, the reclusive Eun-ok (Ban Min-yung) has been blind in one eye since a freak childhood accident. She spends most of her time in sexually charged 'play' with her pet dog, though she does eventually warm up to a drug-abusing US soldier named James (Mitch Malum). All the while, she is oblivious to the feelings that the shy Ji-hum (Kim Young-min) has for her.

Through these disparate characters, Kim weaves a narrative that paints a very bleak picture of post-war Korea, a land marred by violence, cruelty, and despair. As with "Spring in My Hometown", the sentiment is decidedly anti-American, with a number of vignettes that criticize the detrimental effects of American cultural contamination. This is most obvious in the front-and-center relationship between Eun-ok and James, such as the film's disturbing climax in which Eun-ok goes to desperate extremes to stop James from carving his name into her flesh.

Unfortunately, the on-screen brutality is often overwhelming, as every character conflict results in an outpouring of vicious violence. This is particularly noticeable in the film's final act, where the escalating depravity becomes both tedious and unnecessarily exploitative, ultimately diminishing the emotional resonance of what came before it.

Among the cast, Ban, Yang, and Kim turn in the strongest performances, credibly portraying characters that represent the traumatized psyche of a divided country. The supporting cast fares not so well, particularly two performances that end up being distracting and annoying. Pang grossly overdoes her turn as Chang-guk's hysterically insane mother, while Malum is in dire need of acting lessons, as he manages to ruin every scene he is in with his wildly inappropriate emoting and painfully stilted line delivery.

"Address Unknown" has the makings of a hard-hitting drama that depicts the painful legacy of the Korean War and the downside of the American presence in the country. Kim also creates an ensemble of memorable characters and an atmosphere of uncompromising bleakness to tell his story. Unfortunately, the impact of all this ends up being diminished by some irritating supporting performances and the director's trademark proclivity towards the violent and the extreme. Provocative but overwrought, dismal but emotionally cold, "Address Unknown" comes a little too close to being returned to its sender.

One Fine Spring Day (Bomnareun ganda) - 2001

Starring: Yoo Ji-tae, Lee Young-ae
Director: Hur Jin-ho
Availability: Hong Kong-import VCD, Korean-import DVD (Region 3)
Rating: ● ●

Lee Young-ae and Yoo Ji-tae (*image courtesy of Cinema Service*)

After making a splash with his directorial debut "Christmas in August", it would be another three years before director Hur Jin-ho would deliver his follow-up feature "One Fine Spring Day". Though it was one of the most highly anticipated releases in the latter half of 2001, "One Fine Spring Day" ended up underperforming against expectations, and for good reason-- this sophomore romantic melodrama wasn't very good.

The film details the entire life cycle of the romantic relationship between quiet sound recording engineer Lee Sang-wu (Yoo Ji-tae) and lonely DJ Han Eun-su (Lee Young-ae). They are first united when Ji-tae accompanies Eun-su to the town of Kangneung to record some nature sounds for an upcoming radio program. An inkling of their mutual attraction becomes rather apparent as they begin work together, and the relationship begins to take shape after Eun-su shyly invites Sang-wu to spend the night at her apartment.

Unfortunately, such romantic bliss is not long-lived. Living in different cities, the wear-and-tear of the long-distance relationship gradually wears down Eun-su, who comes to the snap decision that they should spend some time apart. Sang-wu, who has become quite attached to Eun-su, finds this unacceptable and tries very hard, even to the point of desperation, to change her mind.

Hur's previous effort "Christmas in August" was rife with internal conflict and tension that sprang from a terminally ill man's unwillingness to admit his mortality to anyone, including a woman he has fallen in love with. However, in the case of "One Fine Spring Day", this sort of emotional intrigue is missing, reducing the poignancy of the on-screen action. All that is left for the audience to hang on to are the on-screen actions of the characters, which are hardly involving, sympathetic, or even of passing interest.

This is most noticeable in the film's latter half, where the story degenerates into a tedious series of vignettes detailing the complete breakdown of the relationship. Eun-su's desire to end the relationship seems arbitrary, as no explanation or rationale is given. Meanwhile, Sang-wu's reaction to such rejection becomes a neverending clothesline of counter-productive behaviors, such as waiting by the phone for calls that will never come, vandalizing Eun-su's car in a jealous rage, and stalking. With two such unsympathetic characters, it is difficult to determine whom the audience should be rooting for. And in combination with the leisurely pacing, "One Fine Spring Day" becomes an increasingly frustrating film to sit through.

However, the film does have some positive points. The most notable is the lensing by Kim Hyeong-gu (who also served as Director of Photography for "Musa"), whose compositions are at times stunning, such as the image of Sang-wu standing amidst a field of tall grass while a breeze gently blows. And despite being saddled with characters that don't really have much to do, actors Lee and Yoo are up to the demands of the material and do share some chemistry, particularly in the film's stronger first half.

It is disappointing to see a film like "One Fine Spring Day" coming from director Hur Jin-ho, especially in comparison to a cinematic masterpiece such as "Christmas in August". Here is a film that represents the shortcomings of traditional Korean melodrama. With emotionally dead material being punched up by arbitrary pathos, "One Fine Spring Day" is a film that is both cold and distant.

Kilimanjaro - 2001

Starring: Park Shin-yang, Ahn Sung-ki, Kim Seung-cheol
Director: Oh Seong-ook
Availability: Korean-import DVD (Region 3)
Rating: ••

Kilimanjaro DVD box art (*image courtesy of Sidus*)

In addition to being one of the few examples of failure in South Korea's nascent 'netizen' film production funding model (where Internet users buy 'shares' in upcoming productions in the hopes of making a return after the film is released), 2000's "Kilimanjaro" has the dubious distinction of squandering a promising premise with aimless storytelling, confusing character motivations, and glacial pacing, making it a disappointing directorial debut for Oh Seung-ook, whose previous accomplishments including scribing 1998's "Christmas in August".

"Kilimanjaro" starts off interestingly enough as police detective Hae-shik (Park Shin-yang) witnesses his estranged twin brother Hae-cheol killing his two children before turning the gun on himself. What could have possibly driven Hae-cheol to such a monstrous act of desperation? Unfortunately, as Hae-shik carries his late brother's ashes to the family tomb in the town of Chumunjin, he gains first-hand experience of the neverending cycle of despair that dominated Hae-cheol's troubled existence.

Upon his arrival in Chumunjin, Hae-shik is mistaken for his dead brother by a local crime kingpin and tortured over some unpaid debts. Luckily, he is rescued by Hae-cheol's long-time friend Beong-gae (Ahn Sung-ki), who agrees to pay the hefty ransom out of his own meager savings. Beong-gae, completely unaware of Hae-cheol's recent death, accepts Hae-shik as his long-time friend and introduces him to his other business associates, such as the gun-crazy and mercurial Jong-du (Kim Seung-cheol) and the god-fearing 'Missionary' (Choi Seon-jung), who all share a common dream of starting their own business. Hae-shik, having completely eased into passing himself off as Hae-cheol, joins Beong-gae and his crew to make their dream a reality. Unfortunately, such deception results in Hae-shik feeling the same heartbreaking hopelessness that claimed the life of his brother.

While a man learning more about his estranged twin brother by impersonating him provides the basis for a fascinating story, director Oh ends up squandering the opportunity with a meandering and confusing script that takes forever to reach its destination. Hae-shik's motivation for impersonating his brother lacks credibility, as is his involvement in Beong-gae's affairs, particularly when they make the questionable decision of vandalizing the local crime boss' car. Oh also indulges himself a little too often, dragging out many of the film's scenes unnecessarily, and taking a number of pointless detours along the way.

About the only interesting aspect of "Kilimanjaro" is probably the film's tension-filled and bloody last reel, as Hae-shik, Beong-gae, and associates find themselves taken prisoner and forced to play Russian Roulette, leading to the story's tragic conclusion. Unfortunately, the emotional resonance of these scenes is somewhat diminished by the questionable actions of the protagonists that got them into such a mess in the first place. Another positive is the welcome presence of veteran thespian Ahn, who is easily the most interesting person on the screen, with his sympathetic portrayal of a man whose loyalties lead him astray to a tragic end. On the other hand, Park is okay as Hae-shik, though the muddled motivations of his character make it difficult to take him seriously.

With the exception of Ahn's dignified performance, "Kilimanjaro" fails in almost every aspect. Instead of scaling the narrative heights established by other films of the latest 'Korean New Wave', "Kilimanjaro" ends up being a chore and a bore to sit through.

Waikiki Brothers - 2001

Starring: Lee Eol, Oh Ji-hye, Park Won-sang, Hwang Jeong-min
Director: Im Sun-rye
Availability: Korean-import DVD (Regions 1 and 3)
Rating: ••

Waikiki Brothers DVD box art (*image courtesy of Myung Film*)

At first glance, Im Sun-rye's sophomore feature "Waikiki Brothers" might appear to be the Korean version of "That Thing You Do!", with the travails of a little band that could being detailed to the accompaniment of old Western and Korean pop standards. In actual fact, "Waikiki Brothers" is the flipside of the Tom Hanks film, a serious drama that depicts the disintegration of a nightclub band that nobody has ever heard of. And like Jeong Jae-eun's "Take Care of My Cat", which also dealt with the pain of broken dreams, "Waikiki Brothers" became the subject of a grassroots re-release campaign after quickly disappearing from theaters. Alas, this slow-moving and mostly humorless account of a band's disintegration quickly sinks under the weight of its uncharismatic and uninteresting characters.

At the center of the implosion is Sung-woo (Lee Eol), who is the leader of the band. Back in the Eighties, when he and his bandmates were in high school, the Waikiki Brothers were seven-strong and dreamed of becoming Korea's answer to The Beatles. However, two decades later, the band has shrunk to Sung-woo, dim-witted drummer Kang-soo (Hwang Jeong-min), and ladies'-man keyboard player Jung-suk (Park Won-sang), and they barely make ends meet by playing at beauty contests and country fairs. After an unsuccessful stint on the road, the band returns to their backwater hometown of Suanbo to play a steady gig at a local hotel's nightclub, which also happens to be named Waikiki.

Unfortunately, things only go from bad to worse. A falling out occurs after Jung-suk steals Kang-soo's prostitute girlfriend, with the former getting killed by a pimp and the latter quitting the band to work as a bus driver. Even the addition of Sung-woo's old guitar teacher (Oh Gwang-rok) to the band ends up being short-lived, as the old man is subject to frequent spells of drinking and fainting (mostly in that order). Sung-woo eventually finds himself reduced to playing in a karaoke bar and being mistreated by its drunk patrons.

However, there is one faint glimmer of hope for Sung-woo. Upon his return to Suanbo, he runs into In-hee (Oh Ji-hye), a girl he once had a crush on. Back in high school, she was the lead singer of an all-girls rock-and-roll band, but now she is a widow who makes a living by selling vegetables. However, she too still has a love for singing.

The passion of youth and the anguish of disappointment are contrasted throughout "Waikiki Brothers". An extended flashback to Sung-woo's high school days is a sharp contrast to the bitter reality that he finds himself in, unable to make ends meet and nothing to show after two decades of hard work. Though his love of music is as strong as ever, it seems that he has been left behind by a changed world. While true talent was recognized in his day, only good looks matter now, as evidenced by a waiter (Ryu Seung-bum) who becomes the hotel's new 'band' armed only with a synthesizer and a haircut. And a scene of youthful exuberance, Sung-woo and his friends streaking along the shore, has been supplanted by cheaply produced karaoke videos of swimsuit models prancing along a beach.

However, as interesting as the contrast between dreams and reality might be, "Waikiki Brothers" has very little else up its sleeve. Though some might call this film a serio-comedy, there is actually very little humor to be found. The main characters also lack depth, other than the obvious caricatures they are-- the impassioned artist, the love interest, the fool, the philanderer, and the grizzled veteran. And if it wasn't for the film's numerous musical numbers, a mix between old Korean pop songs and Western favorites such as "La Bamba" and "I Love Rock 'n Roll", "Waikiki Brothers" would have been intolerably dull.

Perhaps I set my expectations too high for "Waikiki Brothers", as the colorful DVD cover art and music-heavy trailer misled me to expect something bright and bouncy. In reality, "Waikiki Brothers" ends up being similar to films such as Lee Chang-dong's "Green Fish" and "Peppermint Candy", as well as Kim Sun-su's "Beat", in detailing how the dreams of youth can turn out terribly wrong. Unfortunately, even if I was expecting a heavy drama, "Waikiki Brothers" doesn't end up being quite as memorable as these other films, as it is sabotaged by its slow-burning plot and minimalist characterizations.

Real Fiction (Shilje sanghwang) - 2000

Starring: Joo Jin-mo, Kim Jin-ah
Director: Kim Ki-duk
Availability: Korean-import DVD (multi-region)
Rating: ••

Real Fiction DVD box art (*image courtesy of Hyoneung Films*)

Despite what you might infer from the title, Kim Ki-duk's "Real Fiction" has neither the daring real-time execution of films such as Mike Figgis' "Timecode" or the edgy storytelling of Quentin Tarantino's "Pulp Fiction". This disappointing follow-up to Kim's critically lauded "The Isle" may appear to be innovative on the surface, though after the first fifteen minutes, not only is it obvious where it is all going, but the end result is painfully underwhelming.

The concept behind how "Real Fiction" came to be certainly sounds intriguing. The film edits together the footage shot on the streets of Seoul by Kim and 11 assistant directors during a three-hour window. The story, which was played out and captured on traditional film and digital video, follows a struggling street artist (Joo Jin-mo) who apparently suffers a mental breakdown. While sketching a portrait for a customer, he sees a woman (Kim Jin-ah) taping him with a video camera. He then follows her down the street and ends up in a theatre, where he is confronted by his past failures and humiliations-- how the woman he loved was raped by his best friend, how a detective tortured him to extract a confession for a crime he didn't do, or how he was beaten by a junior officer while in the army.

With his anger boiling over, he then wanders around Seoul and commits one revenge killing after another. As expected, anyone who has wronged him gets their just desserts, along with his tormentors in the present, who include a sneaky photography studio owner who takes advantage of him, his cheating girlfriend, and a local gangster who frequently extorts money.

Like his other films, Kim exposes the ugly side of modern Korea through a series of violent vignettes-- sexual exploitation, economic deprivation, police corruption, etc. Unfortunately, as shocking and lurid as these revelations are, there seems to be little point or profundity to what is being presented. Furthermore, the story lacks any suspense as the insane artist wanders from scene to scene-- at least the social outcast in Joel Schumacher's "Falling Down" had a dedicated police detective on his tail. It also doesn't help that Joo, who was more interesting in "Musa", essentially sleepwalks through the entire film with mostly the same dead-eyed expression

Finally, like the material that comes before it, the film's ending is also a letdown, as the artist returns to the park where the film started and (surprise, surprise) it appears that all the killings were only in his mind. And to further let the audience off the hook, someone yells the equivalent of 'cut' and the entire crew applauds the completion of the film. Alas, with its gimmicky conception, brutal violence, exploitative sexuality, and pointless pretentiousness, "Real Fiction" certainly isn't keeping it real.

The Uprising (Yu Jae-su eui nan) - 1999

Starring: Lee Jung-jae, Shim Eun-ha
Director: Park Kwang-su
Availability: Hong Kong-import VCD and DVD (multi-region), Korean-import DVD (multi-region)
Rating: •

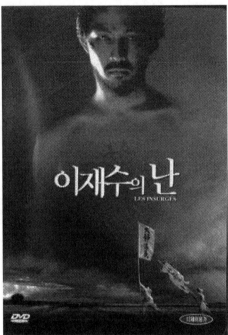

The Uprising DVD box art (*image courtesy of Cinema Service*)

About one hundred years ago, the Choson Dynasty of Korea was in its twilight. As with what was happening in neighboring Asian countries, the Confucianist way of life under Choson rule, which had lasted already over half a millennia, faced increasing external pressure from foreign governments which were aggressively expanding their spheres of influence in the region through diplomatic ties, trade, and even military force. Such political and social turmoil led to lines being drawn between the traditional Confucianists and the growing ranks of Christians, who had been steadily gaining influence since French missionaries began their work in the country over a hundred years before. Though the Confucianists had the upper hand at the middle of the Nineteenth century, by the end of it, their power was slipping to Christian-dominated influences.

In 1901, this political powder keg exploded. The place was dirt-poor Cheju Island and the spark was the declaration of heavy taxes by the Choson government, a move that was ardently supported by French Catholic priests and their followers. In response, a group of Confucian scholars established a rebel army, which eventually came under the command of former government messenger Yi Jae-su, who was only twenty years old at the time. The rebel army then laid siege to the Christian stronghold in Cheju, an act that resulted in the massacre of hundreds of Christians in the span of just a few days.

With "The Uprising", celebrated director Park Kwang-su, who rose to fame on the strength of "The Black Republic" and "To the Starry Island", tries to fashion a historical epic around this bloody incident, which in some ways, is reflective of South Korea's recent growing pains in decades past. Unfortunately, Park's direction of this potentially gripping subject matter is lifeless and uninvolving. And if you thought the pairing of Korean cinema superstars Lee Jung-jae and Shim Eun-ha in 2000's "Interview" was disappointing, their presence in "The Uprising" is downright frustrating. With the former playing Yi Jae-su and the latter as his true love Il Sook-hwa, Park wastes these two bankable stars with a script that is more interested in the dry historic details than actually telling an emotionally charged story. Not surprisingly, this South Korean-French co-production failed to get a rise out of audiences, both at home and abroad.

Chapter 9: Fish Out of Water - Comedies

Korean comedies are some of the funniest in the world and for good reason-- they take the universally appealing 'fish out of water' premise and run with it. Surveying the recent entries in Korean comedies, it seems that the formula is being put to work in a number of interesting ways: a meek bank clerk finds empowerment by becoming a professional wrestler in "The Foul King"; a frustrated college professor who kills noisy dogs must search high and low when his wife's new pooch goes missing in "Barking Dogs Never Bite", while a dim-witted bodybuilder goes in search of his long-lost girlfriend in the savage streets of Los Angeles in "Iron Palm".

One of the more noticable innovations among Korean comedy films has been the emergence of the gangster comedy. During 2001, Korean moviegoers saw gangsters in a completely different light as they were dropped into various 'fish out of water' situations, such as a tomboyish female gangster dealing with love and marriage in "My Wife is a Gangster", a big boss being knocked back down to high school in "My Boss, My Hero", or gangsters and Buddhist monks at each others' throats in "Hi, Dharma". Of the top ten homegrown productions of 2001, four of the top six were gangster comedies, and it seems that the momentum for this new genre is still strong in 2002, with "Marrying the Mafia" being the year's highest-grossing film.

My Boss, My Hero (Doosaboo ilchae) - 2001

Starring: Jung Joon-ho, Jeong Wung-in, Jeong Un-taek, Oh Seung-un
Director: Yun Je-gyun
Availability: Korean-import DVD (multi-region)
Rating: ●●●●½

My Boss, My Hero artwork (*image courtesy of CJ Entertainment*)

Like the other action comedies that dominated the Korean box office in the fall of 2001, "My Boss, My Hero" takes the old standard of Asian cinema, the gangster, and drops him into an absurd 'fish out of water' situation, invoking hilarity out of what are usually mundane cinematic set pieces. In the case of "My Boss, My Hero", a mob boss is sent back to high school, a place that ends up being far worse than life on the mean streets.

Kye Doo-sik (Jung Joon-ho) is the second-in-command of a mob gang. Though he has successfully expanded his boss' territory by defeating a rival gang, he is prevented from moving up in the criminal organization due to his lack of a high school diploma. It seems that all his contemporaries have at least a high school education, with some having even attended college, and Doo-sik's lack of formal education is downright embarrassing-- he is even oblivious to the existence of the Internet and has yet to discover what an e-mail address is. Thus, Doo-sik is given an ultimatum by his boss (Kim Sang-joong)-- he must go back to school and graduate if he wants to continue as a gangster.

With the help of his underlings Kim Sang-do (Jeong Wung-in) and the dim-witted Dae Ka-ri (Jeong Un-taek), Doo-sik poses as a 20-year old student and enrolls at a privately run high school. Unfortunately, he quickly learns that high school life is far rougher and tougher than the life he has left behind. In addition to being beaten by his teachers and robbed by the school bully, Doo-sik quickly learns that the school is rife with corruption. The parents of rich students routinely bribe the school's principal, who in turn coerces the teaching staff into awarding good marks. The principal is also behind the school's problem in retaining female teachers, as he routinely sexual harasses them. Unfortunately, there is little anyone can do about this situation, as the principal is backed up by a local mob. Doo-sik also learns that the lure of getting into a top college is so strong that some students are willing to do anything, as with the case of Yoon-joo (Oh Seung-eun), a female student he befriends, who prostitutes herself after school to pay for her education. Fed up with the corruption and injustice all around him, Doo-sik decides to take matters into his own hands, which leads to an all-out battle on school grounds.

The first half of "My Boss, My Hero" is clearly a 'fish out of water' comedy, as Doo-sik is knocked to the bottom of the food chain at his new school. Coupled with the ineptness of Ka-ri, who consistently gives Doo-sik bad advice about how to fit into his new environment, there are more than a few well-earned chuckles to be had. In addition, the film makes some pointed comments about the brutality of the Korean education system, a sometimes-dangerous place where corporal punishment still exists and the pressure to perform leads to all sorts of abuses and criminal behavior (apparently, the story is loosely based on an actual incident at a Seoul high school). Unfortunately, there are a number of instances where the script strains credibility, such as Doo-sik being bullied by the local toughs, particularly since he easily stands a head taller than them and is almost a decade their senior. In addition, this first half also suffers from some choppy editing, which makes a number of the scene transitions particularly jarring.

However, the film really takes off in the second half, where the story sheds the laughs and presents Doo-sik's heart-wrenching struggle to help the teachers and students overthrow the school's corrupt administration. As the principal's underworld connections arrive to break up a peaceful protest, director Yun Je-gyun pulls no punches in showing the brutality that ensues. In addition, the film's second half also features a beautifully rendered fight sequence that takes place in a torrential downpour, reminiscent of the opening action sequence in "My Wife is a Gangster".

"My Boss, My Hero" was the last entry in the 'gangster comedy' genre from 2001. Though it is far from perfect, the combination of light-hearted laughs and genuine emotional weight make this satirical look at high school life a solid effort. And if the film's closing scene is any indication, I can't wait to see what the sequel has in store.

The Foul King (Banchikwang) - 2000

Starring: Song Kang-ho, Chang Jin-young, Jang Hang-seon, Park Sang-myun
Director: Kim Jee-woon
Availability: Hong Kong-import VCD, Korean-import DVD (multi-region)
Rating: ●●●●½

Kim Su-ro and Song Kang-ho (*image courtesy of Cinema Service*)

The popularity of professional wrestling (a.k.a. live theatre for the masses) is not merely a North American phenomenon. Indeed, people all over the world love enjoy watching grown men and women grapple, throw, and pound each other into submission in intricately choreographed battles for ring superiority (or at least watch someone find new and fascinating uses for a foldable chair). South Korea is no different, and in the 2000 comedy "The Foul King", director Kim Jee-woon's follow-up to "The Quiet Family", a meek bank clerk finds self-esteem and a sense of purpose as a professional wrestler, á la Masayuki Suo's "Shall We Dance?"

At the start of "The Foul King", protagonist Im Dae-ho (Song Kang-ho, who also appeared in "The Quiet Family") is in a sorry state. He is a lowly bank employee who is on the verge of being fired for his incompetence. His boss (Song Yeong-chang), a bully who strongly believes in 'survival of the fittest', likes to put Dae-ho into inescapable headlocks. Dae-ho also holds a torch for one of a pretty co-worker, though he is unable to work up the nerve to ask her out. Even at home, Dae-ho gets no respect with the constant scolding from his father.

However, things begin to change when, on a lark, Dae-ho signs up to be a professional wrestler at a rundown gym under the tutelage of an aging coach (Jang Hang-seon) and his unimpressed daughter Min-yeon (Chang Jin-young). Following the cue of his favorite old-school wrestling champion, Dae-ho becomes the 'Foul King' a masked wrestler with plenty of tricks and cheats up his sleeve during matches. Unfortunately, like his day job, Dae-ho seems destined to remain the underdog-- an upcoming match against current champ Yubiho (Kim Su-ro) is rigged by the local mob, with Dae-ho being ordered to go down and stay down.

"The Foul King" is the typical story of the outcast who finds dignity and empowerment in an unconventional pursuit, such as the Japanese salaryman who uses ballroom dancing to escape the dreary conformity of Japanese society in "Shall We Dance?", a troubled teenage girl proving her naysayers wrong in "Girlfight", or a boy who finds refuge in ballet in "Billy Elliot". What gives director Kim's take on the genre its charm is the off-kilter sense of humor. Given that this is a film set in the world of professional wrestling, the use of slapstick is expected and welcome, particularly in the antics of Dae-ho's dim-witted sparring partners. However, other gags are so 'out there' that Kim seems to be channelling the Coen brothers, such as a hilarious scene where Dae-ho confronts a youth gang on a darkened street and proceeds to don his wrestling mask before kicking their butts.

Lead actor Song is another reason to see this film, as he delivers a gifted comic performance that makes good use of his character's awkwardness. One scene has Dae-ho trying to save face by pretending to talk on a cell phone, only to have a real call come in, while another has him being pinned under a set of weights, though he is too embarrassed to ask for help from Min-yeon. But aside from the film's many laughs, Song also injects the story with some much-needed humanity. This is most apparent in the bout against Yubiho, as Dae-ho is continually brutalized when he refuses to give up what little dignity he has and lose the match.

Song Kang-ho (*image courtesy of Cinema Service*)

Director Kim has certainly outdone himself with this 'self-actualization through professional wrestling' sophomore effort. Funny, full of heart, and just a little off-kilter, "The Foul King" is undoubtedly a comedy classic of the latest 'Korean New Wave', and definitely a must-own for collectors of Korean cinema.

Kick the Moon (Shinlaui dalbam) - 2001

Starring: Lee Sung-jae, Cha Seung-won, Kim Hye-su, Lee Jong-su
Director: Kim Sang-jin
Availability: Korean-import DVD (multi-region)
Rating: •••

Cha Seung-won, Kim Hye-su, and Lee Sung-jae
(image courtesy of Cinema Service)

"Kick the Moon" was director Kim Sang-jin's long-awaited follow-up to his 1999 smash hit "Attack the Gas Station!". A screwball comedy about a bizarre love triangle that develops between a smooth gangster, a strict schoolteacher, and a comely noodle shop owner, "Kick the Moon" doesn't achieve the 'classic' status of Kim's previous effort. Nevertheless, this rambunctious production it still is worth a gander, particularly for the fun performances of its three leads.

The story begins in the early Eighties with a rumble between two rival schools in the city of Gyeongju. Caught in the midst of the youth violence are Ki-woong, a popular student whose exploits that night would become the stuff of legends in the years to come, and the geeky Young-jun, who is probably the least popular kid at school. Fast-forward two decades later and both of these kids have grown into very different young men. Ki-woong (Cha Seung-won) has become a dedicated teacher at his former *alma mater*, while Young-jun (Lee Sung-jae, who also appeared in "Attack the Gas Station!") has become a 'big boss' in the Korean mafia.

However, their paths cross once again when Young-jun is sent to Gyeongju to muscle out a rival gang, and though their reunion is amicable at first, a series of complications lead them to declare war on each other. First, they meet the lovely Min Ju-ran (Kim Hye-su), who owns a small noodle shop, and both men end up being smitten. Second, Ki-woong sees Young-jun as a corrupting influence on his students, particularly Ju-ran's younger brother Ju-seob (Lee Jong-su), who are becoming increasingly enamoured with the gangster lifestyle and beg to become part of Young-jun's gang. Meanwhile, Young-jun's gangland rival is quietly plotting his revenge, placing all of the above in jeopardy. And like "Attack the

Gas Station!", all of these small plot points culminate into a mammoth conflagration of gangsters, students, and police.

The most interesting aspects of "Kick the Moon" are its characters. In contrast to "Attack the Gas Station!", which was a little thin on characterization (probably because there were so many of them), "Kick the Moon" maintains a pretty good focus on its main characters.

Lee is suave as a gangster who, despite his underworld ties, uses his status for good, such as how he convinces Ju-seob and his school chums to become top-ten students with the implied promise of recruitment if they get good grades--something that Ki-woong has tried and failed to do many times before. And speaking of Ki-woong, Cha is fun to watch as a hardworking (not to mention pugilistic) teacher who goes above and beyond the call of duty to make sure that his students stay out of trouble. Rounding out the love triangle is Kim, whose Ju-ran character seems to have taken a few cues from "My Sassy Girl". When Ju-ran first appears, she is demure and humbly apologetic as she begs the police not to arrest her brother. But as soon as she steps outside, Ju-ran exacts punishment on Ju-seob that is even more brutal than what the police are willing to do. Similarly, another great scene has an intoxicated Ju-ran screaming at the top of her lungs that Ki-woong and Young-jun make peace and holds hands as they walk down a crowded thoroughfare. Aside from these three leads, "Kick the Moon" has a number of other interesting supporting characters and the absurd situations they find themselves in, such as an aging detective who has a habit of throwing his wallet and badge to announce his arrival, or Young-jun's gangland rival who must deal with being called back for mandatory military training.

"Kick the Moon" ended up being the third highest-grossing homegrown production in 2001, trailing just behind "Friend" and "My Sassy Girl". And though it isn't quite the home run that "Attack the Gas Station!" was, as it occasionally gets bogged down by some slow pacing and meandering storytelling, it still possesses enough charm, absurd wit, and subversive humor to satiate fans of Kim Sang-jin's 1999 comedy.

Barking Dogs Never Bite (Flandersui gae) - 2000

Starring: Lee Sung-jae, Bae Doo-na, Kim Ho-jeong
Director: Bong Joon-ho
Availability: Hong Kong-import VCD and DVD (Region 3), Korean-import DVD (Region 3)
Rating: ●●●½

Barking Dogs Never Bite poster
(*image courtesy of Cinema Service*)

"Barking Dogs Never Bite" is the odd title to an odd black comedy where man's best friend bites the dust in a number of unsettling ways, such as being thrown off the roof of a high-rise, locked in a cupboard, or ending up in someone's dinner. The chief perpetrator of the canine crimes is frustrated Yoon-ju (Lee Sung-jae), an occasional lecturer who is trying to secure tenure at the local university by any means possible, including bribes. To further add to his pressure, his demanding wife (Kim Ho-jeong) is expectant with their first child. Thus, when a small dog begins barking while he is working from home, his seething frustration spills over and he abducts the dog, locking it in a forgotten part of his apartment building's basement.

The dog's owner reports the purloined pooch to the building manager's office, galvanizing the bored Hyun-nam (Bae Doo-na) into putting up missing posters and conducting her own search. Upon seeing the posters, which state that the missing dog is medically incapable of barking, Yoon-ju realizes that he has abducted the wrong dog and returns to the basement to liberate it. Unfortunately, someone else has beaten him to the punch-- the building's janitor has snatched the dog for a stew he is making.

Yoon-ju eventually does eventually track down the noisy dog, and in an operation worthy of "Mission: Impossible", he snatches it from under the owner's nose and throws it off the roof of the building. However, this dastardly act is witnessed by Hyun-nam, who immediately goes into hot pursuit in a well-executed sequence that even John Woo or Tom Tykwer ("Run Lola Run") would be proud of. Unfortunately, the inopportune opening of a door brings the chase to an abrupt halt, allowing Yoon-ju to escape and keep his identity unknown to Hyun-nam. But in an ironic twist of fate and to Yoon-ju's chagrin, his wife brings home a new pet dog, which Yoon-ju ends up losing while taking it for a walk. With his wife breathing down on him to find the dog, Yoon-ju turns to Hyun-nam, who is still trying to track down the serial dog killer plaguing the neighborhood.

Lee Sung-jae (*image courtesy of Cinema Service*)

Through Yoon-ju's distasteful treatment of man's best friend and his attempts to bribe himself into professorship, as well as Hyun-nam's tireless efforts to rescue dogs, first-time director Bong Joon-ho makes some pointed remarks about Korean society, such as corporate corruption, class struggle, and society's treatment of those at the lower rungs of the economic ladder. Unfortunately, despite some brilliant technical work that spoofs the conventions of action films, "Barking Dogs Never Bite" never amounts to more than a curiosity, as it is burdened by generally unsympathetic and uninteresting characters, laggard pacing, and, of course, subject matter that would make any dog lovers oatmeal hit the roof. Alas, it seems that this film's bark is actually worse than its bite.

Iron Palm - 2002

Starring: Cha In-pyo, Kim Yoon-jin, Park Kwang-jung, Charles Chun
Director: Yuk Sang-ho
Availability: Korean-import DVD (Region 3)
Rating: ●●●½

Iron Palm poster (*image courtesy of Korea Pictures*)

The term 'iron palm' refers to the endpoint of martial arts training focused on toughening the hands through repeated strikes against various materials. The 2002 comedy "Iron Palm" (also known as "Mr. Iron Palm") is about a young martial artist (Cha In-pyo) who has become a master of this technique and now calls himself 'Iron Palm'. Unfortunately, that seems to be the only thing he knows, which creates a whole host of problems when he goes to Los Angeles for the first time to search for his long-lost girlfriend Jinnie (Kim Yoon-jin).

As a testament to his naïvete, Iron is shocked to discover that Jinnie has a job as a scantily-attired 'soju (Korean rice wine) girl' at a local bar and has settled down with a new boyfriend, clothing entrepreneur 'Admiral' Lee (Charles Chun), despite the fact that he and Jinnie have actually not seen each other, spoken over the phone, or even written to each other in the past five years.

At first, Jinnie tries to cover Iron's embarrassing presence by telling Admiral that he is her cousin and that he has come to the United States in search of his college student girlfriend. The arrogant yet gullible Admiral then makes it his mission to help Iron win back the girl with his own brand of business-centric advice and role-playing sessions with Jinnie. Alas, the truth eventually does come out, kicking off an ugly tug-of-war between Iron and Admiral, who are both vying for Jinnie's heart.

The main problem with "Iron Palm" is how most of the humor and the story's major emotional beats are forced. The character of Iron is certainly amusing, as he wanders around Los Angeles completely clueless about everything and turns out to be a pretty crappy martial artist. However, at times, his character ceases to be credible. For example, despite his determination to win back Jinnie at any cost, he keeps his mouth shut during his interactions with Admiral, allowing the 'cousin' perception to perpetuate unchallenged. Another example of arbitrary plotting happens later on in the film, when Jinnie falls off the roof of her building and breaks her leg, necessitating Iron and Admiral to take turns looking after her-- the only problem is that the reason why Jinnie falls is completely unbelievable, and only occurs to service the needs of the story.

Those moviegoers who hate reading subtitles will be pleased to learn that a large majority of the dialogue in "Iron Palm" is actually in English. Iron deliberately speaks English all the time once he arrives in Los Angeles, as he is determined to become an American, as does Admiral and Jinnie, who have both settled down into the American way of life.

Unfortunately, the majority of the weak spots in the film also happen to be when the characters are speaking English. This occurs due to a combination of painfully scripted dialogue and stilted acting, the same problem that plagued the 2001 Hong Kong actioner "Full-time Killer", where the pacing often ground to a halt as the actors gingerly spoke in languages they were not completely comfortable with. This is most apparent with Kim, whose thesping abilities go down a notch every time she switches to English-- a stark contrast to the decent work she did as the conflicted North Korean spy in "Shiri" (interestingly enough, Kim grew up and studied in the United States prior to launching into her Korean acting career). Unfortunately, this problem is not limited to the Korean actors, as the film's most prominent non-Korean cast member, Angelinas Santana, who plays Jinnie's co-worker Gloria, is also in dire need of acting lessons.

However, "Iron Palm" does have its moments. Iron's clueless-ness is often charming, and his 'iron palm technique' involving a rice cooker is worth a few laughs. However, top kudos would have to go to Park Kwang-jung, who plays Iron's older brother Dong-seok and ends up stealing most of the scenes. His acting is head-and-shoulders above the rest of the cast, and his character's poor handle on English and habit of using foul language is a hoot, particularly during the film's climax when he officiates a wedding ceremony at an Elvis wedding chapel in Las Vegas.

With the theatrical run in Korea and the DVD release occurring within the span of a few months, it looks as if audiences did not respond well to "Iron Palm", which is of little surprise. Despite being a quaint fish-out-of-water comedy, its few saving graces, such as the affable charms of leads Cha and Kim and the scene-stealing antics of Park, end up being marred by mediocre English dialogue, below-average performances, and a story that just strains credibility a little too often.

Hi, Dharma - 2001

Starring: Park Shin-yang, Jeong Jin-young,Park Sang-myun, Kim Im-moon
Director: Park Cheol-kwan
Availability: Hong Kong-import VCD and DVD (Region 3), Korean-import DVD (multi-region)
Rating: ●●●

Hi, Dharma poster (*image courtesy of Cineworld*)

Rounding out the 2001 South Korean love affair with the gangster comedy is Park Cheol-kwan's "Hi, Dharma" which was the third-highest grossing entry into the genre, just behind "Kick the Moon" and "My Wife is a Gangster". Unfortunately, in addition to its lesser box office returns, "Hi, Dharma" ends up being the weakest entry in this recent cinematic fad, with an episodic narrative structure that never really gels together.

This time around, gangsters on the lam find themselves in a Buddhist monastery. Following an ambush by a rival organization, Jae-gyu (Park Shin-yang) and his loyal henchman impose themselves on a group of monks at a secluded mountain temple. Luckily for them, the wise chief monk (Kim Im-moon) allows the gangsters to stay out of the kindness of his heart.

Unfortunately, this does not sit will well with his the monastery's second-in-command (Jeong Jin-young), who finds the presence fo the ill-mannered gangsters disruptive to their daily routine of prayer and meditation.

Pretty soon, a power struggle develops between the gangsters and the monks, resulting in a series of competitions to determine whether or not Jae-gyu and his men can stay, ranging from soccer (Korean "Shaolin Soccer"?) to doing 3000 bows to a thinking-man's exercise involving filling a leaking clay pot with water. Meanwhile, on a more sinister note, Jae-gyu gets indications of treachery afoot in the criminal organization he calls home, and thinks his new boss may actually have other designs for him and his men.

The most disappointing aspect of "Hi, Dharma" is how loosely thrown-together the film feels. Compared to the other entries in the gangster comedy genre, the humor in "Hi, Dharma" is rather tame as the story leaps from one comic episode to the next. There are also some gimmicky subplots that seem to have been arbitrarily thrown in to give the film more flavor, such as an encounter with a female monk (Lim Hyun-gung) and a mentally imbalance college student (Kim Young-joon) who wanders in and out of scenes.

As for familiar faces, "Hi, Dharma" offers plenty. Jeong Jin-young is terrific as the paradoxically aggressive monk who ringleads ongoing efforts to push out the interlopers, only to become increasingly frustrated by his failed attempts at removing the unwelcome guests. Park Shin-yang instills a sense of nobility into his role as the chief gangster, while veteran thespian Kim In-moon is fun to watch as the monastery's aged but wise leader. Also making an appearance are Lee Won-jong of "Kick the Moon" and Park Sang-myun of "My Wife is a Gangster".

In the early months of 2002, it was announced that MGM had purchased the U.S. remake rights for "Hi, Dharma", joining a number of other high profile Korean productions to catch the attention of studio heads in Hollywood. Unfortunately, unlike predecessors "My Sassy Girl" and "My Wife is a Gangster", "Hi, Dharma" is hardly a slam-dunk. Aside from some fun comic performances, this gangster comedy is somewhat tame compared to its more rambunctious cinematic brethren. Offering little more than a mere clothesline form some rather unremarkable comic vignettes, "Hi, Dharma" is a 'fish out of water' premise that doesn't quite click.

No. 3 - 1997

Starring: Han Suk-kyu, Song Kang-ho, Choi Min-shik, Lee Mi-yeon, Park Sang-myun
Director: Song Neung-han
Availability: Hong Kong-import VCD and DVD (multi-region), Korean-import DVD (Region 3)
Rating: ● ● ●

No. 3 DVD box art (*image courtesy of Universe Laser & Video*)

Two years before "Shiri" catapulted Han Suk-kyu, Choi Min-shik, and Song Kang-ho into superstardom, these three actors appeared in Song Neung-han's directorial debut, "No. 3". In addition to featuring a number of faces who would go on to become household names during the latest 'Korean New Wave', "No. 3" ends up being a precursor to the gangster comedies that took the Korean box office by storm in 2001.

The title refers to the position of gangster Tae-ju (Han) in his criminal organization, though he insists that he is actually number two. Though he loves his wife Hyeon-ji (Lee Mi-yeon), she becomes tired of being a gangster moll and experiences an emotional awakening by becoming the understudy of a hopelessly third-rate poet named Rimbault (Park Kwang-jung), who is already in hot water over an affair with the sexually voracious wife of Tae-ju's boss (Bang Eun-hee). Tae-ju finds himself in a power struggle with an assassin named 'Ashtray' (Park Sang-myun), so-named because that's what he kills people with, who is brought in after Cho-pil (Song) and his ragged team of wannabe gangsters try to assassinate their big boss. Finally Dong-pal (Choi) is a tough-talking public prosecutor who is determined to throw everyone in jail, even at the risk of his own life.

Irreverence permeates this film as it juggles all these oddball characters and the absurd situations they find themselves in, such as Tae-ju illustrating how ducks swim to Hyeon-ji over breakfast, the use of on-screen text to convey concepts of Sun-Tzu's 'art of war' while Cho-pil negotiates with his boss, or demonstrations on the lethality of Ashtray's weapon of choice. Unfortunately, despite its bizarro genre-bashing take on gangster films, "No. 3" ends up being a few screws loose.

None of the characters are particularly likable, the film unfolds in fits-and-starts, and not all of the gags work. However, it does provide a glimpse at the stars of the latest 'Korean New Wave' before they became famous, and is a fascinating signpost in the evolution of the gangster comedy, both of which might make it worth a look.

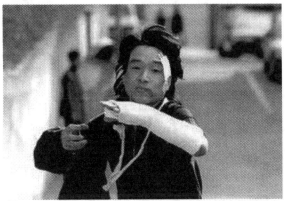

Han Suk-kyu (*image courtesy of Cinema Service*)

Bet on My Disco (Hae-jeok, discowang doeda) - 2002

Starring: Lee Jeong-jin, Yang Dong-kun, Lim Chang-jung, Han Chae-young
Director: Kim Dong-won
Availability: Korean-import DVD (multi-region)
Rating: ●●●

Lee Jeong-jin and Han Chae-young
(image courtesy of A-Line)

The Disco Sound emerged in the mid-Seventies, bringing with it the entire club culture. Bolstered by the introduction of the twelve-inch single, which suited the extended mixes of the Disco Era, club culture crossed over into the domain of mainstream music. Major record labels stood up and took notice of the numerous independent music houses pumping out new records in an effort to satiate the feeding frenzy for new disco tunes.

By mid-1977, there were upscale disco clubs in every major American urban center where the growing masses of disco enthusiasts could dance the night away. Later that same year, with the theatrical release of "Saturday Night Fever", disco fever gripped North America and became an industry unto itself. With high-tech clubs sprouting up all over the place, disco-format radio stations taking over the airwaves, and disco instructional classes preaching to the newly converted, the Disco Sound seemed unstoppable.

The disco phenomenon was not limited to North America, as disco fever quickly spread around the world, infecting the youth of Europe, the Middle East, and of course, Asia. In the bubble-gum romance/comedy "Bet on My Disco", first-time director Kim Dong-won gives us a glimpse of how true love motivates a young man in Korea to become a 'disco king'.

The story involves three high-school friends: the good-looking martial-arts master Hae-jok (Lee Jeong-jin) and his two sidekicks, the rough-around-the-edges Song-gi (Yang Dong-kun) and the dim-witted Bong-pal (Lim Chang-jung). One day, Hae-jok finds himself smitten by a beautiful girl walking down the street and becomes obsessed with getting to know her. What he doesn't realize though is that the girl is Bong-pal's seventeen-year old sister, Bong-ja (Han Chae-young). Furthermore, after Bong-pal and Bong-ja's father ends up in the hospital from a work-related accident, Bong-ja goes to work as a hostess in a new disco club to support the family, despite her brother's protests.

After Hae-jok hears that the girl of his dreams is working as a hostess, he storms into the disco to 'rescue her', only to be beaten down by the hired goons of the club's owner, a powerful mob boss, who has taken a fancy for Bong-ja as she reminds him of his long-lost love and former professional dance partner. Hae-jok is then given a deal-- if he can win an upcoming dance competition being hosted by the disco, Bong-ja will be released. Unfortunately, the competition is only a week away and Hae-jok doesn't know the first thing about disco. Desperate, the three friends turn to a flamboyant dance instructor who has been teaching Song-gi's mother.

Viewers familiar with the Singaporean comedy "That's the Way I Like It", in which a Bruce Lee fan decides to enter a disco competition to pursue the woman of his dreams, will feel a sense of déja vu upon watching "Bet on My Disco". Unfortunately, "Bet on My Disco" doesn't quite hit the heights of the superior "That's the Way I Like It". First of all, the script is bogged down by uneconomical storytelling and it seems to take almost forever before the main story truly gets rolling. In addition, the dance choreography is rather unimpressive, which is disappointing given how disco is the main topic and this sort of film is conducive to eye-pleasing dance routines.

However, the saving grace of "Bet on My Disco" lies in its characters. Despite their one-dimensional trappings, the quirky characters that populate the film manage to be both sympathetic and fun to hang around with. In addition, the budding relationship between Hae-jok and Bong-ja gives the story some much-needed emotional pull.

"Bet on My Disco" is actually based on director Kim's well received short-film "'82, Haejok Becomes a Disco King", which he originally put together in 1998 (this film is included and compared with the feature-film version on the DVD release). Unfortunately, running at almost two hours, "Bet on My Disco" is not as snappy as it should be, as it is bogged down by long-winded storytelling, slow pacing, and some rather unremarkable dance choreography. However, despite such shortcomings, "Bet on My Disco" still manages to be an interesting diversion with enough infectious charm to put a smile on your face and a song in your heart.

Funny Movie (Jaemitneun yeonghwa) - 2002

Starring: Im Won-hee, Seo Tae-hwa, Kim Jeong-eun, Kim Su-ro
Director: Jang Gyu-seong
Availability: Korean-import DVD (Region 3)
Rating: ●●½

Im Won-hee and Kim Jeong-eun (*image courtesy of Cinema Service*)

With "Funny Movie", director Jang Gyu-seong goes where Jim Abrahams and David Zucker ("Airplane"), as well as the Wayans brothers ("Scary Movie") have gone before-- create a parody of an existing genre and machine gun it full of pop-culture references. In this 2002 film, director Jang and writer Son Jae-gon poke fun at the films of the latest 'Korean New Wave' with plenty of scattershot references. Unfortunately, despite a title that indicates otherwise, this parody quickly ceases to be funny.

The film's plot is loosely based on "Shiri", with two South Korean secret agents, Fango (Im Won-hee) and Gabdu (Seo Tae-hwa), trying to stop Japanese terrorists from blowing up the opening ceremonies of the World Cup, an event that will be attended by the leaders of South Korea, North Korea, and Japan. Like the 1999 blockbuster, one of the terrorists, Sang-mi (Kim Jeong-eun), has undergone plastic surgery and has become the significant other of Fango, and faces a crisis of conscience when her leader Murakami (Kim Su-ro) arrives in Seoul to personally lead the mission.

The story unfolds with a clothesline of gags that poke fun at recent Korean films, with almost no stone being left unturned, including references to "Green Fish", "The Contact", "Christmas in August", "The Foul King", "Bichunmoo", and "Attack the Gas Station". Unfortunately, only a few of these actually manage to stand out. Among the better jokes are the film's opening scene in which South Korea's President Kim Dae-jung and North Korea's Chairman Kim Jong-il anonymously chat it up over CB radio à la "Ditto", a couple of nods to "Nowhere to Hide", and a "Shiri"-inspired scene in an Internet café where Murakami's deficient typing skills are an impediment to an online chat with Sang-mi.

However, most of the gags are merely recreations of scenes from other movies in search of a punch line, such as a flashback reminiscent of "Joint Security Area", a run-in with a train straight out of "Peppermint Candy", and a chase through the streets of Seoul that mimics "Friend". And if this middling material wasn't enough, Jang throws in a couple of scatological scenes that are more gross or disturbing than actually funny, such as the S&M extracurricular activities of a Japanese detective and his post-mortem examination.

Though it certainly helps to be familiar with the material being parodied, even die-hard fans of Korean cinema will find "Funny Movie" sorely lacking. For a comedy to be effective, there are two approaches. You either have a very strong script in which the humor organically arises from the quirks of the characters or the situations they find themselves in, or throw out so many zingers that even if one misfires, it won't be very long before a funny one comes along-- "My Sassy Girl" and "My Wife is a Gangster" are examples of the former, while the "Airplane" or "Austin Powers" movies are examples of the latter. "Funny Movie" does neither.

The rehash of "Shiri" is not that interesting to begin with, and it quickly becomes a disjointed mess with all the haphazardly inserted comic bits. Furthermore, at two hours, "Funny Movie" is far too long, the result of too much less-than-sparkling material, and comic set pieces that run far past their expiration date, such as the flashbacks of Fango and Sang-mi's romance modelled

Im Won-hee (*image courtesy of Cinema Service*)

after "My Sassy Girl" or numerous references to "No. 3" as Murakami tries to keep his band of terrorists focused on the mission.

"Funny Movie" has been billed as Korea's very first movie parody, and if the film itself is any indication, it may very well be the last. Other than providing viewers the opportunity to play 'spot the reference', the disappointing "Funny Movie" offers little to live up to its namesake, and even devoted fans of the latest 'Korean New Wave' will find very little to laugh about.

Chapter 10: Most Wanted – Korean Films Without English Subtitles

Despite a steadily growing fan base for Korean films around the world that has encouraged distributors to release back-catalog titles for international consumption, there are still a number of high profile yet older films that still have yet to see a re-release on DVD or VCD with English subtitles. Thus, here is a brief rundown of the 'most wanted' of the latest 'Korean New Wave', listed in alphabetical order:

Just Do It (Hamyeon dwinda) - 2001

This black comedy is the sophomore feature of "Love Wind, Love Song" director Park Dae-yeong. After his business fails and drags his entire family into poverty, Byeong-hwan (Ahn Seok-hwan) strikes gold after being hit by a truck and receiving a huge insurance payoff. Sensing that there is more money to be made, his entire family begins scheming additional ways in which they can deliberately injure themselves to score more insurance money. With its well-conceived and funny characters, as well as its snappy pacing, "Just Do It" has been favorably compared to 1998's "The Quiet Family".

The Letter (Pyeon ji) - 1997

This Korean adaptation of the 1995 classic Japanese romantic weeper "Love Letter" stars Choi Jin-shil of "The Legend of Gingko" as Jeong-in, a female grad student who falls in love with Hwan-yu (Park Shin-yang of "Hi, Dharma") after he returns her lost purse. Unfortunately, Hwan-yu dies some time later and leaves Jeong-in behind. And just when her grief is about to get the best of her, Jeong-in receives a letter written by Hwan-yu…

A Promise - 1998

Despite being the top-grossing Korean film of 1998, Kim Yoo-jin's "A Promise" has yet to see the light of day in an English-subtitled release. Box office draw Jeon Do-yeon, hot off the success of "The Contact", stars as a doctor who falls in love with one of her patients, a gangster played by Park Shin-yang, who made a name for himself in "The Letter". Buoyed by her unforgettable performance, this star-crossed romance sealed Jeon's reputation as one of Korea's top actresses.

The Spy (Gancheob Li Chol-jin) - 1999

Yoo Oh-sung of "Friend" fame stars as a North Korean spy who is sent across the DMZ to steal a genetically engineered pig from a South Korean lab in "The Spy". Unfortunately, he ends up having all his gear stolen by thieves, and is left to fend for himself as a stranger in a strange land, setting the stage for a hilariously absurd fish-out-of-water comedy. Yoo won many accolades for his portrayal of the film's clueless protagonist, a tough soldier who finds himself at a loss when faced with the modern conveniences of South Korea, such as banking machines and fast food.

There is No Sun (Taeyangeun eobda) - 1998

Also known as "City of the Rising Sun", this film was director Kim Sun-su's follow-up to "Beat". Similar to the 1997 film, "There is No Sun" is another tale of the wreckage that ensues when the optimism of youth collides with bitter reality. "Beat" lead Jung Woo-sung returns as washed-up boxer Do-chul, who crosses paths with the Hong-gi (Lee Sung-jae, who earned his first Best Actor award for this role), who dreams of becoming a millionaire, and falls in love with Mimi (Go Eun-han), a model who dreams of becoming a movie star. Like "Beat", loyalties are tested, tragic mistakes are made, and insurmountable odds must be overcome for the characters to find happiness. On a technical note, Kim once again emulates the filmmaking style of Hong Kong's Wong Kar-wai in this film.

Whispering Corridors (Yeogo goedam) - 1998

The predecessor to "Memento Mori", "Whispering Corridors" was the directorial debut of Park Ki-hyung.   Taking place in an all-girls Korean high school, "Whispering Corridors" begins with the murder of a teacher, who is found hanging from the school's roof one morning. This kicks off an investigation by rookie teacher Ms. Hur, who is convinced that it is the handiwork of the restless spirit of Jin Ju, a former student who had committed suicide long ago. Though it is first-and-foremost a horror/chiller, like "My Boss, My Hero", "Whispering Corridors" is also a thinly veiled attack on the Korean high school system that is marked with fierce competition, values stifling conformity above all else, and is rife with bullying and sexual harassment. With a top-notch cast that included Lee Mi-yeon of "The Last Witness", Park Jin-hee of "Love Wind, Love Song", and Kim Kyu-ri of "Libera Me", "Whispering Corridors" became an instant classic, as well as one of the biggest box office hits in 1998.

Chapter 11: The Rising Stars of Korean Cinema

Now that you have had an overview of the films of the latest 'Korean New Wave', you probably noticed a number of the same names keep popping up over and over again, such as actors Han Suk-kyu, Choi Min-shik, and Shim Eun-ha, or directors Jacky Kang Je-gyu, Kim Sang-jin, Kim Ki-duk and Lee Chang-dong. Similar to how Hong Kong cinema made household names out of the former British colony's stars and directors, such as Chow Yun-fat, John Woo, and Jackie Chan, South Korea's homegrown film industry has its own share of superstars, both in front of and behind the camera. And like their Hong Kong predecessors, some of these stars are setting their sights on Hollywood, such as Park Joong-hoon's recent turn in Jonathan Demme's "The Truth About Charlie".

So who are the stars to be watching? Who are South Korea's answers to Chow Yun-fat and John Woo? This chapter will detail a select sample of the rising stars of Korea's film industry are, including what films you can catch them in (films marked with a '*' are reviewed in earlier chapters).

Ahn Sung-ki

Image courtesy of Cinema Service

Ahn Sung-ki is one of South Korea's most prolific actors, having starred in over fifty films since starting his career at the age of 7 in 1959's "The Teenagers' Rebellion" by director Kim Ki-young. His name appears numerous times in the credits of films from the latest 'Korean New Wave', such as a priest with supernatural powers in "The Soul Guardians", the object of Shim Eun-ha's affection in "Art Museum by the Zoo", a veteran soldier in the historical epic "Musa", and as an elusive master criminal in "Nowhere to Hide". Even in his more throwaway roles (such as "Last Witness" or "Kilimanjaro"), there is nothing disposable about this veteran actor's performances, which combine his superlative thesping skills and his impressive screen presence.

Selected filmography:
- The Soul Guardians (1998)*
- Spring in My Hometown (1998)*
- Art Museum by the Zoo (1998)*
- Nowhere to Hide (1999)*
- Black Hole (2000)
- The Truth Game (2000)
- Kilimanjaro (2000)*
- Musa (2001)*
- Last Witness (2001)*
- Chihwaseon (2002)

Bae Doo-na

Image courtesy of Cinema Service

Bae Doo-na may not be as glamorous compared to the likes of Kim Hee-sun or Shim Eun-ha, but she does possess a very down-to-earth beauty. Bae was actually discovered by a model scout while walking down a street in 1998, and from there she began acting in television dramas. 1999 marked her feature-film debut playing a malevolent spirit in the Korean-Japanese co-production "The Ring Virus". From there, her choices in roles have steadily gained in substance and acclaim, including the black comedy "Barking Dogs Never Bite", the erotic romance "Plum Blossom", the coming-of-age drama "Take Care of My Cat", and probably her most demanding role yet, the woman at the center of a vicious circle of violence in "Sympathy for Mr. Vengeance".

Selected filmography:
- The Ring Virus (1999)*
- Barking Dogs Never Bite (2000)*
- Plum Blossom (2000)
- Take Care of My Cat (2001)*
- Sympathy for Mr. Vengeance (2002)*
- Geum-sun (2002)
- Tube (2002)

Chang Yoon-hyun

Unlike most of his contemporaries (and with the exception of Im Kwon-taek, of course), director Chang Yoon-hyun had his start well before the beginning of the latest 'Korean New Wave'. While still in college in 1987, he earned acclaim for his independently produced short film "For the Elite". After studing film producing in Hungary, Chang returned to his native Korea and produced two films, 1989's "Oh! Land of Dream" and 1990's "The Night Before the Strike", with the famous 'Jangsangotmae' Independent Movie Group.

In 1997, he branched into more commercial fare with his directorial debut "The Contact", which ended up becoming the biggest film that year and helped elevate actor Han Suk-kyu to superstar status. In 1999, he reunited with Han Suk-kyu once again to direct the 'hard gore thriller' "Tell Me Something", which also became one of the year's top-selling films.

Selected filmography:
- The Contact (1997)*
- Tell Me Something (1999)*

Choi Min-shik

Image courtesy of Samsung Pictures

Choi Min-shik is Robert De Niro, Al Pacino, Marlon Brando, and Harvey Keitel all rolled into one. His film career truly took off at the start of the latest 'Korean New Wave', with his portrayal of the no-nonsense public prosecutor in the gangster comedy "No. 3". Since then, some of his most memorable roles have been playing 'tough guys', such as the ruthless North Korean general in "Shiri" and a gangster with a heart of gold in "Failan". However, Choi is also adept at dramatic and comedic roles, as witnessed by his hilarious portrayal of the dim-witted uncle in "The Quiet Family" or his tragic turn as a cuckolded husband to Jeon Do-yeon in "The Happy End".

Selected filmography:
- No. 3 (1997)*
- The Quiet Family (1998)*
- Shiri (1999)*
- The Happy End (1999)*

- Failan (2001)*
- Chihwaseon (2002)

Han Suk-kyu

Image courtesy of Samsung Pictures

Considered the 'Tom Cruise' of South Korean cinema, über-popular actor Han Suk-kyu is probably the closest thing to Chow Yun-fat superstardom on the peninsula. Equally up to the task of serious drama and high-octane action, Han's filmography is a diverse collection of roles and genres, such as playing a disillusioned wannabe-gangster in "Green Fish", a man looking for love on the Internet in "The Contact", a dying photo-shop proprietor in "Christmas in August", a dedicated cop in serial-killer chiller "Tell Me Something", and of course, as a secret agent in the explosive "Shiri". And because of the so-called 'Han Suk-kyu effect', whereby almost every film he stars in becomes a box office hit, Han now commands the highest salary in the industry. Not bad for a guy who started his career in the early Nineties as a professional voice dubber.

Unfortunately, Han has been taking an extended breather since 1999's "Tell Me Something". Other than starting his own production company to solicit new screenplays via his web site, Han has not appeared in any new films. In the meantime, the actor's many fans eagerly await his next film appearance in the 2003 film "Double Agent", where Han will play a North Korean spy who infiltrates the South.

Selected filmography:
- The Gingko Bed (1996)*
- Green Fish (1997)*
- No. 3 (1997)*
- The Contact (1997)*
- Christmas in August (1998)*
- Shiri (1999)*
- Tell Me Something (1999)*
- Double Agent (2003)

Hur Jin-ho

Image courtesy of USC Asian Film Connections

Director Hur Jin-ho began his career in 1992, when he began studying film at the Korean Academy of Film Art. From there, he worked as a screenwriter and assistant director to director Park Kwang-soo and cut his teeth in films such as 1993's "To the Starry Island" and 1995's "A Single Spark". In 1998, he debuted as a director with his touching romantic melodrama "Christmas in August", which united the two future superstars of Korean cinema for the first time, Han Suk-kyu and Shim Eun-ha. After sweeping the Korean film awards, including awards for Best Picture, Best Director, and Best Actress, there was little doubt that Hur was among Korea's best and brightest filmmakers.

However, it would be another three years before his sophomore feature, "One Fine Spring Day", bowed into theaters. Despite the film being highly anticipated by Hur's fans, "One Fine Spring Day" ended up underperforming, as it lacked the punch of his debut. Nevertheless, Hur remains one of the most celebrated names in the latest 'Korean New Wave'.

Selected filmography:
* Christmas in August (1998)*
* One Fine Spring Day (2001)*

Im Kwon-taek

Image courtesy of USC Asian Film Connections

With a career that has spanned over four decades and over 100 films to his name, it could be argued that veteran director Im Kwon-taek is the father of modern Korean cinema. In addition to being the most recognized Korean director on the international stage, Im's films have won numerous awards over the years, both at home and abroad, and has given Korean cinema some of its beloved classics, such as 1981's "Mandala" and 1993's "Soponje". And even with the arrival of the latest 'Korean New Wave', Im continues to skilfully plie his trade to this day, such as having the first Korean film to be invited to the Cannes Film Festival ("Chunhyang"), as well as his recent win for Best Director at the 2002

Cannes Film Festival with "Chihwaseon", a film that details the life of 19th-century Korean painter Jang Seung-eop.

Selected filmography:
- Downfall (1997)
- Chunhyang (2000)*
- Chihwaseon (2002)

Jang Dong-gun

Image courtesy of Cineworld

Heartthrob Jang Dong-gun, with his magazine-cover good looks and his top-notch acting, is easily one of the most popular actors in South Korea. Similar to Hong Kong stars Andy Lau, Jacky Cheung, and Lai Ming, Jang's successful career spans both film and music. During the early Nineties, he became a household name by starring in a number of popular television series (including Korea's most highly rated series "All About Eve") and became one of the country's best-known television actors. It was also during this period that Jang began his music career, recording several best-selling albums that have made him a pan-Asian singing sensation. Jang has also dabbled in modeling and work in commercials, including having earned the distinction of being the most well paid actor to appear in a commercial for work in a refrigerator advertisement, which paid him 450 million won ($375,000 US).

In 1997, he branched out into film with a couple of roles, the romance "Repechage", and the Wong Kar-wai-wannabe art film "Holiday in Seoul". However, it was in 1999 that his film career kicked into high gear, playing Park Joong-hoon's dashing partner in "Nowhere to Hide". This was followed up by his channeling of Chow Yun-fat in the 1930s Shanghai actioner "The Anarchists" and his bad-boy turn in the highest-grossing Korean film of all time, 2001's "Friend". Today, the ascent of Jang's acting career seems unstoppable, having appeared in 2002's sci-fi actioner "2009 Lost Memories" and his upcoming appearances in director Kim Ki-duk's "The Coast Guard", as well as Kang Je-gyu's long-awaited follow-up to "Shiri", due out in 2003.

Selected filmography:
- Repechage (1997)

- Holiday in Seoul (1997)*
- First Kiss (1998)
- Love Wind, Love Song (1999)*
- Nowhere to Hide (1999)*
- The Anarchists (2000)*
- Friend (2001)*
- 2009 Lost Memories (2002)*
- The Coast Guard (2002)

Jeon Do-yeon

Image courtesy of CJ Entertainment

Jeon Do-yeon is perhaps one of South Korea's most versatile actresses. Like Gary Oldman, Jeon is able to completely transform herself into whatever character she is playing with her chameleon-like acting skills. As a result, Jeon's film career is chock full of challenging roles and for the uninitiated, she is almost unrecognizable from one film to the next. 1997's "The Contact" was her breakthrough film, where her melancholy character carried on an Internet-based relationship with Han Suk-kyu. However, her reputation as one of Korea's foremost actresses was solidified the following year in "A Promise", a romantic weeper where she played a doctor who becomes involved with a gang leader she treats. 1999 saw her in two diametrically opposed roles-- first as a naïve seventeen-year old schoolgirl in "Harmonium in My Memory" and second with her complex portrayal of a cheating housewife in "The Happy End". Since then, it has become difficult to know what to expect when you see Jeon in a film role, as she was deglamorized into a spacey schoolteacher in 2000's "I Wish I Had a Wife", and vamped up as a trashy gangster's moll in 2002's "No Blood No Tears".

Selected filmography:
- The Contact (1997)*
- A Promise (1998)
- Harmonium in My Memory (1999)*
- The Happy End (1999)*
- I Wish I Had a Wife (2000)*
- No Blood No Tears (2002)*

Jeon Ji-hyun

Image courtesy of Sidus

Despite only having three film under her belt, Jeon Ji-hyun has gained quite a following, and according to the readers of South Korea's monthly movie magazine "Screen", she is the country's most popular actress. In China, the are women and girls, some as young as 12-years old, who are seeking out plastic surgery so that they could like like this Korean screen beauty. Of course, Jeon's superstar success, both at home and abroad, can be attributed to three little words: "My Sassy Girl".

Prior to finding success as the sociopathic but emotionally vulnerable titular character of the 2001 romantic-comedy hit, Jeon started her career as a model and television actress. Her first film, 1999's "White Valentine", tanked, though she made up for it the following year with her moving performance in the time-twisted romance "Il Mare". After the international success of "My Sassy Girl", Jeon now has the pick of the litter in terms of film roles, and she is even scheduled to appear in a Hong Kong film directed by Stephen Chow of "Shaolin Soccer" fame.

Selected filmography:
- White Valentine (1999)*
- Il Mare (2000)*
- My Sassy Girl (2001)*

Jacky Kang Je-gyu

Jacky Kang Je-gyu, the director who forever changed the face of Korean cinema in 1999 with "Shiri", started his filmmaking career as a celebrated screenwriter in the early Nineties, winning awards for his scripts, such as "Who Has Seen the Dragon's Toenails?" in 1991 and "The Rule of the Game" in 1994. In 1996, he was named the 'New Director of the Year' at the country's Golden Bell Awards for his directorial debut, "The Gingko Bed", which was both a critical and commercial success.

In 1999, his sophomore feature "Shiri" broke the country's box office records, sinking the previous numbers achieved by "Titanic", and put him at the forefront of Korea's 'latest New Wave'. In addition, the techniques Kang used to finance and produce "Shiri", gleaned from the business models of Hollywood filmmaking, forever changed how films were put together in South Korea. Since the success of "Shiri", Kang has been busy with a number of productions under his company Kang Je-gyu Films, which has produced films such as "The Legend of Gingko", "Kiss Me Much", and Kang's follow-up to "Shiri", due out sometime in 2003.

Selected filmography:
- The Gingko Bed (1996)*
- Shiri (1999)*

Kim Hee-sun

Image courtesy of Cinema Service

Kim Hee-sun is considered the 'most beautiful woman' in Korea, and not surprisingly, next to Jeon Ji-hyun, she is the actress that many Asian women aspire to be, even to the point of getting plastic surgery. After toiling away on television dramas, Kim made her big-screen debut in 1997 with Jang Dong-gun in "Repechage". From there, she starred in three genre films, "Ghost in Love" and "Calla" in 1999, and the Korean-Chinese *wu shu* epic "Bichunmoo". However, the actress finally hit her stride in the 2001 romance "Wanee & Junah". Unfortunately, to date, that film has been her last appearance on the big screen, and she now spends most of her time working in commercials and advertising.

Selected filmography:
- Repechage (1997)
- Ghost in Love (1999)*
- Calla (1999)*
- Bichunmoo (2000)*
- Wanee & Junah (2001)*

Kim Ki-duk

Image courtesy of CJ Entertainment

The 'bad boy' of Korean cinema, Kim Ki-duk's films are known for their uncomfortable use of sex and violence to reveal the rotten underside of modern Korean society, a reflection of the director's difficult lower-class childhood. Whereas his contemporary Lee Chang-dong will hold back on using disturbing imagery to make his point, Kim seems to revel in it like the Korean answer to extreme Japanese director Takashi Miike-- "The Isle" features a woman using fishing hooks on herself, "Address Unknown" includes numerous scenes of eyes being gouged and characters beating the stuffing out of each other, while "Bad Guy" details a middle-class schoolgirl being turned into a prostitute by a vindictive thug. Given how women end up taking the brunt of the abuse in Kim's films, it is not surprising that he receives the most criticism from feminists and women's groups. And though his films can be extreme, and sometimes even pretentious, they do deal head-on with some of the ugly issues afflicting today's Korea, including police corruption, prostitution, and the persistent treatment of women as 'second-class' citizens.

Selected filmography:
- Birdcage Inn (1998)
- The Isle (2000)*
- Real Fiction (2000)*
- Address Unknown (2001)*
- Bad Guy (2001)*
- The Coast Guard (2002)

Kim Sang-jin

Director Kim Sang-jin is a master at the comedy genre, having gotten his start as an assistant director and scribe under director (and Cinema Service founder) Kang Woo-suk. He came into his own as a director in 1995's "Millions in My Account", but his breakthrough and international following would not come until 1999, when he released the iconoclastic satire "Attack the Gas Station!", in which four bored youths take over a gas station and upset the local social order. He followed this up with the popular gangster-comedy "Kick the Moon" in 2001, and in 2002, he returned once again with "Jail Breakers", where two criminals must break back into prison after escaping in order to receive a pardon.

Selected filmography:
- Two Cops 3 (1998)
- Attack the Gas Station! (1999)*
- Kick the Moon (2001)*
- Jail Breakers (2002)

Kim Yoon-jin

Image courtesy of Samsung Pictures

Kim Yoon-jin, 'the girl from Shiri', actually grew up in the United States and developed her acting skills at the New York School of Performing Arts, Boston University, and Oxford University. After landing roles in legitimate theatre on Broadway and popping up occasionally on American television, Kim was discovered by a Korean television network and cast in a TV drama that was being shot in New York. From there, she landed more roles on Korean television and a small film role in 1998's "A Fantastic Story", which ultimately led to being cast in "Shiri" and changing the trajectory of her career forever.

Since her success in "Shiri", Kim has appeared in another Kang Je-gyu production, "The Legend of Gingko" from 2000. In 2002, Kim appeared in three films, including the sci-fi action film "Yesterday", the romance "Deep Loves", and the comedy "Iron Palm", which was filmed in Los Angeles and had Kim speaking a large part of her dialogue in her almost flawless English.

Selected filmography:
- A Fantastic Story (1998)
- Shiri (1999)*
- The Legend of Gingko (2000)*
- Iron Palm (2002)*
- Yesterday (2002)
- Deep Loves (2002)

Kwak Kyung-taek

Director Kwak Kyung-taek studied film at New York University. For anumber of years, he made a name for himself on the short-film circuit, such as winning the Best Film award at the Seoul Short Film Festival in 1995 for "A Story of a

Military Prison". In 1997, he debuted as a feature filmmaker with the comedy "3pm Paradise Bath House", which was followed by the suspense film "Doctor K" in 1999.

Image courtesy of USC Asian Film Connections

However, in 2001, Kwak struck gold with "Friend", a film about how the bond between four boyhood chums is put to the test as they grow up and apart, which was based on Kwak's own experiences growing up in Pusan. "Friend" went on to become the highest-grossing homegrown film in Korean history, outpacing both "Shiri" and "Joint Security Area". In 2002, Kwak returned to the nation's cinemas with "Champion", a critically acclaimed look at the real-life story of Korean boxer Kim Deuk-gu who, in 1982, went fourteen rounds with Ray 'Boom Boom' Mancini in Las Vegas before falling into a coma.

Selected filmography:
- 3PM Paradise Bath House (1997)
- Doctor K (1999)
- Friend (2001)*
- The Champion (2002)

Lee Byung-heon

Image courtesy of Cinema Service

Lee Byung-heon, a regular fixture on both television and movie screens in Korea, got his big break in the 2000 blockbuster "Joint Security Area", playing a South Korean soldier at the center of a cross-border incident in the DMZ. Prior to that, his most notable appearance was opposite an unrecognizable Jeon Do-yeon in "Harmonium in My Memory". However, since 2000, Lee's career has expanded to include the time- and gender-bending romance "Bungee Jumping of Their Own", lending his voice to the Korean animation "My Beautiful Girl, Mari", and starring opposite Lee Mi-yeon in "Addiction".

Selected filmography:
- Harmonium in My Memory (1999)*
- Joint Security Area (2000)*
- Bungee Jumping of Their Own (2000)*
- My Beautiful Girl, Mari (2001)
- Addiction (2002)

Lee Chang-dong

Director Lee Chang-dong got his start as a playwright, only to become a novelist, and then a screenwriter. After penning 1994's "To the Starry Island" and 1996's "A Single Spark", Lee got behind the camera to direct "Green Fish", which would be the first of a series of compelling films that would peel back the glossy sheen of Korea's political and economic reforms to reveal the plight of the marginalized and disenfranchised members of Korean society. "Green Fish" detailed the corruption and destruction of a soldier who returns to his hometown, while "Peppermint Candy" used a unique reverse chronology to depict the downfall of a man during twenty years of recent Korean history, and his most recent film, "Oasis", deals with the unlikely romance between a parolee and a woman with cerebral palsy.

Selected filmography:
- Green Fish (1997)*
- Peppermint Candy (2000)*
- Oasis (2002)

Lee Jung-jae

Image courtesy of Cinema Service

Like Jeon Do-yeon, Lee Jung-jae is one of the more versatile actors of the latest 'Korean New Wave', having handled a wide diversity of roles throughout his career. Though his film career began in 1994, his breakthrough did not occur until 1998's "An Affair", where he played Lee Mi-sook's adulterous romantic interest, which was followed up by his Best Actor appearance in 1999's "There is No Sun". From there, he has dabbled in all major genres and starred with almost every major Korean actress, from the arthouse drama of "The Interview" (with Shim Eun-ha) and the Korean-Japanese co-production of "Asako in Ruby

Shoes", to the romantic melodrama of "Il Mare" (with Jeon Ji-hyun) and "Last Present" (with Lee Young-ae), the historical epic "The Uprising" (again with Shim Eun-ha), and the high-octane action of "Last Witness" (with Lee Mi-yeon). And when he is not lighting up the big screen, Lee is also a successful fashion model.

Selected filmography:
- An Affair (1998)*
- There is No Sun (1998)
- The Uprising (1999)*
- The Interview (2000)*
- Il Mare (2000)*
- Asako in Ruby Shoes (2000)*
- Last Present (2001)*
- Last Witness (2001)*
- Over the Rainbow (2002)

Lee Mi-yeon

Image courtesy of Jun and Jun

Lee Mi-yeon's film career first got off the ground at the end of the Eighties with the drama "Happiness Has Nothing to Do with Students' Records", and she developed quite a following during the early part of the Nineties. After a brief hiatus in 1995, Lee rode back into popularity on the latest 'Korean New Wave', playing Han Suk-kyu's wayward wife in 1997's "No. 3" and then starring in the horror hit "Whispering Corridors" in 1998. Since then, Lee has stuck mostly to the romance and drama genres, such as playing a love interest to Lee Byung-heon in "Harmonium in My Memory", her portrayal of a woman accused of murdering her husband in 2001's "Indian Summer", and most recently as a woman at the center of a love triangle in "Addiction", though she also appeared opposite Lee Jung-jae in the action-oriented "Last Witness" from 2001.

Selected filmography:
- No. 3 (1997)*
- Motel Cactus (1997)
- Whispering Corridors (1998)
- Harmonium in My Memory (1999)*
- Wife in Romance (2000)
- Pisces (2000)
- Indian Summer (2001)*

- Last Witness (2001)*
- Addiction (2002)

Lee Sung-jae

*Image courtesy of
Cinema Service*

Within four years of his big-screen debut in "Art Museum by the Zoo" opposite Shim Eun-ha, Lee Sung-jae has quickly risen into the ranks of Han Suk-kyu and Lee Jung-jae in the pantheon of Korea's top actors. His filmography is chock full of successful films, which includes his appearance opposite Kim Hee-sun in 1999's "Ghost in Love", playing the leader of a group of hostage-taking ruffians in "Attack the Gas Station!", a tearful performance with Ko So-young in 2000's "A Day", portraying a suave gangster in 2001's "Kick the Moon", and most recently, playing the villain as a 'Patrick Bateman'-style serial killer in 2002's "Public Enemy".

Selected filmography:
- Art Museum by the Zoo (1998)*
- Ghost in Love (1999)*
- Attack the Gas Station! (1999)*
- Barking Dogs Never Bite (2000)*
- A Day (2000)*
- Kick the Moon (2001)*
- Public Enemy (2002)*

Lee Young-ae

*Image courtesy of Cinema
Service*

Thanks to her heartwrenching turn as the selfless spouse to Lee Jung-jae in "Last Present", Lee Young-ae has earned the distinction of being the 'most desired wife' in Korea. However, it has been a long struggle for the actress to reach stardom. Like many of her contemporaries, Lee got her start on Korean television in the early Nineties and gained quite a following. Unfortunately, the small-screen fame failed to translate into big-screen success with her feature-film debut in the 1997 international-intrigue drama "Inch'Alla". It would not be until 2000 that she would land the role that would make her a star-- "Joint Security Area". Despite her difficulty with the film's English dialogue, audiences fell in love with her. The love affair continued in 2001, when she appeared in "Last Present" and Hur Jin-ho's long-awaited follow-up to "Christmas in August", "One Fine Spring Day".

Selected filmography:
- Joint Security Area (2000)*
- Last Present (2001)*
- One Fine Spring Day (2001)*

Park Chan-wook

Director Park Chan-wook got his start in film while studying philosophy in Sogan University, where he founded the 'Movie Gang' film club. After directing a couple of small films, Park's career launched into the stratosphere in the year 2000. In addition to writing the script for Yu Young-shik's 2000 actioner "The Anarchists", Park directed "Joint Security Area", which ended up becoming the highest-grossing homegrown Korean production of all time in 2000. With a major box-office hit under his belt, Park was given free reign for his next film. In 2002, his long-anticipated follow-up to "Joint Security Area", the intense psychological thriller "Sympathy for Mr. Vengeance", was released and was proof positive that this director was certainly no one-trick pony.

Selected filmography:
- Joint Security Area (2000)*
- Sympathy for Mr. Vengeance (2002)*

Park Joong-hoon

Image courtesy of Cinema Service

With his 'big head' and distinctive looks, it is not surprising that he bulk of Park Joong-hoon's filmography prior to the latest 'Korean New Wave' reads as an impressive list of comedies, particularly his claim-to-fame from 1993, Kang Wu-seok's action-comedy "Two Cops". Even his 1999 comeback feature, "Nowhere to Hide", despite being a smorgasborg of genres, had a heavy hint of comedy throughout the proceedings. However, in recent years, the veteran actor, who learned his trade both in South Korea and New York, has been branching out. In 2001, he appeared as a psycho killer that harassed a vacationing couple in the harrowing "Say Yes", while 2002 marks his appearance in a major Hollywood production with a supporting role alongside Thandie Newton and Mark Wahlberg in Jonathan Demme's "The Truth About Charlie" (Park's previous lead role in 1998's direct-to-video cheapie "American Dragons", alongside Michael Biehn and Cary-Hiroyuki Tagawa, doesn't count, as that was also a Korean production).

Selected filmography:
- American Dragons (1998)
- Nowhere to Hide (1999)*
- A Masterpiece in My Life (2000)
- Say Yes (2001)*
- The Truth About Charlie (2002)

Ryu Seung-wan

Considered the 'Quentin Tarantino' of Korean cinema, director Ryu Seung-wan represents the 'can-do' spirit of independent filmmaking in today's South Korea. Ryu learned how to make films on his own using a 8mm camera while in high school and served as a production assistant on Park Chan-wook's production "Three Members" (in 2002, Ryu would also star in a supporting role in Park's "Sympathy for Mr. Vengeance"). In the late Nineties, Ryu put together some award-winning short films, some of which were incorporated into his 2000 feature-film debut "Die Bad", which was mostly shot on 16mm film. Despite the technical limitations, Ryu displayed tremendous talent as a filmmaker and the edgy "Die Bad" quickly developed a huge following among Korean moviegoers. And though his 2002 follow-up feature "No Blood No Tears" benefited from a bigger budget and recognizable stars (including Jeon Do-yeon), it ended up fizzling at the box office. Nevertheless, like his debut, "No Blood No Tears" demonstrated that Ryu had a solid gift for filmmaking, and hopefully, his next film will be both a critical and commercial success.

Selected filmography:
- Die Bad (2000)*
- No Blood No Tears (2002)*

Shim Eun-ha

The name Shim Eun-ha is almost synonymous with that of Han Suk-kyu, as the stunningly beautiful and popular actress has been paired with the 'Tom Cruise' of South Korea in two box office hits, 1998's "Christmas in August" and 1999's

"Tell Me Something". Korea's answer to 'Julia Roberts' got her start in television in the early Nineties, but her popularity really took off in "Christmas in August", with her unforgettably sweet performance as a meter maid who falls in love with Han Suk-kyu's character. Her follow-up feature, the romantic-comedy "Art Museum by the Zoo", and her chilling performance as the only link to a series of gruesome serial murders in "Tell Me Something" further cemented her status as Korea's most popular actress. But unlike her male counterpart, there is no such thing as a 'Shim Eun-ha effect', even with the actress' popularity. 1999's "The Uprising" was a misfire, with Shim almost unrecognizable in the dry and academic period piece, while 2000's "Interview" wasted her talent with a pretentious 'Dogme 95'-wannabe arthouse production.

Image courtesy of Cinema Service

Much to the chagrin of her fans, Shim has not appeared in any new films since "Tell Me Something", and rumor has it that she was planning on getting married and quitting the movie business forever. Hopefully, she is merely taking a hiatus like Han Suk-kyu, and will make a return to the big screen in the near future.

Selected filmography:
- Christmas in August (1998)*
- Art Museum by the Zoo (1998)*
- The Uprising (1999)*
- Tell Me Something (1999)*
- Interview (2000)*

Shin Eun-kyung

Image courtesy of Hanmac Films

Prior to her smashing success as the titular character in "My Wife is a Gangster", Shin Eun-kyung was a familiar face to Korean audiences with her regular appearances on television, both in drama series and as a host of a television game show, and a number of films. However, she truly became a rising star after playing a prostitute in Im Kwon-taek's "Downfallen" from 1997. This was followed by appearances in a number of genre pieces throughout 1999 and 2000, including her lead role in "The Ring Virus" (the Korean remake of the Japanese horror hit "The Ring"), the sci-fi actioner "A Mystery of the Cube", and a supporting role in the Japanese horror film "Uzumaki". Of course, these performances don't hold a candle to her hilarious portrayal of the tomboyish gang leader Mantis in "My Wife is a Gangster", making this actress definitely one to keep an eye on in coming years.

Selected filmography:
- Downfall (1997)
- A Mystery of the Cube (1999)
- The Ring Virus (1999)*
- The Emergency Room (2000)
- Uzumaki (2000)
- My Wife is a Gangster (2001)*
- Out of Justice (2001)*
- If You Know Someone Nice, Introduce Me (2002)
- Blue (2003)

Sol Kyung-gu

Image courtesy of Cinema Service

According to Korea's Screen Magazine, Sol Kyung-gu is the most popular actor in the country right now, even besting Han Suk-kyu, who holds the number-two position. In his breakthrough role in "Peppermint Candy", Sol was downright scary. Violent and unpredictable, he is a ticking time bomb of angst and regret. While most viewers will always associate the actor's rough facial features with this career-defining role, a quick look at his film career reveals a wide range of roles for this versatile actor. Closest to his "Peppermint Candy"-style volatility would be his 'Dirty Harry'-inspired turn as a corrupt but determined cop in 2002's "Public Enemy". However, he was also in the sweet romantic comedy "I Wish I Had a Wife" with Jeon Do-yeon, did some swordplay in "The Legend of Gingko" opposite Kim Yoon-jin, and appeared in Lee Chang-dong's 2002 drama-romance "Oasis", which reunited him with "Peppermint Candy" co-star Mun So-ri. He may not be pretty, but he sure can act.

Selected filmography:
- Phantom the Submarine (1999)
- Rainbow Trout (1999)

- The Bird Who Stops in the Air (1999)
- Peppermint Candy (2000)*
- The Legend of Gingko (2000)*
- I Wish I Had a Wife (2000)*
- Public Enemy (2002)*
- Oasis (2002)
- Special Amnesty (2002)

Song Kang-ho

Image courtesy of Samsung Pictures

Song Kang-ho has been pulling a `Tom Hanks`since his big break in 1997`s "No. 3", where he played an inarticulate gangster, a role that netted him a Best Actor award. Like the Academy Award-winning actor of "Philadelphia" and "Saving Private Ryan", Song honed his thesping skills 'on the job' after getting a start in theatre without any previous acting instruction. In addition, Song's early films were mostly comedies, such as the aforementioned "No. 3", "The Quiet Family", and "The Foul King". However, in recent years, his focus has shifted to more serious fare, starting with his bit role in "Green Fish" and his appearance in blockbuster "Shiri". Now, he is pretty well considered a dramatic actor, based on his memorable lead roles in films such as "Joint Security Area", "Sympathy for Mr. Vengeance", "YMCA Baseball Team", and his upcoming role in Bong Jun-ho's "Memory of Murder" in 2003.

Selected filmography:
- Green Fish (1997)*
- No. 3 (1997)*
- Timeless Bottomless Bad Movie (1997)
- The Quiet Family (1998)*
- Shiri (1999)*
- The Foul King (2000)*
- Joint Security Area (2000)*
- Sympathy for Mr. Vengeance (2002)*
- YMCA Baseball Team (2002)
- Memory of Murder (2003)

Yoo Oh-sung

Image courtesy of Korea Pictures

Yoo Oh-sung is probably best known for his gangster roles, thanks to 1997's "Beat" and the 2001 box-office smash "Friend", two films that finally got this actor the attention he deserves after toiling away in film since 1991. However, Yoo is also quite adept at comedy, as illustrated by his hilarious performances in two 1999 films, the instant classic "Attack the Gas Station!" and the 'fish out of water' espionage parody "The Spy". In 2002, he went the "Ali" route by bulking up for his portrayal of real-life boxer Kim Deuk-gu in Kwak Kyung-taek's follow-up to "Friend", "Champion".

Selected filmography:
- Beat (1997)*
- 2PM Saturday (1998)
- Spring in My Hometwon (1998)*
- The Spy (1999)
- Attack the Gas Station! (1999)*
- Friend (2001)*
- The Champion (2002)

Chapter 12: Where to Get Your Fix for Korean Flicks

Now that you have read about the delights that are waiting to be discovered in the world of South Korean cinema, how does one go about actually getting their hands on Korean movies, especially ones with English subtitles?

Film Festivals

South Korean films are becoming increasingly popular with film festival programmers, and most international film festivals now feature at least one or two, if not more. For example, the 2002 Toronto International Film Festival featured an impressive slate of Korean films, while the 2002 San Diego International Film Festival unspooled "Peppermint Candy" and "Die Bad". In addition, check out film festivals that are dedicated to Asian cinema, such as the Fant-Asia Film Festival in Canada or the San Diego Asian Film Festival, or the regular programs run by New York's Subway Cinema (such as 'When Korean Cinema Attacks' that ran in the summer of 2001).

The Local Theatre

With Hollywood studio execs sniffing around South Korea for the 'next big thing', it won't be very long until Korean movies become a regular attraction at the local multiplex. Over the last two years, a few pioneering Korean films have received limited distribution in North America, primarily through the arthouse circuit. For example, at the tail end of 2000, "Chunhyang" and "Nowhere to Hide" enjoyed limited U.S. releases in select cities. The fall of 2001 saw the release of "Tell Me Something", "Shiri" made its North American debut in early 2002, which was then followed by an autumn release of "Take Care of My Cat".

Home Video

Perhaps the easiest way to get your hands on Korean films is through home video, particularly with the growing popularity of the DVD format. And with the growing popularity of Korean cinema in Hong Kong, film distributors in the former British colony are becoming an important source for Korean films, whose releases typically include English subtitles. And though finding Korean films is considerably easier if you live in a city or town that has a 'Koreatown' or 'Chinatown', this barrier has all but been eliminated thanks to the advent of the Internet, allowing one to browse and buy Korean films with the mere click of a mouse. But before getting into where to start shopping, it is important to know the various formats available: VHS, DVD, and VCD.

VHS

Among all three formats, VHS is probably the least popular, with very few retailers actually selling or renting Korean films in this antiquated format. However, some smaller outlets, such as Korean grocery stores or Korean video stores, might still carry VHS tapes, though in many cases, the films will not have English subtitles. But if you still don't have a DVD player and are fluent in Korean, then buying or renting VHS tapes might be a viable option.

DVD

The DVD (which stands for digital versatile disc) format has grown by leaps and bounds since coming out of nowhere in 1997. In 2002, it is estimated that the penetration of DVD players into U.S. homes will be in excess of 50%, while 2001 statistics show that half of the consumer sales of movies were in the DVD format. With such overwhelming consumer support for this new home video format, distributors of Korean films have been jumping on the DVD bandwagon, creating a rapidly growing library of new releases and catalog titles, many of which come with English subtitles.

However, before you go out and blow your savings on brand new Korean DVDs, you should make sure that they are compatible with both your television set and your DVD player. Television sets come in three 'flavors': NTSC (the standard in North America and parts of Asia, including South Korea and Japan), PAL (used in Western Europe and Australia), and SECAM (France and Eastern Europe). DVDs recorded in one standard (such as PAL) will be incompatible with both the DVD and television set of another standard (such as NTSC), unless both your DVD and television set can support multiple standards. However, most domestically sourced DVD players and televisions will only support the standard in your own country. For more information, HorrorDVDs.com has a nice article on the compatibility of different television standards available at http://www.horrordvds.com/extras/articles/palntsc.

In addition, buyers need to be aware of the region codes on DVDs, which divide the world into eight different regions, such as North America (Region 1), Europe and Japan (Region 2), and Southeast/East Asia (Region 3, which includes Hong Kong and South Korea). DVDs encoded for a specific region (such as Region 1) cannot be played back on a DVD player from another region (such as Region 3), unless your DVD player is a 'region-free' one. You can learn more about DVD region codes from the DVD FAQ found at http://www.dvddemystified.com.

In terms of television standards, all South Korean DVDs are in the NTSC standard, which is good news for Korean film buffs in North America, but bad news for those of you in the United Kingdom and other European countries. With respect to region codes, many Korean DVD releases are multi-region, meaning that they can be played anywhere in the world, particularly the ones released through Hong Kong distributors (such as Modern or Mei-Ah). However, there are some films, particularly the newer releases, which are only playable on Region 3 machines.

VCD

Almost unheard of in North America and Europe, VCD is the most popular home video format in Asian countries, though this may change as DVD continues to make inroads with consumers. Essentially a CD containing one or more large MPEG files (the same type of video compression used on home computers), each VCD holds about 74 minutes of full-motion video with stereo sound. Though the picture and sound quality are not as pristine as DVD, it is still pretty good in comparison to VHS, though the image does have a tendency to 'pixelate' if the on-screen action becomes too intense (for example, this is really noticeable in the VCD release of "Shiri").

However, despite the lower picture and sound quality in comparison to DVD, VCD does have many advantages:

- The VCD format can be played on almost any machine. In addition to dedicated VCD players, many mid-range to high-end DVD players can also play VCDs (for a complete list of VCD-compatible DVD players, visit http://www.vcdhelp.com/dvdplayers.php). The file structure on VCDs can also be read by your home computer, and it is possible to play the giant MPEG files through Windows Media Player or other similar multimedia applications. In addition, there are after-market hardware/software add-ons that allow videogame consoles (such as the Playstation 2 or the Sega Dreamcast) to play VCDs.
- Note that some VCDs, particularly the Hong Kong releases, will contain dual-language tracks, with the original Korean on the left audio channel and a Cantonese dub on the other. While VCD-compatible DVD players allow users to switch between the left and right audio channels to isolate

one of the language tracks, Windows Media Player on your home computer does not, resulting in an 'echo' effect as you hear both language tracks simultaneously. Thankfully, there are many free VCD player applications for Windows and Macintosh operating systems that can help you get around this issue. For more information and links to download sites, check out http://www.vcdgallery.com/help.htm.

- Unlike DVD, it does not matter whether your television set is NTSC or PAL, as VCD supports both standards. Despite the majority of VCDs being recorded in the PAL standard, VCD players, regardless of country of origin, are able to read them properly. In addition, there are no region lockout codes on VCDs, allowing you to watch movies from other countries.

- VCDs are relatively inexpensive, as the going price for new VCDs is in the range of $10-15 US.

- A number of films will come out on VCD first before being released on DVD, particularly for the releases by Hong Kong distributors. However, as a caveat, the Korea-only VCD releases typically do not contain English subtitles.

- Like DVDs and other digital media, the picture and sound quality of VCDs will not deteriorate with time.

- VCDs typically come packaged in the same 'jewel boxes' that hold regular CDs, making them easier to store compared to VHS tapes.

For more information on VCDs, check out Russil Wvong's Video CD FAQ at http://www.geocities.com/Athens/Forum/2496/vcdfaq.html or http://www.vcdhelp.com/faq.htm.

Where to Shop

If there is a large Korean or Chinese community in your city or hometown, you will probably be able to find Korean movies for sale at Chinese or Korean DVD/VCD stores, bookstores, and electronic shops. Though most of the staff at these stores will be able to speak English, some will not, and you should keep the following in mind while browsing and buying:

- DVDs and VCDs will typically state on the package what region/television standard they are for. Practically all DVDs and VCDs for sale in your home country will typically be compatible with domestic standards.

- DVDs and VCDs will usually state whether or not the film contains English subtitles. For Hong Kong releases of Korean films, look for the following Chinese words on the label, which means "Chinese and English sub-titles':

中英文字幕

- Unfortunately, there are a lot of pirated VCDs and DVDs of Korean films floating around, particularly in the Chinese DVD/VCD stores. Though it may be tempting to pick them up, steer clear of them. First of all, it is wrong, and may discourage future film productions, such as how video piracy has been crippling Hong Kong's local film industry for the past decade. Second, the quality is usually poor, as the pirates typically use video footage that someone shot in a movie theater, or the transfer from the original source material is glitchy, with the disc subject to skipping or the image plagued with 'video artifacts'. Third, though the packaging may say that the film has English subtitles, in actuality it will not, leaving you with a low quality copy of a film that you won't understand. So how does one tell if they are looking at an illegal copy of a VCD or DVD? Typically, the box art will be of shoddy quality, as though somebody printed it off on a laser jet printer. The films may also have different names in order to cash in on the popularity of other films, such as "Phantom the Submarine" being labeled as "JSA III" or Park Chong-wan's "Eternal Empire" being called "Bichunmoo 2". Finally, the details on the back of the box will have been cut-and-pasted from another DVD—for example, I have seen illegal copies of "Friend" and "Joint Security Area" with the synopses and cast listings for "Disney's The Kid" or "One Tough Cop" on the back.

Another alternative for browsing and buying Korean films is the growing number of Internet retailers that specialize in Asian films. In addition to carrying only legitimate, high-quality original VCDs and DVDs, Internet retailers provide a wealth of information on the discs they sell, such as plot synopses, the presence (or absence) of English subtitles, DVD region coding, television standards supported, listings of any special features, and even reviews from other customers. The following is a list of well-established Internet retailers that are worth checking out:

- **Poker Industries** (http://www.pokerindustries.com): One of my favorite places to shop on the Internet, Poker Industries is the online division of MC Comics in New Jersey. In addition to carrying a wide range of Asian films on VCD and DVD, including an up-to-date selection of Korean films, Poker Industries carries CD soundtracks to some of the more popular Korean films, such as "My Sassy Girl" and "Bichunmoo".
- **Asian Cult Cinema** (http://www.asiancult.com): The online store of the niche Asian cinema magazine (which I occasionally happen to write articles for) has a moderately sized catalog of Asian genre films,

including a small cadre of the more popular Korean films, such as "Shiri" and "Nowhere to Hide".

- **YesAsia.com** (http://www.yesasia.com): YesAsia.com, which has three separate global sites (North America, Japan, and International), carries a wide range of Chinese, Korean, and Japanese products, including videos, music CDs, television series, posters, videogames, and gifts. Their catalog of almost 300 Korean movies on VCD and DVD is probably the largest online selection of any retailer, including new releases direct from Korea that do not contain English subtitles. One nice timesaving feature of their site is a menu selection that allows visitors to see a listing of only the films that contain either English or Chinese subtitles.

- Rivalling YesAsia's movie selection is California-based **DVDAsian** (http://www.dvdasian.com), which has a pretty good selection of new and old Korean films on DVD.

- **HKFlix.com** (http://www.hkflix.com): This online store for Hong Kong movies also has a decent selection of Korean films, some of which have a 'lowest price' guarantee attached to them. In addition, HKFlix has what is perhaps the most interesting example of cross-merchandising, with links offering packages of instant ramen with your order for the 'complete HKFlix experience'.

- **Amazon.com** (http://www.amazon.com): If you are a loyal customer of Amazon.com, then you'll be pleased to know that the retail conglomerate of the online world has a small but growing selection of Korean films, mostly comprised of North American releases, such as "Shiri", "Tell Me Something", "Chunhyang", and "Happy End".

- **YeonDVD.com** (http://www.yeondvd.com): YeonDVD is the online DVD shop run by the wife of Darcy Paquet, a journalist for Screen International who also manages the Korean Film Page (http://www.koreanfilm.org). The selection is pretty good, however, the site does not yet accept credit cards for payment, and buyers must pay by Paypal, money order, wire transfer, or personal check.

- **Sensasian.com** (http://www.sensasian.com): Buyers in Asia might want to check out this Internet retailer based in Malaysia and Hong Kong, which has a very good selection of Korean DVDs and VCDs.

This list of Internet retailers is not comprehensive, and I'm sure you will come across many more on your own. However, as with any sort of Internet shopping, be sure to do your homework before committing your credit card number, such as understanding where they can deliver orders to and what the associated shipping charges would be, or what their return policy is.

Chapter 13: Hong Kong or Bust – Where Next?

In the fall of 2002, the extent to which Hong Kong's film industry had fallen from its halcion days was revealed by some startling and dire statistics. The number of films produced in Hong Kong in 2001 numbered 126, compared to 242 in 1993, while box office sales dropped from $227 million US to $103 million US during the same period. As a result, funding for new productions has dried up dramatically, while revenue-starved exhibitors are dropping the prices of movie tickets. The reasons for the crisis are many, including the successive economic recessions that have battered the former British colony and rampant piracy that makes first-run films available from street peddlers within days of theatrical release. In addition, industry observers cite increased competition by foreign films, singling out Hollywood and South Korea as leading the charge.

Will South Korea eventually overtake Hong Kong as the mecca for filmmaking in Asia, or will the market forces laying siege to Hong Kong eventually lead Korea's homegrown film industry down the same path to ruin? Right now is a precipitous period for South Korean cinema. One the one hand, Korean films are gaining more international recognition around the world, such as the almost 60% rise in film exports during 2001thanks to hits like "My Sassy Girl" and "Friend", the significant 'coming out' of Korean films during the 2002 Toronto International Film Festival, and the growth in international sales of Korean DVDs.

However, during 2002, there were also some indications that such record growth may not be able to go on forever. With only a limited domestic market and international buyers still in the process of warming up to Korean films, the rising production and marketing costs (which the Korean Film Commission estimates to be rising at 23.3% and 43.1% per year, respectively) are increasingly running up against the capacity of the market to sustain them. For example, 2002 saw some spectacular big-budget failures, such as sci-fi actioner "Resurrection of the Little Match Girl", which was budgeted at $9.2 million US (making it the most expensive live-action film in Korean history), and the time-travel adventure "Yesterday", which was budgeted at $5 million US. In addition, as a result of strong competition from Hollywood imports, such as "The Lord of the Rings: The Fellowship of the Ring", "Ocean's Eleven" and "A Beautiful Mind", Korean films had a harder time cracking into the top ten, and it looks as if it will be a struggle for homegrown productions to beat or even meet the impressive 50% market share figure achieved in 2001 (as of June 2002, the market share of Korean films was lower though still impressive at 46.1%).

As a result, Korea's production houses now seem to be placing greater emphasis on star- and story-driven features rather than ones requiring lavish special effects budgets. Furthermore, audience tastes in Korea continue to demand quality over quantity, as witnessed by the biggest hits of 2002 being modestly budgeted films with strong scripts, such as "The Way Home", which details the travails of a boy who is sent to live with his grandmother in the country, "Marrying the Mafia", a gangster comedy where a young lawyer becomes involved with the daughter of a big boss, and "Public Enemy" (reviewed in a previous chapter) in which a corrupt cop and a ruthless serial killer come to blows. Hopefully, if filmmakers are able to heed the lessons learned in 2002, a greater emphasis on quality will save the South Korea from the fate that has befallen Hong Kong's film industry.

Furthermore, with Hollywood increasingly buying distribution and remake rights, the international profile of Korean films should grow in coming years. It was only a few years ago that Hong Kong filmmakers and stars were all but unknown outside of the British colony. But thanks to pioneering efforts by Jackie Chan, John Woo, and Chow Yun-fat, home video sales of older Hong Kong films blossomed, and the filmmaking techniques of Hong Kong filmmakers have permeated throughout Hollywood. And as the rest of the world warms up to Korean cinema, more export opportunities will allow filmmakers to leverage international sales to ensure steady returns on their productions, thereby ensuring continued overall health of the industry.

There is little doubt that South Korea is walking in the footsteps of Hong Kong. However, the question is whether South Korea will be able to better Hong Kong's failing industry by sustaining its remarkable growth through innovation and an empahsis on quality, or run into the same walls that have befallen what was once the jewel of Asian filmmaking. Only time will tell.

Appendix: Korean Movie Look-up

Title	Year	Genre	Rating	Page
2009 Lost Memories	2002	Action	●●●●	33
Address Unknown	2001	Drama	●●½	191
Affair, An	1998	Romance	●●●●	125
A.F.R.I.K.A.	2002	Action	●●½	85
Anarchists	2000	Action	●●●	79
Art Museum by the Zoo	1998	Romance	●●●●	127
Asako in Ruby Shoes	2000	Romance	●●●	147
Attack the Gas Station!	1999	Comedy	●●●●●	41
Bad Guy	2001	Drama	●●●	181
Barking Dogs Never Bite	2000	Comedy	●●●½	210
Beat	1997	Drama	●●●●	170
Bet on My Disco	2002	Comedy	●●●	218
Bichunmoo	2000	Action	●●●	76
Bungee Jumping of Their Own	2001	Romance	●●●	141
Calla	1999	Romance	●●	149
Christmas in August	1998	Romance	●●●●½	43
Chunhyang	2000	Romance	●●●●	129
Contact, The	1997	Romance	●●●	145
Day, A	2001	Drama	●●●●●	161
Die Bad	2000	Drama	●●●●	163
Ditto	2000	Romance	●●●●	123
Dream of a Warrior	2001	Action	●	91
Failan	2001	Romance	●●●●●	45
Foul King, The	2000	Comedy	●●●●½	206
Friend	2001	Drama	●●●●½	30
Funny Movie	2002	Comedy	●●½	220
Ghost in Love	1999	Romance	●●●½	139
Ghost Taxi	2000	Horror	●	114
Gingko Bed, The	1996	Romance	●●	151
Green Fish	1997	Drama	●●●●	168
Guns & Talks	2001	Action	●●●●½	56
Happy End	1999	Drama	●●●●●	156
Harmonium in My Memory, The	1999	Romance	●●●½	135

Title	Year	Genre	Rating	Page
Hi, Dharma	2001	Comedy	●●●	214
Holiday in Seoul	1997	Drama	●●½	189
I Wish I Had a Wife	2001	Romance	●●●	143
Il Mare	2000	Romance	●●●●½	119
Indian Summer	2001	Romance	●●●½	137
Interview	2000	Drama	●●½	187
Iron Palm	2002	Comedy	●●●½	212
Isle, The	2000	Drama	●●●½	174
Jakarta	2000	Action	●●●½	74
Joint Security Area	2000	Drama	●●●●●	27
Kick the Moon	2001	Comedy	●●●●	208
Kilimanjaro	2001	Drama	●●	195
Last Present	2001	Romance	●●●●½	121
Last Witness	2001	Action	●●●½	72
Legend of Gingko, The	2000	Action	●●	87
Libera Me	2000	Action	●●●	81
Love Wind, Love Song	1999	Romance	●●●●	131
Memento Mori	1999	Horror	●●●½	105
Musa	2001	Action	●●●½	69
My Beautiful Days (aka 24)	2002	Drama	●●●	179
My Boss, My Hero	2001	Comedy	●●●●½	204
My Sassy Girl	2001	Comedy	●●●●●	48
My Wife is a Gangster	2001	Comedy	●●●●½	38
Nabi	2001	Drama	●●●½	172
Nightmare (aka Horror Game Movie, Scissors)	2000	Horror	●●	113
No. 3	1997	Comedy	●●●	216
No Blood No Tears	2002	Action	●●●●	62
Nowhere to Hide	1999	Action	●●●½	64
On the Occasion of Remembering the Turning Gate (aka Kind of Life)	2002	Drama	●●●	183
One Fine Spring Day	2001	Drama	●●	193
Peppermint Candy	2000	Drama	●●●●½	51
Public Enemy	2002	Action	●●●½	67
Quiet Family, The	1998	Horror	●●●●½	96
Real Fiction	2000	Drama	●●	199
Record, The	2000	Horror	●	115
Ring Virus, The	1999	Horror	●●●½	103
Say Yes	2001	Horror	●●●½	101
Secret Tears	2000	Horror	●●½	109

Title	Year	Genre	Rating	Page
Shiri	1999	Action	●●●●½	24
Siren	2000	Action	●●½	83
Sorum	2001	Horror	●●●	107
Soul Guardians, The	1998	Horror	●●½	111
Spring in My Hometown	1998	Drama	●●●½	177
Sympathy for Mr. Vengeance	2002	Drama	●●●●●	158
Take Care of My Cat	2001	Drama	●●●●	165
Tell Me Something	1999	Horror	●●●●	98
This is Law (aka Out of Justice)	2001	Action	●	89
Uprising, The	1999	Drama	●	201
Virgin Stripped Bare by Her Bachelors	2000	Drama	●●●	185
Volcano High	2001	Action	●●●●	59
Waikiki Brothers	2001	Drama	●●	197
Wanee & Junah	2001	Romance	●●●½	133
White Valentine	1999	Romance	●	153
Yonggary (aka Reptilian)	1999	Action	●	93

Korean Cinema:
The New Hong Kong

Bibliography

"DVD player sales take off," *Reuters*, (Jan. 4 2002).

"Korea," Microsoft® Encarta® Online Encyclopedia, 2002

"Korea, South," Microsoft® Encarta® Online Encyclopedia, 2002

"Territory Report: South Korea," *Hollywood Reporter*, (May 11 2002).

"What is a VCD?". *vcdgallery.com*. Website accessed June, 2002.

Alford, Christopher. "Domestic pic prosperity." *Variety* (Dec. 6 1999).

Coppola, Antoine. "Korean Cinema: Story of a Revelation", *FilmFestivals.com*. Website accessed May, 2002.

Elley, Derek. "Local hitmakers eye global breakouts." *Variety* (Dec. 3 2001).

Kim, Mi-hui. "Film industry lures fresh capital—quick returns, high profit, guaranteed success attracts investors." *The Korean Herald* (Dec. 1 2001).

Kwang, Mary. "HK movie world's fortunes take a tumble." *The Straits Times* (Sept. 19 2002).

Lee, Yeon-ho. "Mapping the Korean Film Industry." *Cinemaya* N. 37 (1997).

Marshall, Jon. "A Brief History of Korean Film", *Pusanweb.com*. Website accessed May, 2002.

Paquet, Darcy. "Actors and Actresses of Korean Film", *KoreanFilm.org*. Website accessed October, 2002.

Paquet, Darcy. "A Short History of Korean Film", *KoreanFilm.org*. Website accessed May, 2002.

Paquet, Darcy. "Going to the Movies in Korea", *KoreanFilm.org*. Website accessed May, 2002.

Paquet, Darcy. "Korean box office hit may be the last of the blockbusters." *Screen Daily International* (Oct. 1 2002).

Paquet, Darcy. "Korean films keep up record pace set in first half of 2002." *Screen Daily International* (July 17 2002).

Paquet, Darcy. "Korea's Cinema Service plans own studio and multiplex circuit." *Screen Daily International* (Apr. 14 2002).

Paquet, Darcy. "Korea's film floatation boom yet to materialise." *Screen Daily International* (Mar. 18 2002).

Paquet, Darcy. "Netizen Funds", *KoreanFilm.org*. Website accessed May, 2002.

Shim, Sang-min. "Success factors of the Korean film industry." *The Korean Herald* (Oct. 15, 2001).

Thacker, Todd. "Famous faces - Identifying icons of Korean pop culture." *The Korean Herald* (Sept. 27, 2002).

Index

CPSIA information can be obtained
at www.ICGtesting.com
Printed in the USA
LVHW110012030222
710074LV00005B/390